Anonymous

The Proceedings of the First Annual Meeting of the National Conference

on university extension, held in Philadelphia, December 29-31, 1891, under the auspices of the American society for the extension of university teaching

Anonymous

The Proceedings of the First Annual Meeting of the National Conference
on university extension, held in Philadelphia, December 29-31, 1891, under the auspices of
the American society for the extension of university teaching

ISBN/EAN: 9783337164256

Printed in Europe, USA, Canada, Australia, Japan

Cover: Foto ©Suzi / pixelio.de

More available books at **www.hansebooks.com**

THE PROCEEDINGS

OF THE

FIRST ANNUAL MEETING

OF THE

NATIONAL CONFERENCE

ON

UNIVERSITY EXTENSION,

HELD IN

PHILADELPHIA, DECEMBER 29-31, 1891,

UNDER THE AUSPICES OF

THE AMERICAN SOCIETY FOR THE EXTENSION OF UNIVERSITY TEACHING.

COMPILED BY

GEORGE FRANCIS JAMES, M.A.,
EDITOR OF
UNIVERSITY EXTENSION.

PHILADELPHIA:
J. B. LIPPINCOTT COMPANY.
1892.

PREFACE.

THE first year of Extension teaching in America was devoted to spreading a knowledge of the system and undertaking experiments under various conditions. The results showed the need of thoughtful conference and discussion on the part of those engaged in the work, and at the beginning of the second year, the suggestion for a National Conference on University Extension came to the American Society almost simultaneously from many parts of the United States.

It seems almost incredible, looking back, that within one year of the time when the first centre of Extension teaching was established in Philadelphia, on November 3, 1890, more than two hundred such experiments were being carried on in nearly every State of the Union. We can attribute this only to the well-developed system of Extension teaching which had grown up in the course of more than a score of years' experiment in England, and the possibility of transferring it bodily to our soil.

Another consideration that presents itself is the wide-spread need of exactly such opportunities as are offered in systematic Extension teaching. These two conditions, however, alone do not suffice to explain the phenomenal growth of this movement, and we must look for the explanation to a third fact, well presented by A. E. Winship, editor of the *New England Journal of Education*, in a recent number of *University Extension*.* A careful consideration of many experiments in American education previous to 1890 reveals to us a peculiar ripeness of conditions for this movement; in other words, many had unconsciously been doing Extension teaching in a more or less adequate way. Some had caught one idea of this system, others another, and

---

* Cf. *University Extension*, February, 1892.

each one in his own way was sowing seed which favorable conditions brought to quick maturity.

When the American Society entered upon its educational campaign, it was favored by all these circumstances, and it was possible to accomplish within one year, through the enlightened generosity of many eminent citizens of Philadelphia, more than might fairly have been expected in thrice that length of time. All that could be done by the spread of carefully-prepared circulars and pamphlets, and in more than a dozen States by the personal and active work of its organizers, the American Society achieved. In the course of practical experiments, however, under widely varying conditions, it became evident, as has already been remarked, that the most careful consideration and discussion of those familiar with different sections, could alone lead to the best results.

In answer, then, to many requests, the American Society resolved to issue invitations for a general meeting in Philadelphia during the Christmas holidays. It was felt that there should be a thorough representation, not only of all interested in Extension teaching, and in university and college work, but of all interested in any way in every branch of the public school system and in general education. The truth is gradually becoming more and more evident that education is, and should be felt to be, of the utmost import to every American citizen, and that every effort for the strengthening of our educational system along any line, is of the highest interest to all concerned with it on any other. Especially is this true of the movement for University Extension, since it depends for its success on the most sympathetic co-operation of all our higher institutions of learning, and on the heartiest sympathy and action of the people as a whole, and, it is needless to add, on those educators most closely identified with the masses. We are endeavoring to bring the ideals and the methods of university training, as far as possible, to every American, and in doing this need the assistance of all parties.

Another reason was felt to point strongly to the advisability of general representation at the Conference, and that was the influence of University Extension upon the general education of the country. Experience has invariably shown that wherever a centre of Extension teaching is established there interest is aroused, not only in the particular subject or subjects of instruction, but in the general field of human knowledge and in the great problem of public education. It has been the constant and earnest injunction of the American Society to all its lecturers to advance the interests, not only of Extension teaching and of their own especial subject, but of science and literature, of the public school system, of the American college and American university, and to repeat, of education itself in the broadest and truest sense. Accordingly, the American Society issued its invitation, not only to its own centres and to the affiliated societies in all parts of the country, but to every college and university, to the representatives of the great public school system, to the leading clergymen of all denominations, and, indeed, to all interested in the advance of civilization as promoted by any line of human effort.

The response was gratifying in the extreme. At this first general meeting on University Extension, there were present delegates from twenty States, representing, as will be seen by the list of those present, half a hundred of our best institutions of learning. Every centre of Extension teaching which has so far been established in the country was represented either personally or by a written report submitted to the Conference.

In arranging the programme for the Conference, it was the desire of the Committee to emphasize, in accordance with many requests, the practical side of this work, and to give the opportunity at the same time, in connection with the various papers presented, for the freest discussion of principles and comparison of results. The Society was especially fortunate in the presence of Michael E. Sadler, secretary of the Oxford Delegacy, who, on its invitation, came to attend the Conference and spend several weeks in strengthening the system among us. The Society was thus fulfilling one of its main functions, as was well indicated, at the first session, by Provost Pepper in his address of welcome.

An idea of some of the results of the National Conference may be drawn from the proceedings reported in this volume.

Many, however, defy an effort to put them in such tangible form, and could only be gained by personal conversation with the delegates present, and by seeing with what enthusiasm they expressed their thorough satisfaction with the Conference, and the great pleasure they had in attending and reaping the advantages offered. It is safe to say that no one went home without bearing with him, for the benefit of his own section, a clearer idea of the special principles of this system and a deep impression of the utmost necessity of united and systematic effort on the part of its friends.

Philadelphia has a well-established reputation as a favorite meeting-place of such conventions, and the hospitality of its citizens is far-famed. To the delegates, however, of the National Conference it extended an exceptionally warm welcome, and fairly outdid itself in hospitality. The social features of a National Conference, especially of educators, have ever been a source of pleasure and profit. The evening receptions tendered the delegates on Tuesday and Wednesday at the Art Club and at the Academy of the Fine Arts, were typical of what such meetings should be.

It was the unanimous thought of all present that, in arranging and carrying out the National Conference, the American Society had added one more characteristic benefit to the cause of University Extension in America, and had at the same time secured, in great measure, the success of similar meetings in the future.

CONTENTS.

	PAGE
PREFACE.	3
MINUTES OF THE NATIONAL CONFERENCE	9

ADDRESSES.

ADDRESS OF WELCOME. By Provost William Pepper, University of Pennsylvania ... 15
THE PLACE OF UNIVERSITY EXTENSION IN AMERICAN EDUCATION. By Hon. William T. Harris, Commissioner of Education, United States ... 18
CHAUTAUQUA AND UNIVERSITY EXTENSION. By Bishop John H. Vincent ... 32
THE CHURCH AND UNIVERSITY EXTENSION. By Rev. Dr. John S. MacIntosh ... 38
UNIVERSITY EXTENSION AND THE YOUNG MEN'S CHRISTIAN ASSOCIATION. By Walter C. Douglas, General Secretary, Philadelphia. 45
THE COLLEGES AND UNIVERSITY EXTENSION. By President Charles DeGarmo, Swarthmore College ... 51
A PROBLEM IN UNIVERSITY EXTENSION. By Secretary Melvil Dewey. 54
THE CITY AND UNIVERSITY EXTENSION. By Samuel Wagner ... 59
THE DEVELOPMENT OF UNIVERSITY EXTENSION. By Secretary Michael E. Sadler ... 63
THE UNIVERSITY EXTENSION LECTURER. By Professor Edmund J. James ... 89
THE IDEAL SYLLABUS. By Henry W. Rolfe, M.A. ... 107
THE ORGANIZATION AND FUNCTION OF LOCAL CENTRES. By Secretary Michael E. Sadler ... 113
SOME EXTENSION EXPERIMENTS IN AMERICAN HISTORY. By Professor James A. Woodburn ... 122
HISTORY AS AN EXTENSION STUDY. By Professor Wilfred H. Munro. 130
THE UNIVERSITY EXTENSION CLASS. By Edward T. Devine, M.A. . 135
UNIVERSITY EXTENSION IN CINCINNATI. By Professor W. O. Sproull. 144
THE STATE AND UNIVERSITY EXTENSION. By Ralph W. Thomas, A.M. ... 152

REPORTS.

	PAGE
MAINE, VERMONT, NEW HAMPSHIRE, AND MASSACHUSETTS	157
RHODE ISLAND. By Professor Wilfred H. Munro.	158
CONNECTICUT. By Professor H. E. Bourne	160
CONNECTICUT. By Rev. F. B. Hartranft	162
NEW YORK, NEW JERSEY	167
DELAWARE, PENNSYLVANIA, MARYLAND	168
VIRGINIA. By W. Roy Stephenson	169
WEST VIRGINIA. By Professor Howard N. Ogden	170
GEORGIA. By Professor H. C. White	173
LOUISIANA, TENNESSEE	176
KENTUCKY	177
OHIO	178
INDIANA. By Professor James A. Woodburn	182
MICHIGAN. By Professor Isaac N. Demmon	190
MICHIGAN. By Secretary Henry A. Ford	193
ILLINOIS	193
WISCONSIN. By Professor Edward A. Birge	196
WISCONSIN. By President R. C. Spencer	199
MINNESOTA. By Professor Harry P. Judson	201
IOWA	205
KANSAS AND MISSOURI. By Professor Frank W. Blackmar	206
COLORADO, WYOMING	216
CALIFORNIA	217
CANADA	218
REPORT OF THE AMERICAN SOCIETY. By George Henderson, General Secretary	221
LIST OF DELEGATES OF THE NATIONAL CONFERENCE	265
APPENDIX A.—UNIVERSITY EXTENSION IN NEW YORK. By Secretary Melvil Dewey	269
APPENDIX B.—GENERAL ANNOUNCEMENT OF THE AMERICAN SOCIETY.	288

THE MINUTES

OF THE

NATIONAL CONFERENCE.

THE First Annual Meeting of the National Conference on University Extension opened its sessions in Philadelphia on Tuesday, December 29, 1891, at 4.30 P.M., in Association Hall, corner of Fifteenth and Chestnut Streets, at the head-quarters of the American Society for the Extension of University Teaching. The first session was devoted to a model Extension lecture, the second of a course delivered by Michael E. Sadler, of Oxford, on "The Change in Political Economy." The special topic was the doctrines of St. Simon, and the reaction against critical political economy. The lecture was followed by the regular Extension class.

In the evening, at eight o'clock, a reception was tendered the delegates of the National Conference and the members of the American Society of Biblical Literature and Exegesis, at the Art Club.

On Wednesday, the morning session, at 9.30, was opened by an address of welcome from Dr. William Pepper, Provost of the University of Pennsylvania. He was followed by the Hon. William T. Harris, United States Commissioner of Education, who chose for his subject "The Place of University Extension in American Education." President James MacAlister, of the Drexel Institute, gave an address on "University Extension and the Public School System." The work of Chautauqua in public education was presented by Bishop John H. Vincent, Chancellor of the Chautauqua University. The relation of the Church to University Extension was treated by Rev. John S. MacIntosh, D.D. Mr. Walter C. Douglas, General Secretary of the Philadelphia Young Men's Christian Association, spoke of the Young Men's Christian Association and University Extension. The session was closed by Secretary Melvil Dewey, of Albany, with an address on the work of University Extension as conducted by the University of the State of New York.

At the close of the morning session, a meeting of the Council of the American Society was held, and a report was made of the incorporation of the Society and of the general plan of management under a Board of Directors, chosen by the corporation, and an Executive Committee of twelve, six chosen by the Board of Directors and six by the members of the Council; the Council itself being composed of the President, and one other representative from each college and university co-operating with the American Society.

At three o'clock on Wednesday afternoon the deliberations of the Conference were continued with an address, by Mr. Sadler, on the "Development of University Extension." The discussion* which followed was participated in by President William H. Black, Missouri Valley College, Missouri; President Thomas Fell, St. John's College, Maryland; Rev. Dr. W. W. Newton, Pittsfield, Mass.; Mr. H. H. Hay, Girard College; Rev. Mr. Lamb, Moorestown, N. J.; Dr. James MacAlister, of Philadelphia; Rev. J. Max Hark, Lancaster, Pa.; and Dr. Edward H. Magill, Swarthmore College.

Mr. P. J. McGuire, representing President Gumpers of the American Federation of Labor, gave a short address expressing the sympathy of the trade organizations of America with the purposes and methods of this movement.

"The University Extension Lecturer" was the subject of a paper by President Edmund J. James, of the American Society,

---

* The remarks of those taking part in the discussion will be found in their proper place in the Proceedings, except where there was a failure on the part of the speaker to hand them to the Secretary.

discussed by Mr. Bourne, of the Norwich Free Academy, Norwich, Conn.

Mr. Henry W. Rolfe, of the University of Pennsylvania, read the last paper of the afternoon on "The Ideal Syllabus," which was discussed by Professor Felix E. Schelling and the Rev. John S. MacIntosh.

At 8 P.M., on Wednesday, a reception was given the members of the American Society and the visiting delegates by Bryn Mawr College, Haverford College, Swarthmore College, and the University of Pennsylvania, at the Academy of the Fine Arts. The reception was one of the largest and most brilliant of the season, and was attended by more than a thousand guests.

On Thursday, at 9.30 A.M., Mr. Sadler gave a second address on the "Function and Organization of Local Centres." The discussion was carried on by Mr. Henry W. Rolfe, Rev. John S. MacIntosh, Mrs. Kimball, President Charles DeGarmo, Secretary Melvil Dewey, and Professor W. A. Merrill, of Miami University.

Dr. James Albert Woodburn, Professor of American History in Indiana University, read a paper on "Some Experiences as an Extension Lecturer," and was followed by Professor Wilfred H. Munro, of Brown University, who discussed "History as an Extension Study." The succeeding remarks were made by Professor E. P. Cheyney, of the University of Pennsylvania, Dr. Edward H. Magill, and Mr. Edward T. Devine.

The last session of the Conference, on Thursday, at 3 P.M., was devoted first to a discussion of the "University Extension Class," the leading paper being by Mr. Edward T. Devine, Lecturer of the American Society. Remarks were made on this subject by Rev. Dr. Douglas, of Philadelphia, Professor H. N. Ogden, of the University of West Virginia, Dr. W. Clarke Robinson, Professor James A. Woodburn, Secretary Melvil Dewey, and Mr. M. E. Sadler.

Reports of progress in Extension work were made by President William H. Black, for Kansas and Missouri; Professor Leslie A. Lee, Bowdoin College, for Maine; Professor W. H. Munro, of Brown University, for Rhode Island; Rev. F. B. Hartranft,

Hartford Theological Seminary, for Connecticut; Secretary George Henderson, for Pennsylvania; Professor Howard N. Ogden for West Virginia; Professor W. O. Sproull, University of Cincinnati, for Ohio; Professor James A. Woodburn, University of Indiana, for Indiana; Professor A. V. E. Young, Northwestern University, and President Carl Johann, Eureka College, for Illinois; Professor M. E. Sanford, University of Minnesota, for Minnesota; President D. B. Kerr, University of Omaha, for Nebraska. From the other centres of Extension teaching came written reports, which are printed in their proper place in this volume.

The relation of the American college to University Extension was ably treated by President Charles DeGarmo, of Swarthmore College, and the best form of organization of the movement in a large city, by Mr. Samuel Wagner, of Philadelphia.

The closing paper of the Conference was by Mr. Ralph W. Thomas, Chief Examiner of the University of the State of New York, on the appropriation by the New York Legislature of ten thousand dollars to University Extension, and on the means by which this was gained.

Rev. Dr. John S. MacIntosh, of the Executive Committee of the American Society, moved the thanks of the Conference to the Hon. William T. Harris, Commissioner of Education, for his address on "The Place of University Extension in American Education," and his kindness in presiding at the sessions of the Conference on Wednesday, and to President Edmund J. James, who had, at so much expense of time and effort, secured the thorough success of the Conference. Mr. Sadler remarked that it was certainly the most important and successful meeting on University Extension which had ever been held, either in this country or abroad.

Dr. Edmund J. James closed the Conference with congratulations to the delegates present, on the valuable results accomplished, and with the pledge, on the part of the American Society, to contribute in the future, as in the past, its undivided labors to the furthering of this great cause, and to give its hearty co-operation to all bodies and institutions in their efforts in this direction.

ADDRESSES.

ADDRESSES.

ADDRESS OF WELCOME.

BY WILLIAM PEPPER, M.D., LL.D.,

Provost University of Pennsylvania.

IT is with no common pleasure that, as the representative of the American Society for the Extension of University Teaching, I stand here to announce the opening of its first annual midwinter conference, and to extend to the delegates to this conference, and to all members of the Society, a most cordial welcome. The educational problems connected with University Extension have multiplied so rapidly in this country, and the people are so widely awake to the real importance of them, that a general desire has been expressed for their free discussion at certain stated intervals. The arrangement of such a conference is one of the important functions of the American Society, and the simplicity and broad scope of this organization are well adapted to the purposes it must serve.

It is no longer an assumption to assert that every portion of our vast country is genuinely interested in University Extension, and recognizes more or less clearly that the movement is to play a great part in the higher education of our people in the future. The amount of money expended in the various States will depend upon many conditions, but it is hoped that, owing to the largely self-supporting character of the Local Centre work, a sum of, say fifteen thousand dollars, or even ten thousand dollars, per annum can be made to accomplish large results in any single State. It can scarcely be doubted that such a sum or more can be raised, in each State of the Union, to secure for the community the advantages of well-organized and vigorously-conducted University Extension work. The precedent established by the legislature of the Empire State will doubtless be followed wherever the law permits such appropriations; but experience has already shown that, for the conduct of the General Society, a considerable annual sum is required, which must be derived from sources quite apart from the appropriations for State work. The expenses of the General Offices, which must serve as a bureau of information for the entire country; the management of the Home Study system correspondence; the provision of University Extension literature, which has to be liberally paid for and to be sold at barely cost prices; the publication of the University Extension Journal, which demands, in its editorial department, highly-paid talent and yet must be sold at a rate that brings it within the easy reach of all; the importation of University Extension lecturers of distinction, who may be sent to special fields where their services are most needed,—these and other requirements will necessitate a considerable annual expenditure for the adequate support of the American Society.

The Board of Trustees, consisting of fifteen members, which is provided for by the charter of our Society, is therefore charged with the duty of creating and fostering the growth of a permanent endowment fund; of securing an adequate increase in the membership of the Society; and of maintaining a guarantee fund of proper proportions until, from the growth of the endowment and the increased membership, a permanent income sufficient to defray all working expenses is provided. To the Executive Committee, which is appointed partly by the Board of Trustees and partly by the General Council, are intrusted the executive details. Upon the close and intelligent attention given by this committee to the important work intrusted to it will depend the maintenance of the high educational standard of the Society. The method of constituting this committee will, it is believed, fully insure its object.

The General Council of the Society consists of one representative besides the President of each college in the United States and in Canada, together with the Superintendents of Public Education in each State, who are *ex-officio* members. The regular meetings of the Council will occur during the last week of each year, at the annual midwinter conferences in this city. The plan of organization adopted relieves this Conference of all petty details of business, and thus enables it to devote uninterrupted attention to the scientific discussion of the educational principles and methods which should be adopted in our University Extension work so as to secure the highest standard and the most effective results. The entire country will follow with deep interest the deliberations that occur here now and hereafter. To the suggestions and conclusions which flow from our discussions, all of us will look for light and leading in the new and difficult path upon which we have entered.

One important official act must be discharged, each year, by the General Council of delegates, at their conference. This is the election of six members to serve upon the Executive Committee for the ensuing year.

At the close of this morning's session, a meeting of the Council will be held for this purpose, and all members of the Council are particularly invited to attend the meeting.

It will be seen, from the brief sketch I have given of the organization and functions of the American Society, that it has no aim or pretension to interfere with, to supersede or to take charge of, University Extension work in any State. It holds itself ready to offer advice, information, and assistance to those who are engaged, in any locality, in organizing the work. A bulletin will be issued, within a few days, giving full details as to the manner in which such advice, information, and assistance can be most rapidly and efficiently utilized.

Although the plan of organization of the American Society ..as been promulgated so recently, it is a matter of sincere congratulation that membership in the Council has already been accepted, officially, by the Presidents of over one hundred American colleges.

I shall not detain you longer from the important discussions of special features of the work which are to follow. It is enough to feel assured that the organization which has been effected, comprehensive and flexible as it is, is so well adapted to the work before us all that, with continued cordial co-operation, it will prove equal to the great demands that may be made upon it.

THE PLACE OF UNIVERSITY EXTENSION IN AMERICAN EDUCATION.

BY HON. WILLIAM T. HARRIS,

Commissioner of Education, United States.

LADIES AND GENTLEMEN, DELEGATES TO THE NATIONAL CONFERENCE ON UNIVERSITY EXTENSION,—I have been requested to direct my remarks to the general bearings of the question of University Extension. I shall therefore offer some considerations regarding the threefold structure of our educational system into elementary, secondary, and higher education, and discuss the general features which distinguish each grade. I shall endeavor to show that higher education is the sanest and healthiest form of education, because it gives the student the means of correcting one-sided views. It gives him the method of study which compares one science with another and one branch of learning with another, and always bears in mind the important question, How does this element of knowledge relate to the conduct of human life? From this point of view, I shall explain why University Extension seems to me to be one of the most important movements in our time. An exhibition of the fragmentary nature of elementary education and the necessity which has caused this fragmentary character to adhere to it, will make it evident, I hope, that the directors of higher education have a sacred duty to perform in extending, by all legitimate means, the spirit of their methods into the studies which the adult population carry on by means of the newspaper, the periodical, and the book, throughout life.

Let me ask your attention, first, to the general aspects of our civilization. Let us consider the active means at work to produce cosmopolitan civilization and obliterate local and provincial peculiarities.

The most striking characteristic of our modern civilization is that which has to do with the intercommunication of one people with another. The wonders of modern invention are to be found especially in this field of human activity. In the first place, the facilities for travel by land and by sea bring together a greater and greater number of people in each succeeding year. Think of the increase of the number of Americans that have visited Europe,—of the number of Europeans that have visited America. Think of the increasing number of people residing in the Atlantic slope who have visited the cities of the Mississippi Valley and the far-off Pacific Coast. The personal presence and the humane, friendly interest of foreign people in this country form a perpetual educative influence, converting our people to cosmopolitan views and sympathies. But the educative influence of travel is small compared with that of intercommunication by means of letters and literature. In our time we have seen epic, dramatic, and lyric literature retire into the background before the novel or romance as a literary work of art. The novel has been called the prose epic, or the epic of commonplace, middle-class citizens. But the novel in our time has extended its gamut from the description of society manners and customs and the petty events of courtship and marriage to the all-including scientific and historical movements which constitute the highest fields of intellectual labor. In the modern novel we have Shakespeare's mirror, that is held up to reflect society and the individual. We have the painting of the slums, the *demi-monde*, the processes of the schools, the Church; we have fully-colored pictures of ancient historic life, long buried, and brought to life only by the labors of archæology; we have a series of historical pictures, growing rapidly to a great gallery of paintings, illustrating mediæval times, the beginnings of modern times, and, finally, the events of a century ago,—Tolstoi's Napoleonic wars, the Crimean war, Walter Scott's historical pictures; Victor Hugo, Thackeray, and a thousand writers less significant and still important. Each reading public learns to know the character and motives of its fellow-men in far-off countries or far-off epochs. Out of this comes the feeling of the solidarity of the human race. Every one feels that there is nothing human that he can consider to be entirely strange to him. But even the novel is not to be compared, in its influence, with the daily newspaper and periodical press as an instrument invented by the human spirit to bring about the higher unity and synthesis of all peoples. Not only shall each people combine in itself the best that has been realized by other peoples, but each human individual shall take his morning survey of the daily movement of nations and colossal enterprises.

Here is the significance of our new University Extension movement, which we are here to-day to celebrate by this conference. (University Extension proposes to avail itself of the new inventions and instrumentalities which have been developed in the interests of commerce and the ordinary interchange of opinion, and send the currents of higher thought, higher scholarship, and higher sentiment through these channels, so as to directly influence all men.

In brief, University Extension proposes to itself to gain possession of the organs of public opinion, and it is evident that this enterprise is one of the most important undertaken in our century since the establishment of the common public school.)

In the most advanced civilization we find the completest system of means for the formation and promulgation of public opinion. All persons in the community, by means of the newspaper, look upon the same event, look upon the same sketch of public policy marked out by the statesman, listen to the same arguments, and take sides in view of the weight of argument. The public opinion thus organized is not the public opinion of a village or a province. It is the public opinion of the whole country, and a public opinion which is formed, or secreted, so to speak, by the aggregate action of all the minds in the nation. In fact, this does not state it strongly enough. The public opinion of a newspaper-reading age is an international public opinion, a public opinion which takes into it as a determining element the views and opinions of other civilized nations.

But this kind of public opinion cannot be found in an illiterate community, nor can the newspaper, which is the instrument for forming and disseminating such public opinion, penetrate an illiterate community.

In old times, before the statesman could watch the verdict of public opinion on a proposed measure, he was perhaps obliged to take action. The diplomats found themselves obliged to plunge the nation into war. In our time, with the telegraph, and the newspaper, and a universal reading people, the dial of public opinion is visible to all statesmen and leaders of the people, and it is possible to avoid an appeal to the final court of arms.

It is evident enough that the first requisite for the efficiency of these instrumentalities is a universal diffusion of common-school education, and an ability on the part of all the people to read and understand the printed page. This is given in the common schools. The question arises at once, at this point, Why do not the common schools give an all-sufficient education? Why is not elementary education all that is desired among the people? Is it not true, that if the schools teach the people how to read, and the universal prevalence of periodicals and books furnishes what to read, that the life of the people is turned into a constant education? Will not such reading—such as the elementary school provides for—lead necessarily to the diffusion of all human learning?

In order to answer this question properly, and to see the grounds which exist for the movement known as University Extension, let us consider for a moment the difference between elementary school education and university education. The child who is of the proper age to learn how to read has not acquired an experience of life sufficient for him to understand very much of human nature. He has a quick grasp of isolated things and events, but he has very small power of synthesis. He cannot combine things and events in his little mind so as to perceive processes and principles and laws,—in short, he has little insight into the trend of human events or into logical conclusions which follow from convictions and principles. This is the characteristic of primary or elementary instruction, that it must take the world of human learning in fragments and fail to see the intercommunication of things. The education in high schools and academies which we call secondary education begins to correct this inadequacy of elementary education; it begins to study processes; it begins to see how things and events are produced; it begins to study causes and productive forces. But secondary education fails, in a marked manner, to arrive at any complete and final standard for human conduct, or at any insight into a principle that can serve as a standard of measure. It is the glory of higher education that it lays chief stress on the comparative method of study; that it makes philosophy its leading discipline; that it gives an ethical bent to all of its branches of study. Higher education seeks as its goal the unity of human learning. Each branch can be thoroughly understood only in the light of all other branches. The best definition of science is that it is the presentation of facts in such a system that each fact throws light upon all the others and is in turn illuminated by all the others.

The youth of proper age to enter upon higher education has already experienced much of human life, and has arrived at the point where he begins to feel the necessity for a regulative principle and guiding principle of his own, with which he may decide the endless questions which press themselves upon him for settlement. Taking the youth at this moment, when the appetite for principles is beginning to develop, the college gives him the benefit of the experience of the race. It shows him the verdict of the earliest and latest great thinkers on the trend of world history. It gathers into one focus the results of the vast labors in natural science, in history, in sociology, in philology, and political science in modern times.

The person who has had merely an elementary schooling has laid stress on the mechanical means of culture,—the arts of reading, writing, computing, and the like. He has trained his mind for the acquirement of isolated details. But he has not been disciplined in comparative study. He has not learned how to compare each fact with other facts, nor how to compare each science with other sciences. He has never inquired, What is the trend of this science? He has never inquired, What is the lesson of all human learning as regards the conduct of life? We should say that he has never learned the difference between knowledge and wisdom, or, what is better, the method of converting knowledge into wisdom:—The college has for its function the teaching of this great lesson,—how to convert knowledge into wisdom, how to discern the bearing of all departments of knowledge upon each.

It is evident that the individual who has received only an elementary education is at a great disadvantage as compared with the person who has received a higher education in the college or university, making all allowance for imperfections in existing institutions. The individual is prone to move on in the same direction, and in the same channel, which he has taken under the guidance of his teacher. Very few persons change their methods after leaving school. It requires something like a cataclysm to produce a change in method. All of the influences of the university, its distinguished professors, its ages of reputation, the organization of the students and professors as a whole, these and like influences, combined with the isolation of the pupil from the strong tie of family and polite society, are able to effect this change in method when they work upon the mind of a youth for three or four years. The graduate of the college or university is, as a general thing, in possession of a new method of study and thinking. His attitude is a comparative one. Perhaps he does not carry this far enough to make it vital; perhaps he does not readjust all that he has before learned by this new method; but, placing him side by side with the graduate of the common school, we see readily the difference in types of educated mind. The mind trained according to elementary form is surprised and captivated by superficial combinations. It has no power of resistance against shallow critical views. It is swept away by specious arguments for reform, and it must be admitted that these agitators are the better minds, rather than the weaker ones, which elementary education sends forth. The duller minds do not ever go so far as to be interested in reforms, or take a critical attitude toward what exists.

The duller, commonplace intellect follows use and wont, and does not question the established order. The commonplace intellect has no adaptability, no power of readjustment in view of new circumstances. The disuse of hand labor and the adoption of machine labor, for instance, finds the common laborer unable to substitute brain labor for hand labor, and it leaves him in the path of poverty, wending his way to the almshouse.

The so-called self-educated man, of whom we are so proud in America, is quite often one who has never advanced far beyond these elementary methods. He has been warped out of his orbit by some shallow critical idea, which is not born of a comparison with each department of human learning with all departments. He is necessarily one-sided and defective in his training. He is often a man of great accumulations of isolated scraps of information. His memory-pouch is precociously developed. In German literature such a man is called a "Philistine." He lays undue stress on some insignificant phase of human affairs. He advocates with great vigor the importance of some local centre, some partial human interest, as the great centre of all human life. He is like an astronomer who opposes the heliocentric theory, and advocates the claims of some planet, or some satellite, as the centre of the solar system. In sociology these self-made men advocate, for instance, as a universal panacea for poverty, such devices as the abolishing of all individual property in land, or a single-tax, or a scheme of state socialism; or, on the other hand, the equally negative system of *laissez faire*,—let each look out for himself, and let the government forswear entirely all functions of nurture and provision for the common welfare. In the name of abstract justice, Mr. Herbert Spencer strikes at all of the concrete forms of government in existence, and would fain cut them down to his procrustean standard, protecting free competition without provision for common welfare.

There is a conspicuous lack of a knowledge of the history of the development of social institutions in all this. The individual has not learned the slow development of the ideas of private property in Roman history, and he does not see the real function of property in land. Again, he does not know the history of the development of human society. He has not studied the place of the village community and its form of socialism in the long road which the state has travelled in order to arrive at freedom for the individual.

The self-educated man, full of the trend which the elementary school has given him, comes, perhaps, into the directorship over the entire education of a state. He signalizes his career by attacking the study of the classic languages, the study of logic and philosophy, the study of literature and the humanities. It is to be expected of him that he will prefer the dead results of education to an investigation of the total process of the evolution of human culture. The traditional course of study in the college takes the individual back to the Latin and Greek languages in order to give him a survey of the origins of his art and literature and science and jurisprudence. In the study of Greece and Rome he finds the embryology of modern civilization, and develops in his mind a power of discrimination in regard to elements which enter the concrete life of the present age. It is not to be expected that the commonplace mind, which is armed and equipped only with the methods of elementary instruction, shall understand the importance of seeing every institution, every custom, every statute in the light of its evolution.

Again, the force of these facts is augmented when we consider the enormous development of secondary instruction in this country, not on the basis of the university, but on that of the elementary school. Within one generation the public free high schools have increased from a hundred or less to five or six thousand. For the most part the course of study in these institutions has been largely under the control of men educated only in elementary methods. As might have been expected, this fact has largely determined the character of the studies pursued in the high schools. The classic studies and pure mathematics have been discouraged, and studies substituted for them which have a real or supposed value in the business vocation. The consequence of this has been that the high schools of the country have failed to furnish men of real directive power. Their best representatives have been of the type of the self-educated men that I have just now described.

While I consider it a matter of congratulation that the people of the country are fast establishing throughout the land a system of free education in high schools, yet I find myself obliged to admit that the present and past results of these schools may be summed up as the production of a vast intellectual current of Philistinism. There is not any argument for the importance of University Extension which equals this in strength. The secondary education has largely been diverted from the road that leads to higher education, and turned aside in such a manner as to produce arrested development at the stadium of elementary or secondary methods. The common schools of the people are suffering more from this cause than from all the other causes combined. It is a prolific source of mere mechanical device and methods which lead nowhither. It produces a flippant, self-conceited frame of mind which does not hesitate to attack and tear down institutions which it fails to comprehend. University Extension, as we understand it, proposes to close up this gap between higher institutions and the elementary schools.

In recent years there has been a considerable elevation of the standard of admission to the college, and this has led to an increased development of secondary instruction, especially since the smaller colleges of the country have not been able to follow the lead of the great universities without suffering in the size of their classes. The influence of secondary schools as directors of elementary common schools is not, and never has been, a healthy one. Only the college and university can give this healthy influence.

With University Extension the directors of higher education come at once into contact with the people. The university, through its properly organized faculties, descends into the community and, as it were, takes an inventory of the bright and promising minds that are exercising an intellectual influence upon the direction of affairs. It gathers these into classes and audiences, and discusses with them the living questions of the day. It fascinates them with the superiority of the comparative method of study. It vanquishes the spirit of Philistinism and refutes the theories of cranks.

This process of University Extension, I need not add, has also a retroactive influence of great value upon the university itself. We all know how important is the present tendency towards specialization. We admit, nevertheless, that there is a danger in this, inasmuch as the specialist who does not use the highest or comparative method, and endeavors to bring his specialty into comparison with all branches of human knowledge, —that this specialist, I say, tends to make his branch a hobby, and to set up his local centre as the grand centre of the universe. Unbalanced specialism in education, therefore, tends to the very evils which elementary methods produce. But University Extension will correct this. When the specialist finds himself face to face with an audience collected from people who have received only a common education, he is forced at once into meeting their crude opinions by presenting the comparative history of his theme, and by showing the bearing of other branches of human learning upon it. It is, as I have said, the characteristic of University Extension that it finds its highest principle in the conduct of life, and that it is ethical in its method. The direct contact of university instructors with the people leads to the emphasis of the ethical stand-point.

So much for the reaction of University Extension upon the university itself. But I should not omit to say that the University Extension movement will have another beneficial effect in increasing the number of persons who seek higher education. No sooner does the university enter the field of competition before the common people than it vanquishes the claimants for the cause of secondary education, and the claimants for the cause of elementary education as finalities. The people see at once the superiority of the higher education, and there arises throughout the community an aspiration for its advantages. Even the families of the poor will aspire each to educate one or more of their children for the university. We know that in former times, when the requirements for education had not climbed up to the place they now hold, how often the poorest families in Scotland managed to educate one of the family for the university. The ideal of education, at that time, was university education. This desirable ideal will again prevail in the community, and where we have at present in the United States only one in five hundred of the population enrolled in schools for higher instruction we shall have, as we ought to have, from five to ten times that ratio.

Again, the advantage to the University will appear in the furnishing of direct practical careers to its graduates. In the laboratory and the seminarium the university trains its pupils to the work of original investigation. It sends, therefore, into the community a class of people fully equipped with an intellectual apparatus for the correction and perfection of the political and the economical departments. It focusses a powerful light upon the directive power in the various departments of productive industry and local self-government. Now, University Extension, by reason of the fact that it collects into organized bodies the most enterprising minds of the common people, prepares positions in advance for these graduates of the university. They may take hold of the places where they are most needed without wasting their strength in endeavors to discover such opportunities, and to persuade men in power of the utility of their training for the work.

We have seen how this movement arose in England. With the extension of suffrage and with the increase of means of self-education among the people, and especially with the circulation of semi-scientific information by means of the printing-press, there has been in the past a something of relaxation in the hold which the great universities had upon the people. This has been promoted by the self-educated man whom I have disparaged by calling him a Philistine. The great urban development of England, and, I may say, of all civilization, has produced in the community an aggregation of the weaklings of society,—what we may call the·population of the slums,—a fearful problem for our civilization. It would have been the part of selfish wisdom to establish University Extension in order to recover a hold upon the common people, and in order to grapple successfully with the social problem of the slum element which menaces the rule of law; but, strange to say, the University Extension has not originated in the enlightened selfishness of the university, but rather in the pure missionary spirit,—the spirit of divine charity which has always largely abounded among the directors of higher education. There is no movement, however, which has worked for the perpetuation of the power of the upper classes, and especially of the university educated classes of Great Britain, as has this movement of University Extension.

It is true that circumstances in this country differ from those in England in many particulars, but there are great broad lines of resemblance. In both countries we have what is called local self-government. England is the nation in which local self-government has originated as a complemental element necessary to compensate for the one-sidedness of the Roman principle of centralization. In our government, just as in the home government of England, there is a representation, not only of all individuals but of all interests, and this not only in the legislature that makes the law, but in the courts which administer the law, and in the executive department which enforces the law. The making of laws is determined by the free process of elections and public debates in which all powers and interests struggle for the mastery. The decisions of the courts are determined by the same universal representation of individuals and interests; and, finally, the enforcement of the laws concedes the same rights of consideration for all parties concretely existing in the community. It is evident that in England and in this country—both democratic—there exists a sort of necessity for a free process of influence between the highest and lowest strata of society. In both countries demagogism increases in proportion to the neglect of the lowest stratum by the highest. This argument for University Extension is so obvious that it does not need further expansion here.

There is one incidental effect of University Extension which I think worthy of special mention. The ordinary elementary school, secondary school, or college, seeks to give a general education to the pupil. It wishes to see every one learn the conventional course of study, and not neglect either language, or science, or mathematics, or history. This curriculum, in a certain sense, mistreats those especially gifted individuals, found in all ranks, who have possibilities of the greatest usefulness in certain narrow lines of talent, but who are not attracted by other fields of knowledge outside of their specialty. Their love of one particular branch of human knowledge is so great that all other branches seem to them repugnant. These persons are the stuff out of which genius is made, but our traditional system of education has not known what to do with the candidates for genius. But the new methods of specialization, which the University proper has taken up after the studies of college are completed, has opened up among our university educators an interest in special talent wherever it is found. University Extension provides new channels of communication between the directors of the university and these specially endowed people, scattered here and there throughout the community. The lecturers and class-teachers of the Extension movement are prepared to make an inventory, as it were, of this very important, although not numerous, element in the population. This possibility of saving from waste some of the most gifted of people will occur to every one as a strong reason for the existence of School and University Extension.

The old lyceum course did not provide for the active participation of the audience in the work of instruction. But University Extension provides for discussions between the lecturer and his classes. It provides for reviews, it provides for home-studies and examinations.

In regard to the question of management in this great movement, I suppose that we shall have a full discussion of the question of local centres *versus* one all-including society. It seems to me that we should encourage local centres where there seems to be ambition and ability for successful organization. I think that this matter will take care of itself. The advantages of a great central organization are advantages of finance. There is saved a multiplication of officers and a multiplication of expense by co-operating in one great society. But where local reasons exist for independent societies, let them continue. Let any State whose government provides money to manage University Extension within its boundaries go on and solve its own problems. There are lines of new experiments needed in order to discover the best instrumentalities. The English have developed especially the lecture-course system, with its discussions and written examinations. In many parts of this country the system of home-study and professional instruction by mail has been developed. There are very many other phases, such as, for example, that developed by the Brooklyn Institute, which ought to have full consideration. When we have developed a half-dozen types of University Extension, each local centre may adopt and combine three or four best adapted to it. In the meanwhile we must pay the well-deserved compliment to the American Society, initiated by the University of Pennsylvania, to say that it has made by far the largest step in making a useful and practical application of University Extension in this country; and all new movements in this direction should consider carefully the question whether something cannot be gained by uniting with this great movement already so efficiently organized. Whatever may be the practical conclusion arrived at in regard to these matters of local and central administration, there certainly is but one possible conclusion as to the importance of a national conference with annual meetings for comparison of views. Each movement wishes to understand clearly the aggregate result of the experience of all movements. There should be a national conference, which brings out this experience in all its details, and serves it up for the instruction of all.

I congratulate you, delegates, on your undertaking, which is, in the broadest sense of the term, a missionary movement. It is a movement which holds out the torch of the highest learning, not only for the illumination of all, but for the purpose of assisting each individual to light his own torch at its sacred flame.

CHAUTAUQUA AND UNIVERSITY EXTENSION.

BY BISHOP JOHN H. VINCENT,

Chancellor of the Chautauqua University and Assembly.

THE Chautauqua Idea and Movement deserve a recognition among University Extension workers, because Chautauqua is itself little else than a University Extension agency. To convince you of this, and to secure your confidence and co-operation as University Extension specialists, I accept the opportunity of this hour.

If University Extension as a modern movement meets with something like apathy, if not with pronounced opposition, from certain university men, it is because these men do not understand the movement you represent. If the Chautauqua Movement meets with similar indifference, if not with antagonism, from many universities, and occasionally from a University Extension advocate, it is simply another case of misapprehension.

The opposition in both cases—to University Extension work and to Chautauqua work—is, on the whole, a good sign. I congratulate the cause which both movements represent—that is, the cause of the higher education—on the sensitiveness of the scholars touching these popular devices. True scholars deprecate superficiality. They are anxious lest some easy way be set forth to what they regard as a substitute for culture, power, and honor. Truly great scholars are determined not to degrade the dignity of genuine scholarship; to substitute show for substance; to allow grace of speech to pass for grasp of thought; or a glance at an extended landscape to be as much esteemed among the educators as a patient and persistent digging underground, where the real treasures are hidden. I therefore rejoice when the appointed representatives of thorough and sturdy scholarship look at University Extension with suspicion. It augurs well for the work and the results. The men set to defend the noblest learning and the true power of education are aware of their responsibility. The hesitancy is sure to be followed by heartiness of approval in the end, and their respect is worth something after you have fairly captured it.

I have known and studied the English University Extension scheme ever since 1875. I did not then know, however, that the plans of the English movement and of the American Chautauqua movement were formally laid during the same year. I do know that both beginnings were characterized by the same effort to secure more scientific and thorough work in their respective lines, and that in this attempt both plans provided for systematic lectures, class conversations and drills, printed syllabi and written examinations,—the bringing, in a word, to the out-of-school layman the knowledge, methods, and spirit of the university.

I purpose to present at this time, in as compact and comprehensive a way as possible, a statement of the Chautauqua System, that you may see its resemblance and relation to your own noble, practical, and democratic educational endeavor. Briefly stated, the Chautauqua Idea embraces the following elements:

1. The application of the scientific method in education to religious and biblical instruction, and its illustration in all departments of learning.

2. The recognition by religious teachers of the religious power and value of the "week-day" or so-called secular agencies—commercial, educational, political, and social—in promoting among the people large and worthy views of life, and in advancing among all classes of society the idea of symmetrical education.

3. The introduction of the best representatives of the schools, and especially of the colleges and universities, to the great body of the American people, who now and for long years out of school have a very defective idea of the formal educational processes and too little confidence in them.

4. The provision of popular and practical agencies and methods for promoting the true "popular education" among adults, remembering that, while he begins wisely who begins to influence a generation by labor in behalf of the child in the cradle, he

works more wisely who begins his work of education with the strong hands that make and the tender hands that rock that cradle. Among these agencies and methods long familiar to Chautauqua are the provision of reading-courses, reading-circles, training-classes, lecture-courses, correspondence-teaching, periodical magazines and lesson helps, syllabi, schemes for the most rigid examinations, the employment of local scholars and specialists, winter and summer assemblies in hall, church, or grove, college and University Extension work, etc.

5. The employment of varied devices which appeal to the imagination, gratify the social instincts, and develop personal enthusiasm and *esprit de corps*. These incidental and sentimental features are indispensable to the college life, which emphasizes the idea of *alma mater*. They express themselves in classic halls, in social fraternities, in class loyalty, class rivalries, songs, feasts, and games. Similar expedients have been used by Chautauqua in the interest of the large number of people, representing all conditions of society, and all degrees of culture, who find themselves interested and inspired and strengthened by the class life, the class spirit, the promotions, recognitions, memorial days, vesper services, Chautauqua songs, and other beautiful accompaniments of a fraternity built on a high and holy aim.

6. And, finally, the Chautauqua movement recognizes the value of adults as students, and makes the attempt to enlist grown-up, middle-aged, and even venerable men and women in the worthy endeavor after self-improvement. Adults are popularly supposed to be beyond the limits of educational possibility; whereas their long experience in life and the maturing of their powers render them in many respects better qualified than the immature and inexperienced child for pursuing systematic and varied courses of study.

All these aims unite in a single thought: The application of the highest and most approved methods of education to the out-of-school multitudes,—all of them, at all ages, in all social conditions,—that they may come to appreciate their personal possibilities and responsibilities; that they may see the harmony between things religious and things secular; that they may learn how truly to honor and dignify manual labor; how to despise the frivolity, emptiness, and selfishness of mere wealth without culture and high moral quality; how to bear affliction with fortitude, and how to find the consolation of noble thought in lowly homes; that they may command their children, send them to the public schools at an early age, keep them in school until they are ready for college, and then induce them to pass through college, if not in order to be mechanics or professional men, that they may be, whether mechanics, merchants, or professional men, intelligent, reverent, independent, righteous men and women, true exponents of the Christian idea, and citizens of the nation whom demagogues can never dominate, and by whom in due time all conscienceless schemers, commercial and political, shall be suppressed. Fraud, now possible by an ignorant, selfish, and indifferent people, must fall before popular intelligence, conscience, and purpose.

Chautauqua is not, as some superficial observers have supposed, an evolved camp-meeting. In fact, the Chautauqua Idea, as carried out in many towns and cities of America, and in Oxford and Blackpool in England, and as originally conceived in America, sustains no relation whatever to the camp-meeting or to the grove. Great advantages have accrued to the scheme by the meetings in the grove, but, while these advantages have been appreciated, one of the chief hindrances to the work has been in the prejudice against the camp-meeting among so many people who were perhaps too little familiar with the uses and advantages of that venerable religious institution. The management of Chautauqua has used its most vigorous endeavor from the very beginning to divorce from the Chautauqua work the camp-meeting idea. It has been compelled to say again and again, in a score of ways, that the Chautauqua Movement and the camp-meeting are two entirely different institutions, with utterly different objects,—both useful, but as diverse as an inquiry-meeting on the one hand and a class conference of scientists, theologians, and statesmen on the other.

The influence of Chautauqua on college and university life is to be seen in the results of its practical working during the past seventeen years. The effects are to be found:

1. In the large number of students now engaged in doing Chautauqua correspondence work. Men and women of mature minds, who could not themselves, owing to circumstances beyond their control, leave home and enter any institution of learning, are now engaged under the direction of university men in courses of study equalling those of the best college curricula, and subjected to tests of examination unexcelled in any university.

2. In the large number of summer and winter students now attending the Chautauqua centres north and south, where, under university men, for from two to eight weeks they have the benefit of contact with the living teacher; enjoying methods which are the outgrowths of the most profound theories of teaching, and feeling, for a short time it may be, but nevertheless for all the years that follow, the personal magnetism and inspiration which the gifted teacher communicates to every eager pupil.

3. In the large number of Sunday-school normal pupils, in the sixty or more assembly centres, who, by the university method at its best, have for a long term of years been engaged in biblical, psychological, and pedagogical training work.

4. In the large number of lecture courses on the widest range of subjects, which have been given at these Chautauqua centres, and in towns without number, which by the Chautauqua assemblies have been led to make this experiment.

5. In the large number of readers in that most popular form of the modern Chautauqua work, the Chautauqua Literary and Scientific Circle, who, covering in a four years' course of English reading the college outlook, become familiar with the college world, its topics, its charms, its practical value, and who, being parents or the elder brothers and sisters of the household (there are few members of the C. L. S. C. under twenty-five years of age), are sure to induce the younger people by hundreds and by thousands to resolve upon the high-school and college course. In fact, the C. L. S. C. is a John the Baptist to the college, preparing the way for and announcing the benefits of the college, and appealing to the multitude to patronize the higher centres of culture.

6. In the large number of college graduates who have been

enrolled as readers in the Chautauqua Literary and Scientific Circle. It is a mistake to suppose that only non-collegians are members of this association. The main object of the college being development of intellectual power, every college graduate needs an after course of reading. In fact, it requires a four years' course of special study to enable a man to read with facility and economy of time a single page of good literature. College graduates who have thoroughly understood the C. L. S. C. have availed themselves of this opportunity for reviewing the college horizon in classic English.

7. In the large number of college graduates who now, as teachers and as members of the Chautauqua Literary and Scientific Circle, are able to make the best use of their educational opportunities. They are now able to sit down with less favored fellow-citizens and friends, and, bringing the wealth of their knowledge and the power derived from their intellectual discipline, to help without patronizing, and thus to turn to best account the privileges they have been permitted to enjoy.

8. In the large number of students now in college because of the Chautauqua direction and inspiration. Parents who thought but little of the higher education have through the literature of Chautauqua, through the Chautauqua lectures, through the C. L. S. C. reading, been awakened to the immense importance of a college training for boys and girls, and now, as a result, their children are remaining in the high school, preparing for and entering the college, and all because of the awakening and impetus which the Chautauqua Movement has caused.

Thus Chautauqua recognizes and uses all educational agencies and institutions; commands all scholarship ; plants the seeds of college life in the homes of the people ; prepares young people to make better college students ; supplements the college preparation with opportunities for advanced work after graduating; and, above all, puts college graduates to their best use, that of helping others.

THE CHURCH AND UNIVERSITY EXTENSION.

BY REV. JOHN S. MACINTOSH, D.D.

THE Church, University Extension,—two great aggressive forces,—are they to clash, or to co-operate, perhaps combine? Important and pressing question! The Church is a force; University Extension a new but wonderfully fast-growing force; and it has come to stay, perhaps with change of form and manifestations, but not to disappear as a real existent, penetrative, and changeful force. And these two great forces must touch; but not, I am assured, as foes, but as hearty, mutually respecting, and confiding friends, who are co-workers for the larger common weal, and who have largest interests in common. Marked affinities have they, and they will be bound in closest alliance activities.

The Church,—and observe I use this word in the very broadest possible of broad sense and comprehension,—the Church is, has been, and ever must be democratic, educational, revolutionary, and that for the highest ends and with the finest and the mightiest weapons. And here is a movement pre-eminently democratic, for it says old privileges must be given freely out from patrician hands to the populace; educational, for it takes out not only the school-master but the college professor and the university specialist for the higher and more exact teaching of the people, who are not to be amused by mere popular addresses, but trained by systematic instruction, exact to the last point of accuracy, and yet taking the most seductive garb of all winsome speech; revolutionary of the settled ways of centuries and of ideas fixed seemingly as the hills, and aims that appeared the only possibilities in the case. Startling affinities, verily, between the old mother and the young boy. If there be any one thing more than another that the Church has proclaimed on the house-tops, it is this, that rank has responsibilities, that special privileges have special duties to discharge, and that from him to whom men have given much will they require the more; we get only to give; and, unless I misread it utterly, that lies in the heart of this movement to lift the University out of its sacred seclusion where luxuriantly it has enjoyed its garden of pleasant fruits, and order it to carry its best systems, its best work, its best sons and daughters out to those who are thirsting on the hot fields and fainting by the dusty road-sides of crowding life. The Church working for the people and with the people, working to enlighten, working to turn the world upsidedown that the right side may be brought up and kept up, the Church must and will find one of her best friends and strongest allies in this great popular, educational, and revolutionary movement.

The Church has already taken sides, and that within our lines; she is even now on our side of the fence; not against but for us. Two proofs exist. One of the earliest advances in this educational revolution was made within the lines of the great Methodist Episcopal Church under the magnetic leadership of Bishop Vincent and the dashing flag of Chautauqua. The other took place under the blue banner of Presbyterianism, and in staid old Scotland, where a few years ago "perfervidum ingenium Scotorum" devised a carefully graduated system of "Instruction for Youth" by special text-books, by appointed lectures and lecturers, by class-work, examinations, and certificates, which has in it the very essentials and the vitality of this University Extension Movement. And what, let me ask, has been the special aim in work and the great argument in printed page of that most true churchman, who is in touch with so large a part of the Church-world, and whom I am glad to call my friend, the thoughtful Henry C. Trumbull, but one long struggle and splendid plea for that very union of exact and advancing scholarship fully popularized and of careful, continuous class-work and searching catechetics which, as I take it, are two of the highest ideals and truest glories of University Extension.

And, further, it has been my happy lot, because of my special work in our Society, to get into large and close correspondence with the clergy, especially the junior clergy, all across the continent; and I know how truly sympathetic they are; how their eager eyes are fixed on us in hope, and how many of their lore-loving souls are hungering for some of this living bread. The Church is on the side of this work.

I. WHAT CAN THE CHURCH DO FOR THE MOVEMENT?

That is a practical and a suggestive question.

1. The Church can and should extend to us sympathetic and honorable recognition. Recognition, I say, not patronage and protection, not the demands of a superior nor the dictates of a lord. The first is not needed, and the second will not be brooked. But recognition, frank and friendly, full of true respect and ardent sympathy and unhesitating confidence for a movement which in its own distinctive and appropriate sphere is marked by those very popular, philanthropic, and progressive features that form part of the sweetest charm and strongest claims of the Church herself. Here is an effort honestly made to flood the thick darkness with true light, to sweeten human society by the fresh, clean breezes from the higher hills of truth, and to broaden human souls through healthy, stimulating, but wisely-regulated exercises on the wholesome fields of enlarging thought. The Church can say and show that she appreciates and respects and trusts this undertaking; and I am persuaded that she stands ready everywhere to do this helpful service.

2. The Church can materially aid. Materially, I say; and that in many important directions. To make plain my point, let me choose a definite illustration. Come with me to one of our young, growing, and wide-awake towns; at the very centre of its life, perhaps its very strongest, highest, and most impulsive life, stands a Church of some persuasion; that Church has a great plant, an organized body of zealous workers, a large, fine lecture-room or chapel, a library, with a librarian, a circle of readers, and no small resources in money and appliances, such as magic lanterns, black-boards, maps, and such like. Now, that lecture-room or chapel is exactly what is often needed for local centre work; that library may be easily made, under guidance and realized wants, the storehouse of standard books and works of reference; the treasury may be fairly drawn upon for a part

of the cost of working; and the bands of ardent youth may become the active propagandists and the wise gray heads the shrewd advisers and steady supporters of this church-helping work. What is possible there is easily possible in countless other points, both urban and rural.

3. The Church can lend moral assistance. Here is one of the finest allies the Church can desire in her own stern fight for the brighter days and the better hearts. A voice, a new voice, has been lifted in the waste; a young, clear voice that, with fresh tones and with varied phrase, tells the old message of human inspiration and uplifting "the kingdom of heaven has come nigh unto you," and the common people are hearing gladly. Into the arena where the fight is against the lower and the lustful for the higher and the holier, against the bestial for the spiritual, for the mental and moral against the material, for thought that may master passion, for reason that may keep under the flesh, for the school and the book against the saloon and the brothel,—into this arena of life against death has leaped a young and lusty champion who, skilful of hand and daring of soul, flashes his fresh, strong blade in the front and the thick of the fray. Let us, gray in the battle, cheer him. Ay, that we will, and with all our heart!

4. The Church can render intellectual help. She has a host of trained teachers in touch with and trusted by the people, whose special professional duty it is to make highest thought so thoroughly their own that they make it level to the work-dulled brains of the hard-pushed masses; whose reason of protected existence is partly found in the ability to gather the most fine gold and mint it into the serviceable coin of daily use; and whose life-work is to "go speak all the words of this life to the PEOPLE;" and these trained men are University men, who for six or eight or more years even have been facing University teaching, familiar with University methods, and have been fashioned by University moulds; and these University men are in not a few cases specialists in languages, in science, in history, in antiquities, in economics, in philosophy, or hygiene, or social matters; here is a disciplined force of fighters for sweetness and

light, who need only to study the new weapon and practise some new drill to be effective soldiers in this new crusade,—a crusade which ought to appeal to them more than most others, because they daily feel the need of taking the University down from its heights and its isolation to the hurly burly of the thickening contest of the multitudes that the battle for truth and righteousness may not be a sad succession of defeats, but a shining series of greatening victories.

II. WHAT CAN UNIVERSITY EXTENSION DO FOR THE CHURCH?

Much, every way.

1. University Extension may be the supplement of the school and the complement of the Church. That were efficient help to the Church.

If there be one thing which the State and the Church, the civitas populi, and the civitas Dei, alike need more than another, it is a body of educated citizens, of thoughtful supporters of quick intelligence, of cultured minds and calm, judicious spirits, able to appreciate arguments, appropriate truth, and swiftly adopt safe methods. The common schools, with their noble staff of self-denying teachers, have done much, and will yet do more, magnificent work for both State and Church; but, alas! the stress of human want and the strain of human life take away our boys and girls just when the mind has begun to be truly quickened, when habits of attention have been formed, when the primary lessons have been imparted, and the first fertilizing thought-germs have been implanted; and the mournful consequence is that the state has not her supreme bench of final judgment filled by the fully-taught and highly-trained intellects that are needed by her for her storm-defiant permanence and for her swifter and secure progress; and the Church must needs keep to the first principles of the vast realm of special truth which God and humanity have intrusted and conceded to her. The school wants a supplement; and this University Extension may and should step into the gap and fill up the void.

With this supplement of the school the Church needs her own complement. If she is to do in her own proper field her very best and her highest work, then the men and the women she deals with need to know many things and much of some of the things which she has neither the time nor the best methods of teaching. To use a common phrase and yet a true one, "the man who reads only his Bible will not read very much out of that;" he will not step into that heavy-laden and varied harvest-field so equipped that he shall bear away the many and richest golden sheaves. That book is a library, and needs an increasing library to explain it. All ways in the old world have led to the Imperial City, and each road brought a new student to the Seven Hills, who for himself saw what none other eye had taught; and every pathway of real knowledge and clean, clear truth leads to the golden City of the Sun; and it is the souls of varied wants, of fresh thoughts, and newly-quickened powers, who will find and carry away most of the divine culture. The Church needs to have her own work complemented by work without the sacred walls; and the University Extension along with other educational forces may and can be this necessary complement.

2. University Extension can and will help the Church by enabling her younger clergy to carry on their studies systematically without giving up their parish and pastoral duties. For such extra-university assistance and guidance there is already, and there will be daily growing, a strongly-felt and widely-expressed need and want. Upon this matter I can speak with a good deal of definiteness and personal knowledge. To me, as Chairman of the Home-Study department of our common work, letters have poured in from all parts of our lands and all sections of the Church eagerly asking how, in what ways, with what graduated systems of study, in how many different branches, and on what terms we were preparing to deal with the junior clergy who might desire to carry forward to further points of knowledge their old studies, or who might wish to push investigations out on new lines. An immediate answer to such questions can be seen in the department of Sacred Literature, now made a part of our general work. Another answer may be found in special courses for special students at local centres. And still another in a carefully-prepared course with correspondence for separate and home students.

And 3d, University Extension may tell beneficially on the Church by the introduction of its popular methods and peculiar features into the older ways and systems of Church instruction. This direct and positive influence has already proved itself. In this city, my learned and wide-awake friend, Dr. Henry C. McCook, as devoted a churchman as he is distinguished a scientist, conducted last winter a series of church lectures on Hebrew Prophecy and Prophets on the exact plans of University Extension, with popular lectures, printed syllabus, subsequent class work, and final examinations; and all with distinguished honor to himself, success in his work, and signal advantage both to the ordinary hearer and the actual student. On successive winters I have myself carried on courses on Biblical Introductions and Biblical Theology whose essential features were those of this system. Let then there be no strife between us, we are brethren of the light and of the day; let the effort be the mutual stimulation and the common good; and the only rivalry and struggle be who can do the most for our common land and common citizenship, and who can do it best and quickest.

UNIVERSITY EXTENSION AND THE YOUNG MEN'S CHRISTIAN ASSOCIATION.

BY WALTER C. DOUGLAS,

General Secretary of the Philadelphia Young Men's Christian Association.

THE object of the Young Men's Christian Association is defined to be the physical, intellectual, social, and spiritual improvement of young men. In other words, its high ideal is the development of the entire man. To develop the young men intellectually, it uses libraries, reading-rooms, literary societies, lectures, and evening classes.

Any young man of good character, of any race, religion, or condition in life, may join it, and hence it has all classes of young men in its membership, but, with the exception of quite a large student element, its ranks are filled mainly with clerks and mechanics. In some sections of this city the latter predominate, in others the former. They mingle in all its buildings in varying proportions. They are, of course, all working during the day for a living. The Association seeks to provide for their wants in their leisure hours. The Association aims not only to develop the young men along all the main lines of their lives, but also to ward off things that would degrade and injure them. A young man at work is all right. It is the manner in which he spends his leisure time that gives moral coloring to his life and decides his future value to home, to his employer, and to the state. His avocation is as important as his vocation, and every young man should have some good occupation for leisure as well as business hours. Robert J. Burdette half humorously but altogether wisely puts it in this way: "My son, you complain of hard work killing you, of long business hours. But it is not the hard work that is hurting you, it is not the long hours from 8 A.M. to 5 P.M., but it is the interval, my boy, that is killing you. It is the interval between 6 P.M. and midnight."

The Association steps in at this point, takes hold of young men in the critical period from sixteen to twenty-five years, and seeks to lead them to use means that will help and strengthen them physically, mentally, and spiritually. It is not enough to say to young men, "Thou shalt not," but we must fill their lives with better things. In other words, it is an adaptation in practical things of Dr. Chalmers's famous use of "the expulsive power of new affections."

The educational work of the Association has grown greatly within the past thirty years. In my judgment, to-day it is the greatest of all our agencies in drawing young men into our membership. To me this is profoundly gratifying, and refutes the charge sometimes made that the young men of to-day are frivolous. The Associations are offering great social attractions and many healthful recreations for the tired brains and bodies of young men; but, after all, that which requires most work, hard study, and application is the thing which draws the largest proportion of young men from mill, shop, and office to our buildings in the evenings. The practical talks and historical or scientific lectures of the Philadelphia Association have for years been attended by an average of eleven hundred young men, while in our educational classes last winter there were enrolled twelve hundred and eighty-eight young men. In point of mere numbers it compared favorably with the undergraduate departments of many of our large universities.

But these studies relate almost entirely to business life. They aim to prepare clerks and mechanics for better and more useful lives in their respective occupations. This is good, but there is something more important,—viz., to prepare young men for higher and better citizenship. In the words of the English leaders of University Extension, "to make good workmen is important, to make good citizens is more important." For years there had been a growing sense of need in our more advanced Associations in this respect. With their hundreds of thousands of members all young men, they may become, and indeed are, great training-schools of American citizens of a higher type. Our experience has shown us that in our American cities there are thousands of young men of as bright minds and eager, ambitious spirits as ever matriculated in the colleges of our land. But they have had no advantages. They are poor, or their parents died when they were young, and they have had to go to work early. They are at a disadvantage in life through lack of mental equipment. They are not only fighting its battles with one hand tied, but they are also shut out from worlds of enjoyment known only to the student.

The majority of these young men, it is true, have come to us seeking only for "bread and meat" education,—*i.e.*, for that knowledge which will help them to advancement in their daily business. But there has been a minority who have come asking how they might prepare themselves for college or get higher literary culture. We have been unable as yet to do much for this class.

It was just at this moment that University Extension came before us with its magnificent promise. And its coming has been hailed with joy by these eager, earnest young men, who were brain-hungry and had been crying out for supply in this direction.

The reasons why the Young Men's Christian Association should co-operate in University Extension may be summed up under two heads. The first is because it has the facilities for doing the work. Three things are considered important in the establishment of a local centre for the Extension of University teaching, —viz., an existing organization of some kind to afford a nucleus of attendance, a suitable hall or rooms for lectures and classes, and reference libraries or conveniences for handling books. The Association possesses these requisites. In the second place, University Extension being clearly a movement of the highest public good, and placing educational privileges heretofore denied them within reach of multitudes of young men, the Association should gladly co-operate with it on these accounts. It should do so to that extent that will not interfere with its other work or diminish what it offers to young men. This I take to be the only limitations upon it. The Association aims to give to the world as the final product of its work a young man intellectual as well as spiritual, and there seems no reason why its cooperation with University Extension should not prove a union of forces that will greatly advance its efforts to realize this high ideal of an all-around man.

The extent and method of co-operation we think may be readily and satisfactorily defined. Our experience in Philadelphia has been entirely free from difficulty or embarrassment. The extent and method of co-operation in Philadelphia have been as follows: representative Association men are serving upon the committees of the various local centres. A centre has been formed at the Central Branch of the Young Men's Christian Association, at Fifteenth and Chestnut Streets, which is known as Association Local Centre. The Association puts at the service of this centre office facilities, attention from office help, library, and free use of committee- and class-rooms, so far as its own work will permit. The trustees who hold Association Hall for purposes of revenue have granted the free use of it for the opening lecture of each course, and have made a special rate for such lecture-courses as required this large hall. The Committee of Management of Association Local Centre has no organic connection whatever with the Young Men's Christian Association in the same building. There are upon it two or three representative Association men interested in our educational work, but the committee is made up of other interests, and is representative in the widest sense of all other elements of the community. As a matter of fact, religiously it represents Roman Catholicism, Protestantism, and Judaism, while in other respects it is equally omni-representative.

As will thus be seen, there is no organic connection between the two bodies, as there is none between any other of the fourteen or more University Extension centres of this city and neighborhood and the various universities, societies, and institutes in or with which they are held. It is a matter of co-operation without any such relation as would interfere with the full development and free action of each institution.

The managers of Association Local Centre have voluntarily put all University Extension tickets at half-rates to young men who have already paid their membership-fees in the Young Men's Christian Association. They are also generous in making provision for young men whose resources may be too slender for a double tax even as slight as this.

Two questions will present themselves to managers of Young Men's Christian Associations. The first is as to whether young men have availed themselves of these courses to any extent. Clearly if, by co-operating with other institutions that have educational features, we can bring to deserving young men the priceless advantages of university culture we ought to do so.

The objection has sometimes been made to University Extension abroad and here that it reaches and benefits women much more largely than men. There is no apology for it on this account in England, and there will be none here. If this movement touches, quickens, and broadens the intellectual life of the mothers, wives, and daughters of our nation, if it irradiates our homes with high intellectual joys, if it pervades the womanhood of America with its magnificent culture, then so much the better for University Extension and for our country.

Yet as managers intrusted with a definite work for young men, we must consider the question of the effect of this upon our efforts in behalf of young men, and whether it reaches them as a class to any valuable extent. To this we answer that it is reaching young men, though not to the same extent as others, and more in the evening than afternoon lectures. This has been true both last winter and this. History, literature, economics, and science have all had a number of young men present. A class in higher mathematics for two winters has had an average attendance of nearly one hundred, the most of whom were skilled mechanics. In the evening classes upon socialism now being conducted in this holiday season by Mr. Sadler (of Oxford University), I have seen many intelligent, earnest students that at other times I have seen in the class-rooms of this Association.

The general effect of the introduction of University Extension into our work may be briefly summed up. It has quickened intellectual aspiration among the young men in our membership. It has opened unexplored mines of literary wealth and revealed a new world of beauty and truth. It has stretched before young men a continuation of study and mental growth beyond the more limited and so-called more practical studies of our own class-rooms. It has put within the reach of thousands of them that greatly-coveted but heretofore denied boon and blessing, liberal culture and university instruction of the very highest order. Attendance upon such lectures, by such teachers, for a few seasons, will give any young man a truly broad and liberal culture; and who can estimate the ever-increasing power of such young men for future years in their own social and business circles? By co-operation with this movement, University Extension may be made the fitting crown and completed perfection of that educational effort into which the Young Men's Christian Association puts so much genuine sympathy and vigorous work, because it believes, as it avows, in the intellectual, the physical, the social, and the spiritual development of the young man, —that is, in the development of the whole man. This is its ideal, and in University Extension, while it can properly aid a great progressive and uplifting movement for the good of the general public, it can incidentally but effectually advance its efforts in behalf of that special class for whom it exists and labors,—the young men of our country and the world.

THE COLLEGES AND UNIVERSITY EXTENSION.

BY CHARLES DEGARMO, PH.D.,

President of Swarthmore College.

THE idea is sometimes advanced that only large institutions, able and willing to contribute considerable sums of money to the cause, can successfully prosecute this new method of education. It is argued that this work can never pay for itself, so that much missionary effort must be exerted to keep the movement alive. If this is true, the smaller college would seem to be barred out, for its internal needs are usually so numerous and so imperative that the trustees do not feel that they can contribute much pure missionary work, or invest much capital in advertising, whose return must be slow at best, even if discernible at all.

When the smaller college attempts to embark on University Extension work, it will meet two species of difficulties, one pertaining to finance and the other pertaining to lecturers. It is expensive business to arouse and inform a community regarding all the phases of the University Extension movement. There must be much printed matter, and not a little correspondence. A clerical force is often necessary. The American Society for the Extension of University Teaching has spent many thousand dollars in gathering, collecting, and disseminating knowledge and experience in this field. In one way only does it occur to me that a small college can efficiently and cheaply do this necessary work, and that is by allying itself with some central society that has made a business of doing just this thing. Were the experience and knowledge of the American Society, for instance, at the service of Swarthmore College, we could by this means inform and stimulate the public in a way and to an extent quite beyond anything we could possibly do at our own expense and from our own experience. The United States mail service is cheap, rapid, and efficient, so that no real difficulty seems to arise when we consider colleges remote from the head-quarters of a society. At Swarthmore the central society can stir up and inform our neighboring communities for us. But, though they might find this difficult to do at a distance, it is clear that with plenty of printed matter of the right sort a committee of the college faculty could soon arouse an adequate interest in the subject.

The next great difficulty in the small college is the lack of the right kind of men to do profitable University Extension work. Three lines of action are open, with possible combinations. In the first place, members of the present faculty may do all the outside teaching. But the objection is near at hand, that they are already taxed to the extent of their ability, so that any increase would either overburden them or render some of their work superficial. The next plan is one suggested by Mr. Dewey, of New York. It is that the college should employ new men, who shall do a part of their work in the college and a part in the field, former members of the faculty doing the same, both classes looking partly to the college and partly to the public for their salaries. This sounds feasible, and has some considerable advantages. The plan has, however, a serious financial difficulty. With all due regard to the missionary spirit that may be burning in college professors, I have little doubt that the chance to eke out a slender salary by a little extra money over and above the salary already fixed is one of the largest factors in the enthusiasm with which the college professor goes into this University Extension movement. Two hundred dollars is often the difference between poverty and plenty to such a man. Abolish this incentive to extra work, and I shall expect to see a marked diminution of the present zeal for carrying education to Philistines. If the college can be induced to add another man or two to the faculty out of benevolence or advertising enterprise, there is no reason why even a very small college may not accomplish a great good to the community, and eventually to itself.

A third method might be that of fellowships for recent but able graduates of the college, a part or all of the remuneration to come from work in the University Extension field. These young men might pursue their chosen studies in the college, and at the same time do some lecturing and a considerable amount of clerical work. It would be needful for some older professor to guide their efforts, criticising their lectures both as to matter and delivery, to find them adequate ideas of how to conduct the class and correct the papers. These young men would succeed much better with subjects of positive knowledge, such as chemistry or physics, than they would with social sciences like economics, history, ethics, socialism, politics, etc., for their statements in the former could easily be verified, whereas in the latter only the man of wide knowledge and developed skill could hold his own against the men who would probably oppose him.

My conclusions are that the small colleges need not be ruled off the field entirely by the large and wealthy universities, since by co-operation they may all do that each working alone would be unable to do; and that, aside from what the regular professors may be able to do for a little extra compensation, the most feasible plan seems to be an extension of the work by the employment of young men who are seeking a new career and are willing to work for small pay while winning their spurs.

A PROBLEM IN UNIVERSITY EXTENSION.

BY MELVIL DEWEY,

Secretary of the University of the State of New York.

NEW YORK is the only State which maintains a department devoted entirely to the interests of higher education. From that department I wish to enter an earnest protest against what seems to me a serious mistake on the part of certain men, both in and out of the universities, who urge that the general administrative work of University Extension should not be done by the colleges, and that its instruction should not be given by members of the faculty. Such a theory seems to me to strike at the very essence of University Extension in its best sense, and to deprive the people on the one side and the universities on the other of great benefits to which they are entitled, and on which I hope they will jealously insist.

One of the greatest gains of this modern movement is that it brings the people and the universities closer together, and this proposition of independent work would only tend to create rivalries and drive them farther apart. Experience has shown that Extension students develop an affection and interest for the institution from which they get their instruction, supervision, and guidance. The universities cannot afford to let this affection go out to other agencies when they themselves need it so much in increasing both the moral and financial support of the public.

There has been proved to be a demand for this higher education which we call University Extension, for which the people are willing to pay. All are agreed that the demand must be met. The issue is as to which of two methods will accomplish most good with the available means. We all know that, in the development of the man, residence in a university plays almost as large a part as the actual studies. Our theory is that we are to carry the university to those unable to go into residence. It is an essential of the system that the lecturer, who week by week goes not so much to instruct as to inspire, shall bring with him as much as possible of the university atmosphere, and this can be done only if he is intimately connected with university life. It is not enough that he may be well versed in his subject, for University Extension means the carrying of the university spirit and methods and ideals. To have this work done by men who are not themselves connected with universities is like a city water-supply in which the pipes run not to a great central reservoir, but to hundreds of independent scattered springs.

Outside this main consideration, which people will not always understand, they greatly prefer to have a teacher from the university. There is a certain dignity and public confidence inseparable from the *imprimatur* of our great institutions. A lecturer on the faculty of a great college carries not only all the weight connected with his own learning and personality, but also that important addition which comes from public knowledge that the management of that great institution has, after careful investigation, found him worthy to stand as its official representative. It is like a certified check, in which the indorsement of the bank is worth more than the original signature.

Both university and public will get better teaching from a man who does both kinds of work. There are exceptions to all rules; there are men destined by nature for research alone who would have little value in Extension work, and some who are doing much to advance science that have little value in class work in college. These men ought to be in a place like Clark University at Worcester, where there are few students and the whole time is given up to research and production. There are other men who have in a pre-eminent degree the inspirational qualities that would make them specially valuable in Extension work, but who would be of little worth in research. The majority of college professors, however, by going out for Extension courses, will broaden their view by coming in contact with different students, and by following different methods, and will bring back to their college classes a freshness and breadth of treatment which they could not attain if they remained constantly in the academic ruts. Who can doubt that a professor who is in constant contact with classes which are giving their whole time to the study of a subject will be able to handle the Extension classes more successfully than one without this wide experience. Therefore, I insist that the colleges and the public will both get better teaching for their money if Extension and college work is done by the same men. A speaker just now urged that the public wanted lecturers with more of modern life and spirit than the dull, uninspiring college professor. Very well; but as representing officially the interests of the colleges of our great State, I want to say that the colleges object just as much as the public to these undesirable professors. If a man is not good enough to take charge of a class giving only a third its time to the study, he certainly is not good enough to have in charge men who at large expense are giving their entire time to college work. The fact is, that we wish to rid ourselves of the mediocre and inferior professor both in college and Extension work.

The college president says, "My faculty is already overworked; it is impossible for them to do any of this outside teaching." But this is one of the strongest reasons why the colleges should not allow the money for this outside teaching to flow into other channels. There is hardly a college in America which would not be improved if some, if not all, of its professors could limit themselves in teaching to fewer subjects or to fewer phases of one subject. Within a few days I have chanced on two specific illustrations of this point. Professor A—— said, "I am teaching both physics and natural history in our college, and my time is so crowded I cannot get an hour for anything else."

"Which subject do you prefer?"

"Physics; my interest is all in physics. I am teaching natural history simply because we haven't money to employ a professor in that subject. It is a burden that takes the time and strength I ought to use in developing my own specialty."

"What would be the effect if, instead of teaching natural history in the college, you could teach physics both in college and with Extension classes outside?"

"Why, I could do vastly better work for the college in physics, and should greatly prefer this method."

Then somewhere is another man in similar circumstances whose heart is in natural history, and who would be equally delighted if he could teach natural history both in college and in his Extension classes. The problem is, shall Prof. A. teach both subjects in college and Prof. B. teach both subjects with Extension classes, each of them prevented from doing his best work because his energies are divided and his time taken where no heart goes with it, or shall we put both men on the college faculty, greatly improving the college instruction in both subjects, and let both men do Extension work, improving that just as much. Both men are to be paid; the college has the money for its work, the Extension centres have the money for their work, and I can think of no greater folly than for the colleges to neglect this opportunity of strengthening and enlarging their faculties and taking into their treasuries the money which the public is ready to give for college instruction, which it prefers shall come from the established institutions, and not from a kind of higher education peddler who has no abiding place.

The same principle, I believe, is going to be extended among the colleges themselves. For instance, I know three colleges, no one of which can afford a full professor in economics, while each is very anxious to have one term's instruction in that subject, and, as it must appear on the curriculum, it is attached to some overworked chair and taught in a perfunctory way without inspiration or adequate results. The time is near when those three colleges will learn a lesson from business men, from organizers of trusts and combinations. Each will contribute one-third the salary, and together these colleges will employ a satisfactory professor of economics who will give a third of his year to each institution, and, by putting them on the right track and so inspiring them with an interest in the subject that they will continue to study it in after-years, will do more for the students of those colleges in a single term than would an inferior man in giving his whole time. The churches and the schools are beginning to learn that if they are to succeed in the great work before them, they must recognize the necessity of co-operation and organization, just as corporations and firms do in the business world, and I venture to predict that the colleges that recognize this principle, and even at the cost of temporary embarrassment meet the demands of the public for Extension teaching, will be the colleges that in ten or twenty years will have strengthened their faculty and forces, have increased their hold on the public, and have received in return ample funds with which to pay the expenses incurred by their broader conception of educational work and educational duty.

THE CITY AND UNIVERSITY EXTENSION.

BY SAMUEL WAGNER,

Chairman of Philadelphia Committee on Courses and Centres.

THE practical operations of University Extension in a city involve many interesting problems, upon the solution of which will depend very largely the permanent value and success of the whole movement; for it is in the cities that we must seek to establish those strong centres in organization and administration from which the work may extend to every part of the country. Especially is this the case in cities having one or more well-established institutions for higher education, for these are the storehouses of the food which is to be brought within reach of all the people. A brief consideration, therefore, of the best method to secure a good organization and thorough development of the work may not be amiss at a conference like this.

The question which confronts us is not so much the form of organization, for that is simple enough, but rather at what point in the development of the work organization on very clearly-defined lines should be adopted. There are two views of this question, both of which have many considerations of weight in their favor. One view is that complete organization should follow, and not precede, the development of the work,—that the movement should be allowed at first to have free play, that the formation of local centres should be encouraged at any and every point where there may be found those willing to undertake their establishment, and that it should be determined by actual experiment where local centres are really needed. The other view is based upon the converse of this proposition, that thorough organization, in the form which the work is ultimately to take, shall be adopted at the start, that the work in the whole city shall be mapped out in advance, and the location of local centres be determined with reference to the size and shape of the city and the supposed requirements of the people in each part of it.

As the object in view is very clearly defined, namely, that facilities shall be afforded to all the people of the city to secure continuous, graded, and systematic instruction in those branches which constitute the curriculum of a college course, the practical question is, how far each of these two views shall be adopted as a guide to reach that end. Let us sum up, briefly, what each has in its favor. As to the first, it may be said that it recognizes the fact that the University Extension movement, while strictly educational in its character and in its aims, is radically different, as regards the conditions surrounding it, from the systems of higher education with which we have heretofore been familiar. It is an *extension* of university teaching, and takes the shape of a co-operative movement, the co-operating parties being the people, on the one hand, and our universities and colleges on the other. These universities and colleges are great storehouses of learning, and aggregations of skilled teachers, and by means of this plan the facilities for liberal education are offered to all who wish to use them. It would seem to follow, therefore, that the people themselves should decide when and where this educational work should be done, and that local centres should be established by them in such places as they may demand them. Also, it may be said for this view that the scheme, being co-operative, should be protected in such a way that the people should feel resting upon them the obligation to do their share of the work, and this can best be effected by allowing the fullest freedom in the choice of location for local centres, and in the local management of them. On the other hand, the second of these views has to support it the well-recognized rule that all educational work should be done upon accurate and clearly-defined lines; that those who are to be taught are by no means the best judges of what they shall learn, or in what order they shall learn it; and it may well be urged that any departure from this rule would result in desultory and disjointed work, having no educational value.

Now, we have been engaged for the past year and more in working out this problem in Philadelphia, in the hope that in working it out here we shall be able to do so for the whole country. Under the conditions we have found existing here, the arguments for each of these views to which I have referred seem to be so conclusive that, upon careful reflection, I think they will be found in practice to be entirely in harmony, and not conflicting or divergent views. It will be found that the very character of the movement as an educational scheme will require the utmost freedom in its operations until such time as it shall be fairly and fully projected and its meaning and value impressed upon the minds of the people, and that, when this is accomplished, the strictest rules of educational work should be applied to it in order to give it real educational value. In Philadelphia, and within a circle with a radius of forty or fifty miles around it, there are now established and in operation nearly fifty local centres, formed by the people themselves in each locality. They have been organized with the encouragement of the American Society, and with its assistance in the way of information and advice, but they are all self-supporting. How many of them will become permanent centres for continuous and graded instruction has yet to be seen, but I think it is safe to say that a very considerable number of them will. In the mean time, every one of them is, in deed as well as in name, a centre for proclaiming the good news of University Extension, and every student, at every centre, is a missionary in the cause. So great, in the aggregate, is the number of earnest students, that there is every reason to feel assured that, in the near future, a great many of these centres will undertake and carry on successfully continuous, systematic, and graded work. The American Society is preparing, under the direction of the best experts, outlines and details of complete courses for continuous and graded instruction, and I think it is safe to say, in advance, that a certificate of the Society that a student has successfully pursued any one of these courses will be entitled to the same respect as if the course had been pursued at a university or college.

So far as we have gone, therefore, the conclusion as to the lines on which University Extension work in the city should be conducted would seem to be this: to make the subject known to every inhabitant of the city, and arouse interest and enthusiasm in it in every possible way; to let the movement have free play, and encourage and assist in the formation of a local centre whenever there may be found people ready and willing to form one; to encourage, in every possible way, the establishment of continuous courses giving complete instruction in each particular subject; and, unless all the signs of the movement at its present stage are very misleading, assuredly it will follow that out of all this eager desire of the people already so clearly made manifest, there will come a well-organized and thorough system of liberal education, within the reach of every man and woman in the country.

THE DEVELOPMENT OF UNIVERSITY EXTENSION.

BY MICHAEL E. SADLER,

Secretary to the Oxford Delegacy for University Extension.

No friend of University Extension can visit America without watching with interest and admiration the energy with which the movement has been carried on in this country; and those of us who are engaged in promoting the system in England will derive much benefit from the experiments which you are making, and stimulus from the enthusiasm with which you are developing the system. An earlier speaker at this conference has asked whether, after all, University Extension will enjoy more than a transient popularity, whether it is anything more than a novelty of merely passing interest. The long history of the movement seems to me to allay all suspicion as to its permanence. Its development has been natural, and part of a larger movement in University life.

In the middle ages, we find that large numbers of students flocked to the great Universities from all parts of Europe. Rich and poor, gentle and simple, these students passed along the public highways to the great centres of learning, and so destitute were many of them that we find in the English statute-books old laws empowering University students to beg for their subsistence. But the invention of the printing-press and the diffusion of books made the attendance of large numbers of these poor students at the Universities comparatively unnecessary. Instead of the learner having necessarily to come to the teacher in order to realize his hope of obtaining knowledge, it became more economical to send to the pupil the printed works of his distant teacher. A third stage was, however, reached when it was discovered that, as for almost all learners, books alone are inade-

quate instruments of culture, the pupil needs the stimulus of the living teacher to rouse his interest in the printed book. The development of the railway system at length made possible the widest diffusion of the two elements of the highest instruction, namely, the book and the instructor of the book. Railroads enable us to extend the privileges of the most inspiring instruction to a wider circle of students than in the early days of imperfect communication could enjoy these educational advantages.

Turning to another chain of changes in University development, we find that in its earlier days Oxford suffered from the somewhat indiscriminate attendance of students, old and young. William of Wykeham took, however, the important step of relieving the University from the attendance of young scholars by establishing in connection with his new college at Oxford a subsidiary college at Winchester, where the lads intended for subsequent University training might obtain the elements of learning. It is significant that this first movement for University Extension, which aimed at the establishment, in connection with the University, of a training or preparatory college in another town, was in itself a part of the movement for University intension. The college at Winchester was designed by William of Wykeham, both to extend the influence of the University, and to relieve the latter institution from certain branches of teaching which were more appropriately done outside, and it is to be noticed that the later movement for University Extension has been similarly accompanied by a concentration and development of the higher studies within the University itself. The movements of University Extension and University intension are concurrent elements in the history of the University. As the University becomes more sensible of its duties towards extra-mural students, so also it becomes more sensitive to the claims of those higher studies which it is its noblest privilege to prosecute. Both movements, in short, are signs of a quickening of University life, a sensitiveness to two related duties, an aspiration towards a higher and more perfect efficiency. And by itself superintending the wider diffusion of knowledge, a University familiarizes the public with the idea of, and so protects the higher interests of, research.

The movement for University reform began, so far as Oxford is concerned, towards the close of the last century, when the efforts of a few eminent graduates, notably of Dean Jackson, of Christ Church, and Provost Eveleigh, of Oriel College, were directed towards raising the University from the slough of intellectual despond into which it had previously fallen. The introduction of the system of examination for an Honor Degree roused the energy of the best students. This great change was followed by the purifying of the social life of the University, a change honorably associated with the famous Oxford Movement, the great leaders of which were John Henry Newman and his contemporaries. Thus quickened, the University became sensitive to the claims of further duties, and the middle of the present century saw the abolition of the chief of those religious tests which had shut out from the University much of the best life of England. The influx of new blood into the University system, due to this great change, naturally led to a still further awakening to the educational responsibilities of a national University, and there followed within a few years efforts, on the part both of Oxford and of Cambridge, to raise the standard of education in the schools of the country, by sending out accredited examiners whose duty it was to test the results of instruction in any schools voluntarily submitting themselves to this test. This, as Mr. James Stuart has said, was the first step in the later movement of University Extension. For the first time, the University thus recognized its duty towards students who, technically, were not members of its own body, and postal facilities were the material agency which permitted the new effort.

In 1872, the University of Cambridge, to its lasting honor, took a still further step along the road of educational reform, when, at the instance of Mr. James Stuart, it offered to supply the towns of England with capable instructors in the various departments of knowledge under the supervision and with the sanction of the University itself. Just as postal facilities enabled the University to introduce local examinations, so the new railway facilities enabled the University to establish local lectures, and thus the University Extension system, as we now know it, was begun. It began, as it were, by accident. Mr. James Stuart was invited to deliver some courses of lectures to an audience of women teachers in the north of England. In his private capacity as a University graduate, he accepted the invitation. The first lecture was a success, but the young teacher found himself so embarrassed by having to address a large audience consisting entirely of women, that, in lieu of the catechetical instruction which he had designed as a supplement to the lecture, he suggested to the students that they should write him exercises, and send these essays by post to him at Cambridge. Thus was invented that important element in the University Extension system,—the essay. A second feature in this method of instruction, the syllabus, was imitated by Mr. Stuart from the methods of Professor Ferrier, of St. Andrews. The popularity of Mr. Stuart's first lectures induced a working-men's co-operative society at Rochdale to ask him to address its members. He chose a scientific subject. At the end of his first lecture, some workingmen in the audience asked him to leave the diagrams, with which he had illustrated his discourse, on the walls of the lecture-room until his return to Rochdale, in order that they might explain their meaning to a number of fellow-artisans who had not been able to be present at the first lecture of the course. He acceded to their request, and offered to come to the second lecture before the appointed time, in order to meet for purposes of informal discussion those who wished to talk over the substance of the first discourse. Thus he stumbled upon the principle of "the class" which has ever since been regarded as an essential element in the University Extension system. The development of University Extension was thus essentially practical. Each feature in the system was suggested by practical needs and tested by practical experience. A little later the University of Cambridge officially recognized the efforts of Mr. Stuart and his colleagues; and, after a period of protracted effort, during which Mr. R. G. Moulton rendered invaluable service to the new movement, the system was established as a permanent feature in English education. There followed in London a successful attempt to found a Society for the Extension of University Teaching in the metropolis, and this association, which has played a distinguished part in the history of the movement, owed much to the zeal of Mr. Goschen, now Chancellor of the Exchequer, and to the efforts of its successive secretaries, Mr. E. T. Cook, Mr. Myers, and Dr. R. D. Roberts, the latter of whom has devoted many years to the cause of University Extension.

In 1878, the University of Oxford entered the field, its adhesion to the movement being largely due to the efforts of Professor T. H. Green and Professor Jowett. Not much, however, was done in the University of Oxford until 1885, when its work was revived through the instrumentality of Dr. Percival and of Mr. Arthur Acland, who were aided by the posthumous influence of Mr. Arnold Toynbee, himself an earnest advocate of University Extension. At the present time every University in England is engaged in the work. During the present winter, not less than sixty thousand different persons are attending the lectures. Of these about fifteen thousand are writing papers for the lecturers, about five thousand will probably enter for the final examinations held at the conclusion of the course, and about three thousand will obtain certificates. Several hundred centres of University teaching have been established by the spontaneous efforts and at the expense of local committees, working in almost every district of the country, and comprising almost every element in English life.

The official recognition of this movement by the Universities is of fundamental importance. Their cordial acceptance of its principles has been accompanied by an increasing devotion to the claims of the highest research. The same activity which shows itself in one direction in the diffusion of learning, shows itself in another direction in the accumulation of knowledge, both are phenomena of quickened life, both testify to the increasing activity of the Universities in the discharge of different but equally appropriate duties.

In the earlier stages of the work, perhaps one of the greatest dangers is a certain jealousy between various University bodies, but jealous rivalry is soon converted into generous emulation by intercourse in friendly conference and by the recognition of the width of the new field of educational effort into which the Universities are entering.

Great, however, as the success has been of the work in which we are interested, it is still in the stage where doctrinaire criticism assails it. And our frankest critics press three questions upon us. Who are the students, they ask, for whose benefit good teaching is provided? Next, granting that you find students, is it after all worth while taking trouble to supply them with higher education? In the third place, assuming that it is worth while, are the Universities the right bodies to essay the supply of it?

Each of these questions implies more than appears on the surface. Those who ask the first question often mean that any student who is sincerely anxious for higher education can get it already; that public schools and colleges exist in bountiful profusion; that no man or woman need perish of intellectual starvation in a country where books are cheap, newspapers and magazines widely circulated, public libraries efficient and plentiful; that you can pauperize a people by heedless bounty in teaching as easily as by indiscriminate distribution of alms; and that by making educational opportunities of too easy attainment, you may cut the nerve of energy and self-help which are saving graces in the affairs of mind as in the affairs of business.

Those again who ask whether it is worth while straining every nerve to diffuse higher education mean by their question to suggest the doubt whether the nobler kinds of culture can ever become matters of common currency; whether there is not one education, as the Greeks said there was one aphrodite of heaven and another of the market-place; whether the problems with which higher education deals,—problems of history, of criticism, of philosophy, of evidence,—can profitably be discussed by those who lack preparative training, or assimilated by minds which are biassed by ingrained preconceptions; whether the attempt to popularize culture may not merely multiply prigs or spread superficial accomplishments as a veneer over once-healthy ignorance, or breed discontent with hard lots, or add fuel to revolutionary indigestion; whether it is prudent to vulgarize the vision of the higher learning; whether by increasing book-learning you will destroy the originality of mother-wit as in Britain the village school-masters are scolding the historic dialects out of the remotest villages; and whether there is any foundation for the old idea that by educating one generation you are storing up accumulations of refinement which will be transmitted, as a sort of educational capital, for the outset and outfit of the next.

And those who ask whether, if it be granted that the diffusion of higher teaching is desirable, the Universities are the right bodies to undertake such diffusion, mean by their question that a University exists to protect and to increase the highest learning, to accumulate rather then to distribute, to investigate rather than to popularize, to save rather than to spend, to specialize rather than to edify; that they are the factories of learning rather than the salesmen of it, or, if salesmen at all, dealing only in a wholesale way of business and recognizing as their customers only the advanced students or teachers, whose function in turn it is to pass over the fruit of their education to the wider circle which lies beyond them. The University, it is hinted, exists in its true capacity for research, not for the reproduction of knowledge in attractive forms; it has a mission, but not to be an intellectual missionary. If you associate it in the public mind with the idea of popularization, the time will come when the ignorant crowd will refuse to recognize its truer, though now secret, function of knowledge-making, and when the professors, wearied out of the claims of perhaps distant popular audiences, will begin to neglect their more essential but less prominent duty of patient investigation, forsaking the nobler but more private task of research for the emptier but more ingratiating pursuit of public exposition. They would remind us of Cardinal Newman's words, that "to discourse and to teach are distinct functions; that they are distinct gifts and not commonly found united in one person; that he who spends his day in dispensing his existing knowledge is unlikely to have either leisure or energy to acquire new." In short, that the proper division of labor assigns one function to the public lecturer and to the University another, and that to seek to unite those separate functions in one man or staff of men is to retrogress in intellectual economy. Moreover, that a University is dedicated to a liberal education, while the public task is for useful training, and that therefore for the University to seek directly to save the public is to sacrifice for immediate and more vulgar results what is priceless in distant or fruitful consequences.

These are the arguments which it is for us to meet. They can be met, and met triumphantly, but it would be a mistake to despise or ignore them, to pass them over as prejudices, or to scorn them as selfishness.

Happily, however, we are not compelled to meet *a priori* criticisms by merely *a priori* answers. We can turn to facts, and the facts are on our side. The students are there for any one to see and question them. They are numerous, grateful, enthusiastic. But, in all their variety, four special types of them appeal to our sympathy and justify our work. How many are there not whom sudden loss or harsh turn of fortune has deprived of the very privileges which we have enjoyed? who, on the very threshold of University life, have been called back by claims of domestic duty or stopped by sudden loss of means? To how many does not the very word "University" recall the bitterest act of renunciation, the giving up of the most cherished hopes? In how many lives has there not been some secret unselfishness which pushed aside, in deference to duty, the bright ambition of study, which sacrificed—though no one knew the bitter cost—the one chance of higher learning? Have we no pity, no help for these? Must the gate be always barred against *them*, the vision of knowledge be to *them* never more than a distant Pisgah view? Those in whose eyes you can still see regret, whose faces still bear the sign of "unhappy far-off things"?

Then, again, there are the vast numbers of busy people who cherish the desire of combining with the education of business the education of books. Those, too, welcome the stimulus and encouragement which lectures give, and need, in the midst of jostling engagements and other importunate claims of daily life, the punctual reminder of the weekly lecture-night. "Any one," said the venerable master of Baliol, "any one who regularly devotes half an hour a day to liberal studies, deserves to be called a student." But even so small a fraction of the solid day as this, —great as are the accumulated results of so brief a daily contribution, is with difficulty set aside by men and women whose lives have been for years, as some one put it once, "like an interrupted sentence." Day follows day without bringing the quiet breathing-spaces which we need to collect ourselves for study. Business cares leave a ground-swell of agitated thought behind them, and the waters of life never seem calm enough to mirror intellectual truth. What Sunday is to the religious life, the lecture-night may become to the intellectual, an orderly, appointed breathing-space set aside by practice for the duties of a liberal education.

And yet once more how eagerly those lectures have been attended by women anxious to equip themselves either for equal converse with cultivated people or for the better discharge of the duties involved in the education of children. The claim of women for higher teaching is one of the most significant features of our time. That claim it is our duty to satisfy, and these University lectures are one convenient method of meeting it. It is not given to every woman to go to college, and, even when college work is done, education, so far from being ended, is only just beginning. In a progressive age each generation is almost necessarily separated from its predecessors by some change in point of view. Our individual thoughts are all colored by the new generalizations, the new experience common to our contemporaries. Malthus's father thought with Godwin that all human failings were due to defects in human institutions; Malthus himself, growing up in the chill of the anti-revolutionary reaction, realized that much of human wretchedness was due to defects in human nature itself; men of our own time again are beginning to perceive that Malthus too much ignored the awakening or repressive influences of an eager or stolid environment. Steadily from generation to generation the normal temperature of thought rises or falls, and fathers and sons have to allow for one another's surroundings. But to do so implies sympathy enlightened by education, and involves the possession of an historic sense which does not come without knowledge of history. How many pitiful estrangements, how many harsh misunderstandings, have sprung from merely ignorant want of imagination? We need education, as well as filial tenderness, to bridge over the gulf which sometimes yawns between children and their fathers, and the mother, equipped by education, may become the interpreter of the son to his father and of the father to his son.

But behind all these lie the great mass of the people, tired by the day's work, fagged by the insistent anxieties of bread-winning, and yet each year more directly charged with the ultimate settlement of great problems, each year feeling a greater need for knowledge and for the judgment which comes from knowledge. Pericles, speaking of the Athenian democracy, said that they regarded "the want of the knowledge gained by discussion preparatory to taking action the great impediment to (wise political) conduct." Just as Wesley and Whitefield spread the knowledge of religious truth among the miners and laborers of England, and so steadied the national character before it entered the exciting period of the industrial revolution, so we need others, imitating their devotion, to diffuse civic wisdom among the wage-earners and workmen of civilized countries as a preparation for the anxious period of sound adjustment, of the coming of which the signs may be even now discerned. "A cultivated intellect, a delicate taste, a candid, equitable, dispassionate mind, a noble and lustrous bearing in the conduct of life." These are by no iron law of necessity the prerogative of any one section of the community. The riches which they represent may be diffused in generous measure throughout a nation, and, as Newman said, being "the objects of a University," they are therefore the probable results of a full extension of its work. True as it is that profuse and heedless almsgiving may be hurtful, methods of wise charity need commending by the very persons who would be its most desirable recipients. The danger of pauperizing people does not justify us in keeping our pockets always buttoned up. And no offer is less likely to slacken the energies of a people than the provision of noble teaching, for it is of the essence of learning that it cannot be obtained without the exertion, toil, and attention of the student co-operating with that of the teachers. You cannot stuff men with culture as they stuff Strasburg geese.

Similar reflections are aroused by the second kind of criticism, namely, the question whether, even if the students attend our lectures, it is worth while seeking to furnish them with higher education. No one pretends that every busy man or woman can become a mine of learning. Cultivation of the mind, however, is not to be measured by mere volume of attainment, but by the mental temper and attitude of the student. We may not be able to make our students experts in obscure readings of the classical texts or authorities on Greek inscriptions; but we *can* make them appreciate the poetical beauties of the Athenian drama and conscious of the pregnant significance of classical history. They may not care for the niceties of criticism or for the disentanglement of the involved sentences of Thucydides; but they can be brought to share in the scholar's enthusiasm for Æschylus and Sophocles, to treasure the memory of Pericles, to know the serene philosophy of Plato. For them, too, the glories of the Renaissance may be revealed. The eternal antithesis between the Puritan and the Greek ideal has its open lessons for them as well as for us; Homer, Dante, Shakespeare, Goethe need not be the private possessions of a few, but may become the intellectual treasuries of the people. Pedantry is the vice of an exclusive knowledge rather than of broad and human culture. It would be a false antithesis which made pedantry and superficiality the necessary alternatives. We do not propose to diffuse either. The vain conceit of intricate but narrow knowledge is as far removed as the impertinence of shallow smattering from our ideal of a liberal education which, in becoming popular, need not cease to be liberal. The actual volume of a man's knowledge matters little as compared with the way in which he carries it. It is the quality not the quantity of it that is of vital concern. The effect on his judgment, on his powers of observation and comparison, is what we have chiefly to think of in providing higher education for the people.

Nor will such education blunt originality. As Sir Joshua Reynolds told the students of the Royal Academy a hundred winters ago, "A mind enriched by an assemblage of all the treasures of ancient and modern art will be more elevated and fruitful in resources in proportion to the number of ideas which it has carefully collected and thoroughly digested. . . . There can be no doubt," he adds, "but that he who has the most materials has the greatest means of invention. . . . The addition of other men's judgment is so far from weakening our own that it will fashion and consolidate those ideas of excellence which lay in embryo, feeble, ill-shaped, and confused." "The mind is but a barren soil," again to quote Sir Joshua, "and it will produce no crop, or only one, unless it be continually fertilized and enriched with foreign matter."

So far, indeed, from its being not worth while for us to diffuse the higher education, it is our duty to do so for the economic, the solid, and the religious welfare of our country. Considering only the remotest ends of material welfare, we cannot afford to waste genius, or even talent. We need, to use Professor Huxley's phrase, "capacity catchers." We must leave, as Mr. Ruskin said, no Giotto among the hill-shepherds. Who knows what potter's son may be a Wedgwood, what butcher's son a Wolsey, what barber's lad a Richard Arkwright, what engine-fireman a Robert Stephenson. And for one man of genius who forces his way to eminence and public service, how many are not done to death in the struggle for recognition and for training. Chatterton was sent home from school as a fool of whom nothing could be made; Clive was shipped off to India as a scapegrace; Sir Walter Scott's professor dubbed him dunce, and said that dunce he would remain. Genius is democratic, and we must seek to find, to guard, to help it in both high and lowly places. To do this we need many agencies, but few are more suited to our hand than University Extension. Its teachers will penetrate everywhere and may reach everybody. The two best essays which reached me in a recent competition came from a duke's family and a village billiard-marker. This is a typical result which follows from greater equalization of intellectual opportunity.

Nor is the social advantage of our movement less than its economic. What greater bond has attached to one another the members of the English-speaking race than the love of their common Bible? What stronger tie is there between strangers than the associations of our native region, common memories of a common home? In the same way we may promote the unity of a people by giving it a common background of great thought, a joint and conscious inheritance in one intellectual birthright. St. Simon pointed out how inventors were aided by a class of popularizers. They help the public to understand and appreciate inventions. Far more might a staff of brilliant lecturers enable a nation to enter into the enjoyment of its intellectual heritage, too often ignored or forgotten. In an age when, as Emerson said,

"Things are in the saddle
And ride mankind,"

we need organized protests on behalf of a spiritual, as distinct from a material, ideal of life. Too many men are apt to say of literature and history what Locke said of Latin verse-making, that "it is very seldom seen that any one discovers mines of gold or silver on Parnassus. 'Tis a pleasant air, but a barren soil." Locke forgot that the common passion for these bare mountains and native air have often fired the patriotism of heroic peoples, but the Parnassus of culture is a vineyard on a fruitful hill. And the effects of culture may, as Sir Joshua Reynolds said of art, "extend themselves imperceptibly into public benefits, and be one of the means of bestowing on whole nations refinement of taste; which, if it does not lead directly to purity of manners, obviates at least their greatest depravation by disentangling the mind from appetite and conducting the thoughts through successive stages of excellence, to be that contemplation of universal rectitude and harmony which begun by Task may, as it is exalted or refined, conclude in Virtue."

Nor, even if the education of one generation does not lead to the transmission of acquired aptitude to its successors, does it therefore follow that we are not, by diffusing education, improving the character and talents of our descendants. For an educated nation permanently improves its own surroundings, and the pressure and stimulus of those improved surroundings may educe the hidden potentialities of men and women yet unborn, and rouse into activity secret gifts and powers which, in a less favorable environment, would have perished before development. The ideal of University Extension is the ideal of Plato, who would have so placed the citizens of his ideal commonwealth that their "young men, dwelling as it were in a healthful region, might drink in good from every quarter whence any emanation from noble works might strike upon their eye or ear like healthful breezes from salubrious lands, and win them imperceptibly from their earliest childhood into love of, and into harmony with, the true beauty of reason."

And, as the work of diffusing higher education is thus of supreme and national importance, it is one which the Universities, if they have the means at their disposal, are called upon directly or indirectly, singly or in concert, to push forward and promote. For they are the true leaders of educational progress. The truest culture is not exclusive. For if the pleasures and benefits of culture are such that their diffusion in proper measure is impossible, the time may well be coming of which it was foretold that "the prophet shall be ashamed of every one of his visions." But the essence of true culture can be diffused and in due season will be; just as the Celtic drama was once the means of public inspiration; just as was the great picture of Cimabue which the Florentine citizens bore from the painter's house to the Church of St. Maria Novella with such gladness that the quarter of the city through which they passed was afterwards called the Joyful Quarter; just as were the carvings which Giotto set round the base of his famous tower, and just as were the masterpieces of the French and English builders in the twelfth and thirteenth centuries.

But to diffuse higher education you need something more than books; you need men with strong personalities to expound the books; you need not only a library, but a guide to the library. Now, what bodies can command more readily or train more easily the right kind of guide than the Universities which receive and educate the young men and young women of the country? Either from among their own graduates, or by the exercise of their ready access to men of ability everywhere, which is a privilege of their position, they are able to find and provide the very kind of teachers which the public need. A University can equip two staffs of teachers; one for its own internal duties of research or specialized instruction; a second for the different but not less honorable service of diffusing the results of such instruction or research. There need be no overwork, no unwise confusion of function. It is rather a wise division of labor for which we ask. And just as private munificence or public aid support the internal teachers of a University, so will individual liberality or public contribution maintain those who are engaged in its extra-mural work.

Anything which separates the Universities from the public is to be deplored. But happily such separation is becoming every day more impossible. The University Extension lecturer is bringing into relation with University life large numbers of teachers, of women and of workingmen, all of whom long for the stimulus of higher instruction, but have hitherto been practically outside the pale of University influence. The attendance of elementary teachers at the University Extension lectures in England is the most encouraging. University courses are being made a part of the curriculum of several Normal Colleges. The Inspectors of Schools recommend teachers to attend University Extension classes, and, at our Oxford summer meeting, the central idea of which we consciously imitated from the successful Assembly at Chautauqua, a considerable number of elementary teachers enjoy a brief period of University life by means of small scholarships offered by friends of the movement. It is, however, among workingmen that perhaps the most striking results of University Extension have been seen. For four years at Oldham in Lincoln, six hundred artisans have attended the lectures on historical subjects delivered by Mr. Hudson Shaw. The zeal shown by these workingmen is remarkable. The lecture begins at seven o'clock, is followed by an animated class and brisk discussion, and closes only at a somewhat late hour. For three years artisans from Manchester have come to reside in Oxford during August for a brief period of study, and there have been few more touching episodes in University life than the company of these Manchester artisans gathered under the shadow of the spire of John Henry Newman's church, living in under-graduates rooms, studying in the University buildings, reading in the University libraries, and meeting morning and evening in the College chapel as members of the collegiate community. In different parts of the country, farmers, potters, masons, and weavers attend these lectures, some of them walking at the end of their day's work as many as five miles to attend the lecture. Dr. Roberts, in his book on University Extension, has told some pathetic tales of the enthusiasm of the Northumberland miners; and one of these students has written to Miss Gardner, of the American Society, a remarkable tribute to the moral and intellectual influence of University Extension teaching as established in his district by the University of Cambridge : *

". . . Do you ever get a thoroughly ignorant man interested in University Extension?

" In reply to this I may say that thorough ignorance is rather a misnomer in these days of Board schools and compulsory education. Twenty or thirty years ago, thoroughly ignorant men might be found in scores among the miners, but in this generation every miner's son has the opportunity of getting the elements of education, which he may or may not increase as he gets older. There is a sense, however, in which your question may be understood as applying to the miners of to-day. A number of boys, after they leave school, and commence work at the mines, easily forget nearly all they have learned, and only retain sufficient ability to write their name, or labor through the pages of a book. These, I think, although not thoroughly, may be termed ignorant men. I will, therefore, understand your question as applying to these. When I had the pleasure of seeing you at Backworth, I mentioned one or two that I thought might belong to that category. A better instance has, however, recently come under my notice. We are at present having a course of lectures on 'The Problems of Life and Health,'

---

* Cf. *University Extension*, December, 1891, p. 187.

with special reference to sanitation. The subject is an interesting one, and has provoked a good deal of discussion. At the beginning of the lectures two of the miners, at the mine at which I work, bought two tickets for the course. One of them I knew to be a very intelligent man, and he has supplied me with some interesting facts concerning his companion. He says that when he first knew him he was a dissolute, degraded man, caring for nothing but drink, gambling, fighting, and every other thing that belongs to an evil life. They lived near to each other, and occasionally had some conversation. By and by they took walks together, and questions of interest were discussed in a simple way. One by one he dropped off his evil habits and sought the society of his intelligent friend. He abandoned drink and devoted his money to the purchasing of books. He took every means that was likely to afford him information, and sought knowledge wherever it was to be fonnd. And now he is a student at the present course of lectures, and has already earned first-class marks for his exercises. This I think is a typical instance of what you require, and when I tell you that this man travels a distance of over five miles every Saturday evening in order to attend the lectures, and often does his exercises after a hard day's work at the mine, you will readily understand how keen is the interest which has been aroused. . . ."

This is going far towards the reconciliation of culture and labor. It is significant that among our English University Extension students are counted a princess near the throne and an Oxford chimney-sweep.

Another encouraging feature of our work is the steady rise in the quality and attainments of the audiences. Each year we notice that the students at well-established centres attend more regularly at the lectures and classes, write better essays, and reach a higher standard in the final examinations. The value of the certificates awarded in these examinations is also becoming more generally recognized. At Oxford the standard required for a "pass" certificate is that which has to be reached by an undergraduate in answering the questions set in an examination for a "pass" degree; in order to obtain a "certificate of distinction," the student must write a paper of such a quality as would entitle that paper to be accepted in one of the final examinations for Honors in the University. It should be pointed out, however, that, whereas the candidate for Honors in the University has to write ten or twelve papers, the University student generally does only one. But the standard required in the two examinations is *pro tanto* the same. It is natural, therefore, that employers should be increasingly willing to regard the possession of a University Extension certificate as a recommendation when presented by an applicant for some appointment; that teachers should seek to obtain these certificates in order to improve their qualification; and that some of the best schools in the country should include University Extension courses in their curriculum. Mr. Hudson Shaw, for example, has lectured this autumn at Rugby School on one day, and on another to the workingmen of Oldham; and Mr. Mackinder, who with Mr. Shaw has done so much to advance the University Extension movement, has visited during the same term one of the greatest schools in the country and other centres where his audiences' consisted largely of elementary teachers and artisans.

It must be admitted, however, that in the early years of the history of each centre, much remains to be desired in point of sequence of studies. History is apt to follow literature, and science history without much regard for strict connection of subject-matter. But we must remember that there are two kinds of sequence—sequence of good teachers and sequence of the subjects taught. When a centre is new and weak, the first kind of sequence is often of more practical importance than the second, and if any one of us looks back on the landmarks of his own intellectual life, shall we not find that the influences which in turn have affected us have often been wanting in any formal sequence of educational development. We are now, however, succeeding in gradually remedying this want of sequence in University Extension work, and much has been done by the arrangement of the courses of study at our summer meeting in cycles extending over four years.

I desire to say a few words as to the formal relation between the Universities and the University Extension movement. It is of essential importance to the success of our work that the Universities should either directly or indirectly take a formal part in it. At the beginning of the work especially, the aid of the college professors is extremely valuable; but many of these professors are overworked men, who cannot permanently undertake a large increase in their educational duties. Where this is the case, no one can rightly expect that they will be able permanently to take a large share of the work. Under their guidance, however, a special staff of teachers may soon rise, as has already been the case in England, for the discharge of this important duty of University Extension teaching. But it is important that these teachers should be in official and accredited connection with the Universities and the faculties of higher teachers, for, as Sir Joshua Reynolds has said, "Every seminary of learning is surrounded with an atmosphere of knowledge where every mind may imbibe something congenial to its own original conceptions. Knowledge thus obtained has always something more useful than that which is forced on the mind by solitary meditation." In other words, we desire, through the University Extension movement, to extend the spirit of each University taking part in the work.

And the discharge of its duties towards University Extension reacts favorably on the University itself. It makes the academic mind recognize more clearly than before the intellectual importance of business ability. It provides for the academic economist easy access to those scenes of industrial activity which are the laboratories of economic study; and it encourages and helps those who desire to see in University life a combination of plain living and high thinking.

Our aim, however, in University Extension is not intellectual communism, but the greater equalization of intellectual opportunity. And our experience in England leads us to appreciate the importance and the value of such an association as the American Society for the Extension of University teaching. Such a society is able to provide a bureau of information on University Extension matters. It can secure lecturers and retain the services of promising graduates. It can also gradually accumulate an endowment which will be required for the higher development of University Extension teaching, as well as for that of other kinds of higher education. We need in University Extension a millionaire, and the chance is now offered to a man of wealth to associate his name forever with the history of one of the most striking educational movements of our century.

A difficulty which is pressing upon us in England is the best means of recognizing the attainments of the most advanced University Extension students. To most of us, it appears in the highest degree undesirable to offer the same grade or degree to a student who has resided in a college as to one who has only attended University Extension courses. But it is clear that the latter will, before long, emulate the former both in the extent of his studies and in the standard of his intellectual attainment. What, then, should be the recognition given to such a student by the University? In my own judgment, it will be possible for a group of Universities to go further in recognizing the merits of the best University Extension students than would be possible for any single University acting on its own account. Is it, therefore, out of the question that a number of Universities might unite to offer, under strict provisions and on specified and arduous conditions, a special diploma to such University Extension students as might, after attending a long series of graded courses, pass a searching examination with credit? If such a group of Universities were formed and were found to comprise the leading institutions of higher learning in America, in England, and in Australia, such a diploma, as that at which I hint, might become the symbol of the intellectual federation of the English-speaking world.

REMARKS.

IN reply to the questions addressed to him by members of the Conference, Mr. Sadler explained that in the Oxford branch of the Extension system no student was allowed to enter for the final examination on any course unless he had qualified himself by attending not less than two-thirds of the lectures and classes of the course, and by writing, to the lecturer's satisfaction, not less than two-thirds of the weekly essays. The final examination paper was set by a member of the University appointed by the delegates, but, in accordance with English methods, the lecturer never conducted the final examination on his own course. The examiners were instructed by the delegates to require, from all candidates receiving a *Pass* certificate, the quality of work which would be required from a candidate in any one of the final *Pass* examinations for the degree of B. A. in the University. For the higher certificates of distinction, the Examiners were instructed to require work which, if done in one of the final University Honor examinations, would *pro tanto* entitle the writer to Honors. But Mr. Sadler pointed out that, whereas a candidate in the final Honor Schools of the University was required to reach this Honor standard in at least eight papers out of twelve or fourteen, the University Extension student had only to do one paper on each course. The time allowed for the final examination on each course was three hours. Certificates were permitted by the University only after courses of twelve lectures and classes. Examinations were allowed on courses of not less than six lectures and classes, but, in lieu of certificates, successful candidates received printed statements of the Examiners' award. In answer to other questions, Mr. Sadler explained that about two-thirds of those attending the lectures in the centres were women. There was a slightly larger proportion of women among the students attending the summer meeting held in Oxford in August. He desired to take this opportunity of cordially acknowledging their obligations, in the arrangement of summer meetings, to various American summer schools, and especially to the Assembly at Chautauqua. The University Extension authorities in England warmly supported the work of Chautauqua and of the National Home-Reading Union, regarding it as preparative to University Extension teaching. With regard to the attendance of working-men, Mr. Sadler said that artisans came in large numbers to courses of lectures arranged for and paid for by themselves. But the cost of the lectures made it difficult for working-men in England to establish courses except through the agency of their own organizations. The working-men's Co-operative Societies, wealthy and useful associations, had done much for many years to further the cause of University Extension, and in several centres in the crowded districts of the North there had been large audiences of hundreds of working-men attending University Extension lectures with profit and sustained enthusiasm. Answering further questions, Mr. Sadler stated that the University of Oxford contributed £550 a year (two thousand seven hundred and fifty dollars) to the University Extension department, and, in addition to this, furnished many facilities in respect of printing and the provision of rooms for the summer meeting, etc.

President Fell, of St. John's College, Annapolis, Maryland, said:

Having personally participated in the earlier stages of the movement in England several years ago, and having witnessed the mode of its development in this country, I was for a long time very doubtful of its ultimate success in America. Great contrasts are presented to view to one who is intimately acquainted with the movement in each country. The rapidity with which it has spread in America is in striking contrast with the slowness of its progress in England. Again, the conditions of the public whom it is intended to benefit are distinctly different. In England a University education is for the most part possible only to the wealthy; consequently, outside of this class, there existed a large body of men and women who craved for the blessings of higher education. The democracy cried for culture. Here in America we have already a cultured democracy, and higher education is offered to all, is easy of access, and can be obtained for a slight cost. In England, the Universities of Oxford and Cambridge are in locations not easily accessible to the masses, so that it was necessary for the University to go to them in order to convey instruction; whereas in America we have in nearly every town or city, possessing twenty thousand inhabitants, a college or university offering higher education. We find, therefore, for the most part, as yet, that the Extension lectures have been attended by the cultured of both sexes, and not by the mass of artisans, trades-people, inferior school-teachers, and others, who petitioned so eagerly in England for higher education. And as a result of this a disposition is manifested on the part of those who attended such lectures in many centres to relax interest in a movement, which was merely responded to by them because it appeared an agreeable and novel mode of filling up time. It became a fashionable "fad." In order, therefore, to make a success of the movement, we must not be discouraged if the fervor aroused by a novelty appears to be on the wane, but a strong and united effort should be made by all institutions interested in the movement to adapt and present their methods of instruction to those who have not already enjoyed the benefits of higher education. Such an effort would then secure the success of the movement, the regular and continuous attendance of a class of students, and direct advantage for the institutions themselves.

Rev. Dr. William Wilberforce Newton, of Pittsfield, Mass., gave a short account of a small attempt made on the part of some of the churches among the Berkshire Hills, to reach the working-men in the mill-towns in that region by ten-cent readings on Saturday afternoons on various subjects in English literature. He showed great interest in the movement of University Extension, and expressed the conviction that it is opening a new field of activity for the energies of the Christian Church.

Mr. H. H. Hay, of the Girard College, thought that the colleges ought to lead the movement of University Extension, and inferred from the presence at the Conference of so many college presidents, that they were prepared to do so. He referred to the interest attaching to this system of teaching in its influence on working-men, and by a question gained from Mr. Sadler the information that a large number of the working-classes are following Extension courses in England, and that, out of sixteen hundred who presented themselves for examination, a fair percentage was of the working-people. In this connection Mr. Sadler quoted a special and crowning incident of a working-man, whose essay on Milton, by the beauty of its diction, called forth special praise of the examiners of the University. In response to a further question from a delegate as to how continuity in Extension work can be secured, Mr. Sadler answered that this is largely possible through an active Students' Association. The members of the Students' Club form the really permanent nucleus of an Extension centre, and are largely influential in the determination as to the choice of courses. Their interest is almost invariably in favor of well-ordered sequence in study, and through their efforts much has already been accomplished in this direction. There is, however, an abiding danger from those who, following Extension courses only as a means of amusement, desire a variety of subjects rather than a helpful following out of special lines of study.

Professor Edward H. Magill, of Swarthmore College, said:

MR. CHAIRMAN,—When the faculties of our colleges are criticised for not entering at once, and heartily, into the University Extension work, it must not be forgotten that the reason may not be any lack of sympathy with the movement, but because they are, in so many cases, already worked to the full extent of their ability. This difficulty was seriously considered at the recent meeting of the College Association, at Cornell University, where many of the leading colleges of "The Middle States and Maryland" were represented. We felt the great desirability of our doing our part in this work, and various means were suggested by which it might be rendered practicable. This, I am sure, will be found to be the general sentiment of the colleges, and I have no doubt that by some rearrangement of their work, and a readjustment of it secured by the appointment of some additional professors, or by training the young graduates or fellows to enter upon it, both universities and colleges will, in a few years, adapt themselves to the situation, and be taking that leading place in University Extension work throughout the world which should naturally fall to them. You may depend upon it that it is through no narrow principle of exclusiveness, and no unwillingness to assume all added burdens, that the public good may require, but simply that there is a limit to all human effort, that has kept, thus far, many college men aloof from University Extension work. We all well understand that such work, when it can possibly be undertaken, reacts for good upon the professor himself, and really makes him more valuable in his own college for the specific work in which he is there engaged. To this rule there will be found to be few exceptions, and they will grow fewer every year as the work advances.

Superintendent Charles D. Raine, of Mount Holly, N. J., said:

MR. CHAIRMAN,—Much has been said by persons connected with colleges and universities, but from the public-school teacher, the educator nearest to the so-called masses, nothing has been heard. University Extension is no doubt a good thing, containing possibilities for beneficial results. But, thus far, the effort to reach that great portion of the people whose opportunities for education and mental culture have been limited, has failed. And there are reasons for this. The average American citizen, especially the working-man, is intensely practical in his views and wishes. To engage in a project, he must be convinced that it will yield positive profit and benefit. Those sent out to organize centres often fail to show him the utility of the movement. Associating with persons of a considerable degree of education and cultivation of mind, and accustomed to instructing such, the lecturers naturally present the matter in a form appreciated only by persons of that class of society. It will not do to go before the people with heavy Johnsonese utterances, and a cold, formal, perfunctory manner, crushing and freezing them; nor will it do to send them a callow student,—a penny hand-glass dimly reflecting the thoughts, researches, and expressions of a superior. To make this movement a success, the lecturers must be teachers, true teachers, fully realizing that those they hope to benefit most have not learned to give voluntary attention to study and to literary subjects, as have students in a college or a university. The teaching should be interesting and instructive, imparted by earnest, enthusiastic teachers, in pungent, Saxon-worded speech, that will not only catch the attention involuntarily, but hold it, and inspire the listener to seek more light upon the subject. It has been said here that in a building used for University Extension purposes, the lecture-room should be on the ground-floor, and the library in the topmost story. I would not have it so. The library should be in the next room, side by side with the lecture-room, and the teaching should so sharpen perception, invite comparison, and develop thought, that, at the close, the library would at once be in demand to satisfy the hunger and thirst for more knowledge. Being made attractive, interesting, and instructive, the work, begun as a pleasure, will be pursued as a duty and esteemed a privilege. Then, and not till then, University Extension will benefit the people, improve our citizenship, and accomplish its aim.

THE UNIVERSITY EXTENSION LECTURER.

BY EDMUND J. JAMES, PH.D.,

President of The American Society.

It is, of course, an idle matter to spend time trying to decide which, of a number of elements in a given combination, is the more necessary when all of them are really essential. It is like trying to decide which is the more important part of a pair of shears. In this University Extension work, there are several elements, each of which, however insignificant it may appear, is at bottom really essential to produce the desired result. But, certainly, among them all, no one is of more fundamental importance than the University Extension lecturer himself, the man who actually does the work for which all the rest of the machinery exists, the man upon whom the successful working of the machinery depends to a larger extent, perhaps, than upon any other individual in the whole system, the man without whose continuous and devoted attention University Extension will accomplish but a very small portion of the sum total of the good which lies within its possibilities. So, while we cannot say that it is of more importance than any other element, yet it is certainly essential to the system. It naturally acquires a certain prominence in our consideration by the very numerous points of contact between it and all the rest of the work of the system. So, on this occasion, I feel that we can certainly well devote a very considerable portion of our time to a study of what the University Extension lecturer should be and what he should do.

We rely, in the first place, of course, upon the lecturer to prepare the course of lectures, to prepare the syllabus used in connection with it, to deliver the lectures, to prepare the questions for paper work, to set the lines along which the paper work must be done, to criticise the papers and, finally, to conduct for his part an examination of his own work. Let us then look first at the lecture itself. What should the University Extension lecture be? An analysis of the circumstances under which it is given, of the audience to which it is given, and of the results which may be fairly expected from it under favorable conditions, will give us at least some of the more important points to be considered in connection with it.

I think we may say, in the first place, that the University Extension lecture cannot be the sort of lecture which is given to college students. We may lay it down, I think, as a fundamental principle that the educational problem involved in University Extension is, at bottom, a very different one, after all, from that involved in university instruction itself; or, at least, that so many of the incidentals connected with it are so different from those connected with university instruction as to make it essentially a different thing. So fully has this been recognized by the more thoughtful men who have taken part in the University Extension movement and who have given thought to its possibilities and its circumstances that many of them have maintained that the expression University Extension, itself, is an entirely misleading one, and ought to be discarded for a more appropriate term. I shall not go so far as this, for I think the question of nomenclature, while having a certain importance, is not by any means fundamental. I think, moreover, that the term University Extension has acquired a certain right to be applied to this particular sort of education. And yet it may well be worth our while to call our attention to the fact that the problem after all is different from that involved in university instruction from several different aspects.

In the first place, the university lecturer who comes before an audience of university students knows what to presuppose in the way of previous training. He knows, pretty exactly, if he is a thoughtful and observant man, the general grade of maturity which has been reached by his audience. He knows what they have studied and how thoroughly, on the whole, they have pursued their studies, so that he is able to take up their education, so to speak, very directly and immediately where he finds it and to continue it in connection with the subject which he has in hand. The University Extension lecturer, on the other hand, has a very different condition of things to meet, in this respect. His audience, while made up, as a rule, of people who are interested in the work and are interested in improving themselves intellectually and æsthetically, is yet a mixed audience. It consists of people of various ages, of old and young, of people of different sexes, and, often, of different nationalities, and, what is more important than all, of people of very different degrees of education and training. The University Extension lecturer, therefore, can suppose, one might almost say, next to nothing in regard to the knowledge and training of his audience. He is in very much the same position as the clergyman who comes before audiences made up on very much the same lines as those of the University Extension lecturer; and certainly no one who has studied the problem would doubt, for a moment, that the clergyman's problem, so far as it is educational, is fundamentally a different one from that of the university professor. Those of you who have busied yourselves especially with the pedagogics of college and university courses, are fully aware how carefully and closely, as a result of centuries of development, our educational system has been knitted together. You will very often hear a professor, for example, say it is impossible to teach Greek to a boy who has not studied Latin. You will hear a professor of Assyriology say it is impossible to teach Assyrian to a boy who has not studied Hebrew. What he means, of course, at bottom, is not that it is actually impossible to do so, but that he, by his whole training and by his whole previous education as a pupil and a student and a teacher, has got thoroughly into the habit, in his presentation of Greek and Assyrian, of presupposing a knowledge of Latin and of Hebrew. So, it has not been so very long since men maintained that, in order to teach English literature, a knowledge of Latin and Greek, on the part of the people, was essential; and, of course, to a certain method of teaching, that is undoubtedly necessary and, perhaps, to accomplish certain specific results in the widest and broadest sense it may always be necessary; but no one would claim that English literature, to-day, cannot be taught and well taught to people who have little or no knowledge of the classical languages. Now, if university and college men find it so difficult to adapt one or another element of the traditional curriculum to some other condition than traditional conditions, how much more difficult the problem, and how different, in some respects, must the problem be, when he is thrown entirely out of these ruts and placed face to face with the pressing problem as to what he can do, from an educational point of view, with an audience in regard to whose training and scholarship he can make none of these presuppositions, to which he has always been used in the case of college students.

There is another condition to my mind almost as important as that which I have just described, and which serves to distinguish very particularly the possibilities of the work in University Extension from those in college and university work itself, and that is the length of time at the disposal of the university lecturer and the University Extension lecturer respectively to produce their various impressions. Real education is a result of time as well as of effort. The time element in education is almost as important, if not quite as important, as in economics; where it forms the fundamental element in the conception of capital. You cannot secure culture and training, you cannot secure those specific things which we connect with the idea of a liberal education within a brief period, no matter how great the effort the individual may put forth. It takes time, in other words, to educate the human being. It takes time to educate and discipline along intellectual and æsthetic as well as along moral lines. Not even the warmest believer and adherent of the momentary and sudden revolution in character which may come from religious conversion has ever maintained that anything more can be accomplished than a mere facing about of the individual, a turning of the mind and thought and action from one direction to another. Moral culture can only come as the result of time, of long-continued as well as of vigorous effort. So the university man has, under ordinary conditions, certainly in our modern institutions of learning, whatever may be true of their English counterparts, a certain length of time, a certain period, during which he has his audience directly and immediately under his control. If he does not succeed in making an impression the first hour, he can take the second hour to present the same thought in a different way. He may take a third hour, if necessary. If he does not succeed in doing in it one week, he can take a second week or a third week. If he does not accomplish it in one month, he can take a second month or a third, or even a fourth or fifth. He can make a study, to a certain extent, of the individual students he has before him and with whom he comes in contact and adapt his work, to a certain extent, to the wants of individual members of his class. The University Extension lecturer has not the same advantage. He can meet his audience for a dozen times, or, as experience shows, perhaps twice that often, in a given subject within a given year; but experience, both in England and in this country, shows that we cannot hope to get hold of the same audience on the average for more than a dozen times for the presentation of a certain subject; or, under very favorable conditions, for more than twenty-four or twenty-five times. The cases in which more than this can be accomplished, at least at present, are rare, and I am inclined to think, from my observation of the circumstances, are likely to continue to be rare for some time to come. The Extension lecturer must, therefore, face the problem of getting a certain number of points before an audience, which he meets, say, once a week for a period of twelve or eighteen weeks. The mere statement of the case shows how different the problem involved in the University Extension lecturer's work and in that of the university lecturer.

There is another side in which the work of the two men is very different. The university lecturer has before him, presumably, a set of men or boys who are giving their entire time and attention to the work laid out and required by the college or university. They are supposed to be giving themselves up completely to this educational process which is involved in the curriculum of the institution of learning which they are attending; and, if the claims of society and of athletics or of indolence are sometimes too great to allow the actual realization of this pre-supposition, yet, on the whole, the university lecturer may fairly count on the bulk of the time of his students being devoted, if not to his work, at least to the general university work of which his branch forms a part. The University Extension lecturer, on the contrary, has before him a class of people in whose lives his work forms—even if it become what we hope to make it—a permanent feature, yet, after all, only one element and, perhaps, as far as time and attention are concerned, by far the smallest of several elements which enter into combination to make up the life of the individuals composing his audience. He finds there the busy man who gives the bulk of his time and attention during the day to the speculations on the street or the working of his factory or the manipulations of politics. He finds the woman whose chief attention is absorbed by her household duties, by her charitable works, by her religious offices. He finds the young man or woman, or the boy or girl whose day is spent in the shop or counting-house or the factory, and who, therefore, under the most favorable conditions with the greatest desire in the world to accomplish something valuable and definite, can only give a modicum of his time to this particular work, and, even if we succeed in making by our University Extension movement in alliance with all the other educational movements of the time, education a serious business of life, comparable in the time and attention which it takes to that which is given to amusement, to the church, to politics; yet, after all, it cannot even become more than one of these elements, and with this fact the University Extension lecturer must reckon.

I have not stated these differences in their conditions and methods of work for the purpose of discouraging, in any sense, those who believe thoroughly in the valuable educational aspects of University Extension work. I belong to this class myself, and I should certainly not desire to discourage myself and those who are working with me in this very important field. But I have said these things so as to secure a clearer idea of the conditions under which the University Extension lecturer must work, as compared with those under which the university lecturer is privileged to work. Now, I think it follows, without stopping to draw the conclusion, for any one who has followed me in this statement of the case that the University Extension lecture must be a very different sort of lecture in order to accomplish the highest educational result under the circumstances from the kind of lecture which would do the same thing in the university work itself. In the first place, details must be left very largely out of sight, except so far as detail is necessary in order to emphasize and throw into strong and clear relief the general features of the subject. I say, except so far as detail is necessary. One of the greatest dangers to which the University Extension lecturer is liable is that of dealing simply in formal statements, in fundamental propositions, in glittering generalities. Any teacher knows that such a method of presenting the main features of a subject is foredoomed to failure, for the bald statement of general principles is something which conveys but very little idea to the untrained mind. The general feature or general principle which the lecturer is trying to emphasize must depend far more on the skilful way in which it results as the crowning conclusion of a given presentation, far more upon its being put in such a form that the student himself, out of the details which have been given, shall be in a position to formulate the general principles himself than upon any formal statement, no matter how skilfully and accurately it may be made. It would take a very skilful man, indeed, to give one lecture upon the history of the world, which should contain any valuable matter for the average college student or average man or woman. It takes almost as much skill to treat the whole field of Greek or Roman, or French, or German, or English, or American history in a course of six lectures, so as to produce any abiding result. But it is feasible for the man properly prepared, in a period of six or in a course of twelve lectures, to present one century or one-half century or one special period of English or French or German history in such a way that it shall leave a permanent and indelible impression on the minds of some of his hearers. It is plain, moreover, that the University Extension lecture must, after all, rely for its permanent success upon its ability to interest the audience in the subject in such a way as to lead them to read about it immediately, thoroughly, persistently; in other words, that the object of each individual lecture, as well as of the course, should be very largely to stimulate an interest in the subject as distinct from imparting knowledge on the subject, which latter may very properly be a leading characteristic of the university lecture.

And so I might go on to set forth the peculiar conditions and to analyze the peculiar problem which confronts the University Extension lecturer and to discuss the methods by which he may accomplish his ends. But I have said enough to emphasize the point which I wish to urge upon you especially on this occasion, that the University Extension lecturer must not suppose that the simple lecture which he gives to his college and university students is the proper one to give to his University Extension audience, and to pronounce the opinion that if the lecture is successful in the highest sense before the University Extension audience, it will not be the one which, in the highest sense, will be successful before the university students, and *vice versa*. We have found from our experience in the short time we have been at work, that our college and university men are very prone to fall into this error, and the result is very noticeable in cases where they have done so, in what may be called comparatively inefficient work, judged by the reasonable standard which we may set up on University Extension subjects.

But there is another error into which the university professor is very liable to fall, and that is the error of giving simply what he calls a popular lecture. Nearly all our college and university men in this country do more or less popular lecturing on their subjects and allied branches, before literary societies, teachers' institutes, and similar organizations, so that nearly every college professor has what he calls a popular lecture. It is oftentimes very, very far from being so, but it is at least an attempt in that direction. When these lectures are really popular, under ordinary conditions they are very likely to be simply specimens of the class known as lyceum bureau lectures. This is a very valuable class in its way, and one upon which I should be the last in the world to wish to throw any slur or odium; but it is a class which will not serve the purpose of Universal Extension at all, and which, if introduced into this field, will rapidly give us, in University Extension, poor lyceum bureau lectures by college professors instead of good ones by the present lyceum lecturers. The ordinary popular lecture of the college or university professor will not serve the purposes of University Extension any better than the ordinary lecture by the same party to university students.

Enough has been said, I think, upon this point, to bring clearly before you the proposition stated above, and which I wish to reiterate here, that the kind of lecture which will accomplish the highest results in University Extension work is a very different sort of lecture from that which will accomplish the highest results, on the one hand, in the university, and on the other, in the lyceum bureau. I would urge, therefore, upon the college or university man, who thinks of taking up University Extension work, that he, in doing so, has a new educational problem before him, a problem which will not be thoroughly well solved without the most careful and continued attention upon his part. The fact that university men have not kept this circumstance in mind will account, to a very large extent, to my mind, for those numerous failures, in one form or another, of the University Extension work which the history of this movement, in England and in this country, has to chronicle, and to the large percentage of attempts, which, while we cannot perhaps denominate them as absolute failures, are certainly not calculated to encourage us to put forth long-continued and renewed efforts along these lines. So much for the University Extension lecture. The University Extension lecturer is in so far the man who can give us a lecture which is suited to the conditions we have sketched above.

There are, however, other elements than the mere lecture in the scheme of University Extension instruction. In immediate connection with this lecture is the syllabus or outline of lectures, and in the construction of that syllabus the University Extension lecturer has an opportunity to show all the qualities, except the mere one of pleasant and effective address, which he needs to employ in the preparation and delivery of the lectures themselves.

No one can help being struck, who has taken the pains to read over the syllabi published in England by the various men who have lectured in this field and the same efforts made on this side of the water; I say no one can help being struck by the fact that the average syllabus is a poor affair; that it contains but little help to clear consecutive thought, and that it contains but little help towards following up the lecture and the lecture course in a systematic way; that it has but little to do in inspiring the student with the interest in the study which is fundamental to any great success along these lines. A mere summary of headings which the lecturer proposes to discuss has, of course, its value. A mere series of statements of principles, which the lecturer proposes to develop and illustrate, has, of course, its value, but if that is all which the syllabus contains, it falls very far below the level of efficiency which is easily within the reach of the skillful and successful lecturer. The syllabus should be a sort of guide to the study of the subject which the lecturer proposes to present, a sort of cord which shall lead the student through the labyrinthine windings of the mass of literature which exists on all these subjects, and lead him carefully and steadily and constantly to the wide outlooks, to the important views, to the soul-stirring altitudes which should make up and mark his intellectual and æsthetic progress, so far as it is aided and directed by this particular course of study. It should give to the person who has it some definite knowledge as to what books on the subject and what portions of what books are best worth his reading, if he wishes to view this field as the lecturer views it, if he wishes to get the same outlooks, if he wishes to pass through, to a certain extent, the same experience. It goes without saying that it should be systematic, as far as possible suggestive and interesting and inspiring; and, in short, should be a sort of guide to the study of the particular subject which the lecturer is treating. That means, of course, very much more careful and thorough work on the syllabus than most University Extension lecturers, either in England or in this country, have thus far been willing to give it. It means, alas! more ability to pick out the salient things and put them in an impressive and salient form than the average lecturer in this field possesses; but we can, at least, all of us within the range of our ability, as far as possible, approximate towards the best and most successful thing in this field which can be given.

In close connection with the syllabus should be mentioned the paper work of students, the questions which are presented to them to stimulate and stir their interest and inspire them to take an active part in the work, and not to be content with the mere passive rôle of listener. The preparation of these questions calls for care and attention, if they are to be successful; it calls for skill and ability and a close adaptation and study of the conditions under which these University Extension lectures must be given. Just in proportion as the lecturer is able to get the members of his University Extension audience to take an active and interested part in the pursuit of the subject, in that proportion will he be able to produce permanent and valuable results. I do not mean to say, of course, that the lectures would be valueless, even if the people should not write the papers, but simply that the whole work will be of an enormously greater value, to all those who do actually take part in it, than it would be without it. Now, I am sorry to say that, if any of you will take the syllabi which have been prepared, either in this country or abroad, and go through them carefully, you will be rather struck by the careless way in which this work, on the whole, has been developed. I need not stop on this point longer, except to venture the general remark that, if the largest and best results are to be got from this paper work, the questions must be carefully thought out and must be carefully graded, so that every person who attends the course of lectures and pays close attention will feel that there is some question or questions in the list, on which he may present an acceptable paper, if he will only put forth the effort. There should be other questions which will call for the largest and fullest exercise of the ability to study and to present which the lecturer is likely to find in his audience.

Finally, the class work is the other element in the distinctively technical or educational work of the University Extension lecturer, which calls for special mention. To conduct a good class, even in college and the university, where you have your picked men, your men of a homogeneous training, your men of thorough training, your men who devote all their time to the work; I say, to conduct a good class, even under such favorable conditions, calls for the exercise of one of the highest forms of ability which the teacher possesses. You all know how unutterably "tedious and tasteless the hours" that you have spent in many a college professor's rooms, in the so-called recitations, where there seemed to be, as you look back upon it now, no plan or method of work, no stimulus and little or no searching out of the hidden things in the minds and hearts of the students, no inspiration or stirring up to higher levels, to higher thoughts, and to more vigorous action. The conditions of successful class work in the University Extension audience are, many of them, more unfavorable than those in the college and university. In the first place, you have an audience which is very likely, indeed, to possess some rather obstreperous individuals, who are inclined to take all the time of the class, and whom you cannot dispose of so summarily as you can of a college student of the same kind. You are apt to have very many, a much larger number, of a retiring disposition, who are too timid to say anything, who are frightened if you call upon them to express their opinion, or, if you try to draw them out by questioning. This class includes oftentimes the most valuable element in your audience, and, if you persist in drawing them out by questions and showing up their ignorance, the result is very much more likely that they will leave your work and give up the whole class than that they should be brought to take the same view of the subject that you do.

In the second place, in an audience of this class, you are even more likely to have your time frittered away by an infinite number of questions, some of which have a possible relation to the subject in hand, but most of which have nothing to do with it. You are all well aware, of course, how completely a class of college boys can waste the time of the class and the teacher by asking idle and profitless questions, either on purpose or from ignorance. You can imagine how much more completely a popular audience, such as the University Extension lecturer obtains, may do the same thing, and how easy it is for a question to shunt the whole consideration away from the point that the lecturer is trying to make and into a wilderness of idle and profitless debate. If the lecturer were to undertake to answer all the questions which his class might ask, he would simply use up an hour and produce almost no beneficial result whatever. Consequently, there is no greater opportunity of showing his skill open to the Extension lecturer than is open to him in the conducting of a classs, to draw out the diffident, to squelch the boisterous, to get such questions as will enable him to be helpful and to direct the course of the discussion so as to emphasize and throw into still stronger relief, bring out more thoroughly, to impress more fully upon their minds the fundamental points of its presentation. To do thoroughly efficient work in the class, calls for careful and long-continued attention on the part of the instructor, and nothing will be more helpful to him along this line than the papers which he will succeed in obtaining from the individuals who make up his class. If he can get a large number of them, it will enable him to size up his class, so to speak, to find out the lines along which they are working or reading, to find out how far he is carrying them with him, how far he is inspiring them with an interest in the subject, as a class, as this is one of the most difficult tests of the lecturer's ability, so it is the occasion in which most of our average university and college men fail to come up to the standard. And I may say, in a general way, that in our short experience here in the work that is carried on immediately under the auspices of the American Society we have had more complaints about the inefficient class work of our lecturers than upon any other point. Our communities feel, in an instinctive way, and I think the feeling is the correct one, that the class, if properly conducted, is the one element which will bring more thoroughly educational work into this movement than even the lecture itself.

I think, perhaps, enough has been said to emphasize what I may call the educational aspect and educational function of the University Extension lecturer. The University Extension lecturer should be the man who can give us the kind of lecture which we have described in a general way, who can give us the kind of syllabus, who can give us the kind of class work, who can set the kind of questions, and who, at the end of his work, will leave his audience and his class and his community in a blaze of enthusiasm for the subject which he has been presenting, and for the great field of human science of which it forms a part.

This, however, is not by any means the sole function of the University Extension lecturer. As I said above, the success of this work depends upon the University Extension lecturer at more points than one. The large success of the work is going to depend, not merely upon the success of any one subject; not merely upon the interest excited for any one period of English literature for example, nor upon the interest excited upon English literature as a whole, but upon the interest which is excited in human science as a whole and in its relations to all the other sides of human life. Now, it seems to me that, having regard to the conditions of our American life, and having regard to the nature of this movement, the University Extension lecturer should do two things in addition to the particular work which we have already outlined. He should be an apostle and an evangelist for the University Extension movement as a whole, and above all, for the cause of education in general. He should not feel that, after giving his course of lectures, even if he be thoroughly successful in it, that he has done all that may fairly enough be required of him. This movement cannot be made general, it cannot be made permanent, unless the men who are doing the actual work of lecturing will take it up in their hands and bear it steadily and persistently to the front, in connection with all of their University Extension work. This, we all agree, is one of the great educational movements of the age. We shall derive great help from it from every point of view, if this fact be kept persistently before our notice; if every occasion be taken by the university lecturer to excite interest in the general cause of University Extension; if he consider that he never goes out of his way when he can score a good point for the general movement itself; that, on the contrary, it is a part, a fundamental part, of his duties to keep the cause in mind, and, wherever he sees an opportunity to advance it, to do so. In other words, the Extension lecturer should look upon himself as a man, one of whose special duties it is to enlighten the audience that meets him night after night, to enlighten the community from which his audience is drawn, as to the scope and functions, aim and methods of the University Extension work as a whole. In a word, he ought to leave his Extension audience, he ought to leave the community in which his course has been given, perfectly ablaze with enthusiasm, not merely for Shakespeare, if that be the part; nor for English literature, if that be the whole of his subject; but for University Extension itself, which is carrying out not merely Shakespeare, and not merely English literature, but art and science and mathematics,—education, training, culture,—into the life of the nation.

Now, the ways in which this can be done are numerous. In the first place, of course, there is the local committee, the element in whose hands is the management of the local centre, the people under whose auspices, looking at it from one point of view, the man is giving his lecture. If we are to succeed in carrying through and emphasizing the educational as well as the popular sides of this work, we can accomplish it only with the sympathy and hearty co-operation and support of these local committees. We shall get that for the higher and better sides of the work only if we continually and persistently urge the higher and better sides of the work upon their attention, only if we enlist their interests in the higher and better aspects of the movement. Nobody can do this so persistently, nobody can do it so directly as the University Extension lecturer. He is sure to meet one or another member of the committee upon every occasion he goes to lecture. There is nothing in the way of his getting the committee together for the purpose of giving them a special talk on how this movement is progressing, and how it is being taken up in different localities, and how the most successful centres conduct their work, and everything which will tend to heighten their interest in the movement and clear their understanding as to its correct methods. In a word, the University Extension lecturer should look upon himself as the apostle of the movement, and as having a special call to educate and enlighten the local committee and the community in such a way as to further most efficiently the permanent interests of the cause.

But I do not think that the University Extension lecturer should stop with this. University Extension is not going to accomplish its fullest mission unless it succeeds in interesting the committee not merely in literature, in art, in science, as branches of human knowledge, but in education as one of the great fundamental interests of society, in education as a branch of human life and institutions which stands side by side with religion, with politics, with business, and with amusement as a great and fundamental category of social existence. I believe that we have, in this movement, the greatest machinery for enlightening the public upon educational questions, the greatest opportunity for getting public attention to the importance and significance of educational problems that has ever been offered to us in the history of the world. If this work be properly organized and fitted into the other educational interests and agencies in the community, it may enormously increase the efficiency of them all by directing public attention and interest to the subject, as a whole, in a way which has been hitherto unknown. Now, the man who is to do this for us, and the only man who can do it, is the University Extension lecturer. Surely we have the right to expect from the university and college man an interest in education as such,—an interest in the great department of which his particular work forms a very small, an almost infinitesimal part. It is not too much to expect, it is not too much to demand, that he should put forth a portion of his effort to assist the cause as a whole, to help education as a whole, as distinct from other interests of life, into that place of prominence which it may fairly demand in modern life by its importance and significance for modern civilization. The University Extension lecturer can do this in an incidental way, and in such form as to immensely heighten and stimulate the interest in University Extension and the interest in the particular subject which he is teaching.

It is hardly necessary for me to go into the description of details as to what the lecturer may do and as to how he may do it, in the direction I have indicated. It may not, however, be out of place to suggest some possible things and then ask the individual lecturers, here and elsewhere, to let us know about the work they are doing in this direction, and to pour in their suggestions upon us. For example, suppose the University Extension lecturer has under consideration the subject of literature. Suppose he takes a few moments, five or ten minutes, at the beginning of his lecture, or preceding the close, for a little discussion of educational topics in one form or another. He will find the public very much interested in them, if he will take a little pains to put them into proper shape. He will find that people will go home and talk about them, and, from that time, they will take a new interest in everything pertaining to education. Suppose, for example, on one occasion he were to talk about the function of the university in the life of nations, give them a little historical sketch of the rise of universities, of the place they have occupied in ancient and modern times, with some of the interesting incidents connected with the development of these institutions, and such instances are innumerable. Suppose he were to follow that, upon another occasion, by a brief discussion of the rise of the modern university, of what it is in England, France, and Germany, and of what it is in the United States to-day. Let him give an account of the rise and development of the American college, of the changes which it has undergone, of what its specific function is. Let him take up his own subject, English literature, give an account of its first introduction into the universities as an individual discipline, of its development and of its present state, of the way it is organized, of the methods of instruction, of its relation to other branches; following that up by a discussion of the University Extension movement as such, as the last and latest outgrowth of colleges and universities. It would be perfectly feasible for him, by giving a few minutes each evening, at the opening of his lecture, to some of these general topics, to increase immensely the interest in his lecture course, without in any sense interfering with his educational work, thus interesting the community in higher institutions, in the University Extension movement, and, briefly, in higher education as a whole.

Some one may say that this is too much to ask of the college or university man, that he does not know enough about education in general, that he does not know enough about the colleges and universities, that he does not know enough about University Extension, even, to speak intelligently upon these topics. If this be so, and, alas! I am afraid there is too much truth in it, surely it is a sad state of affairs, and one that ought to be remedied. Men who are engaged in a great educational work ought certainly to be willing to take the time to learn something of the history of that work itself, what it means in the present, what it has meant in the past, if not to give some thought and reflection to the question of what it may mean in the future. I do not hesitate to say that the men who are going to do the most useful work in this field are men who will be able to do the particular things which I have outlined above. I would not, however, say that no one could do successful work in this line who could not accomplish all the things just described, but certainly his work will be more successful in proportion as he is able to measure himself up more nearly to the standard indicated in the above description.

THE IDEAL SYLLABUS.

BY HENRY W. ROLFE, M.A., S.C.,

University of Pennsylvania.

THE aim of the University Extension lecturer is not so much to instruct his hearers directly as to stimulate them to independent study of their own. His work is largely a failure if he does not lead them to think for themselves, and moreover to think thoroughly. In writing the lectures, therefore, in conducting the class, in criticising the weekly papers, the thing that he must especially have in mind is the necessity of developing thoroughness and independence. And of course this holds good of the making of the syllabus as well. It likewise must be constructed with careful reference to these two results. Consequently it may be said that the best syllabus is the one which makes thorough study seem desirable and easy, and so tempts the Extension student to undertake it; but which refrains, on the other hand, from guiding his steps with such great care that he shall have nothing to do but follow, and so shall lose all independence of judgment.

Permit me to take up these two considerations somewhat in detail. And first, the question of thoroughness. What must the syllabus comprise if it is to help the student to do thorough work?

For one thing, of course, it must give him full and accurate information in regard to the best books on the subject in hand. This information, moreover, must be well-ordered, discriminative. I cannot think that a mere list of titles can ever be sufficient. The student should be told plainly what works are absolutely essential, what stand next in importance, and what finally are good but yet of minor interest, or perhaps special in their nature, so that they should be used only by those who wish to undertake comparatively exhaustive investigations. He should be told, too, in what order the books of each of these classes should be taken up, what prejudices and prepossessions on the part of their authors are to be guarded against, how one volume may be made to supplement the deficiencies of another, and so on. In a word, the lecturer should, in the syllabus, freely give to his pupils, as far as it is possible to do so, the full benefit of that knowledge of the literature of the subject which he himself has slowly accumulated. In my opinion, he may well go so far as to specify editions and mention prices. And I certainly would have him, in addition to the general hints of which I have been speaking, or in connection with them, sketch out both a major and a minor course of reading, somewhat in detail; that is, both a leisurely rambling path and a short cut through the great field of study that he has mapped out in his preceding recommendations.

Consider for a moment how the syllabus will be used, and you will not accuse me of having laid too much stress upon this matter of a bibliographical introduction to it. Many intending students will turn to it, long in advance of the lectures, for hints in regard to preparatory reading. Students' associations will be guided by it in the purchase of their works of reference. Libraries will avail themselves of its suggestions in their efforts to use their resources for the benefit of local centres. And, most important of all perhaps, the syllabus is likely to become, in some cases at all events, the handbook of the solitary students, who, after being awakened by the lectures to a deep interest in some subject, will strive to continue its study by himself, for months and perhaps years, during which time he certainly will need all possible assistance.

I pass now to the lecture outline. This has varied very much, sometimes being a mere skeleton of the lecture, in the form of a few short sentences or a series of bare catch-words, sometimes, on the other hand, presenting a careful condensation of everything essential in the whole discourse. The former method, that of short sentences or catch-words, would do very well if the object of this outline were simply to spare hearers the labor and distraction of taking notes in the lecture-room, it being

The Ideal Syllabus. 109

understood that they would carefully write out the substance of what they had heard as soon as they reached their homes. But, if the syllabus is to save them from all note-taking whatever, after the lecture as well as doing its progress, if it is to be made, as I believe it should be, a substitute for such task-work, serving to recall at any time, however remote, all that the lecturer deemed of special value; then it should be fairly full, should be an epitome, a synopsis, rather than the barest and briefest summary. It will in that case go far towards insuring that thoroughness of work upon which I am now dwelling; for it will render it almost impossible for the lecture, which is the first step in Extension work and thus in certain respects the most important, to be dealt with superficially and imperfectly by a student who is at all in earnest.

I would ask your consideration now of a third feature of the syllabus, the questions in answer to which the weekly papers are written. Upon the skill with which these are chosen depends very largely the value of the paper work; and upon that, in turn, depends more than upon anything else the final worth of the entire course of study. So the questions should be contrived with the utmost care. They should not be so difficult as to repel the student nor yet so easy that he may answer them without some measure of earnest thought. They should cunningly tempt him to read, consider, compare. They should suggest to him the many aspects of the subject, its large possibilities, the deep underlying philosophy of it. In fine, the questions are of the very greatest importance, and demand in their preparation all the lecturer's art.

Up to this point I have spoken of the necessity of making the syllabus of such a character in every part that the student will be helped and, indeed, almost compelled by it to be thorough and careful in his work. Allow me now to call your attention to the necessity of developing within him independence as well. The lecturer will render his hearer but a poor service if he teaches him to be ever so thorough, but in so doing represses his originality. Hence great pains must be taken to leave room for the free play of his judgment. So in the syllabus, as in the lecture, one must sedulously avoid dogmatic assertions, or a one-sided presentation of the matter; must persistently maintain an attitude of inquiry and a spirit of fair investigation and free discussion; or, to be less general in statement, one must refrain from giving too much advice about books and reading, too full an outline of the lecture, questions too searching and exhaustive. Leave the pupil something to find out for himself. It is better, even, to let him make frequent mistakes than to guard him with too much care against making any.

The task, then, to sum up our conclusions, is to reconcile in the syllabus as well as may be two somewhat conflicting requirements: the necessity of so guiding the student that he shall not find it easy to be superficial, and the no less imperative necessity of leaving him so free from guidance that he shall be forced to be somewhat independent and original in his work.

I am well aware that a syllabus which should satisfy those requirements must be very difficult to construct. But so are all forms of Extension work difficult. And it is a fortunate thing that it is so. If they were easy for either teacher or pupil, this movement could not accomplish the great results that we hope from it. For strenuous effort alone can develop one's powers.

It is not to be regretted then that the syllabus is found to require much time and much study. And it is plain that the lecturer cannot be altogether successful who allows himself to think of it as a slight task, something that can be thrown off in an hour or two, perhaps even before the lectures are written. He should rather look upon it as one of the three important steps in the preparation of his course. He should feel that he has first to master his subject; then to construct his lectures with all his skill; and then, finally, to devote unlimited time and pains to the making of his guide, this hand-book, this representative, always present with the student, of himself, and his efforts.

And now, as I close, permit me to commend to your notice certain concrete illustrations of what a good syllabus should be. I may not refer, of course, to the work of any of our American lecturers, lest I should seem to make comparisons and distinctions; but I can and do suggest that all who are interested in the matter study the syllabus of our English visitors of last year and this.

REMARKS.

Professor Edward H. Magill, of Swarthmore College, said:
As the syllabus is an essential part of every well-organized University Extension course, it seems to me that the manner in which it is given is a subject for our serious consideration. And first of all, let me say that I do not present my own views upon this subject as the only correct views, or those which I would urge upon others. Nor can I speak, as others can, from experience in University Extension work, but what I shall say is based upon my experience in my own college classes. For myself, then, let me say that I should consider it a serious error to follow the usual practice of giving out to classes the syllabus before the beginning of a lecture. I desire to have the undivided attention of a class to the various parts of the subject which I present, and not to have that attention divided nor distracted by endeavoring, while listening, to follow the printed syllabus before them. An instructor presents his subject under the most advantageous circumstances when he can ask his classes, in the beginning, to give him their undivided attention, without being burdened by taking notes, and that all notes needed for the home study of the subject will be given them at the close of the lecture.* I know that it is sometimes said that taking notes is a useful practice, and that it is not well for classes to be relieved from it. This is doubtless true, but there will be other occasions when this practice may be acquired, and the University Extension lecturer who desires to give his classes the maximum amount of knowledge in his necessarily limited time, will be careful not to burden them with anything that is unnecessary. This argument reminds me of the old familiar one that mental discipline, being the chief

end of all study, whatever will add to the difficulty of a study is so much added to its value. We all know that in these latter days, when so many studies are clamoring for a place in our curricula, this purely mental discipline claim has lost a large portion of its significance. I would then say, print the syllabus of each lecture on a separate sheet, give it out at the close, and open each lecture hour by a brief examination upon the last lecture, sometimes conducted *viva voce*, and sometimes in writing. And at the close of the course, while I would give a final written general examination, in determining the success of the student I should also give much weight to the result of these briefer examinations given from week to week.

These are my views upon this important point, and for myself I am sure that they are correct, although they might not prove to be so for another member of this Convention. If there is one lesson which, more than others, has been impressed upon us by these meetings (if such lessons were needed), it seems to me to be this: That in the science and art of teaching, there is no truth more important than that we must, as teachers, be ourselves, preserving our own individuality; and that any attempt to follow implicitly in the footsteps of others can never secure the highest results, but only a low and uniform order of mediocrity.

THE ORGANIZATION AND FUNCTION OF LOCAL CENTRES.

BY M. E. SADLER,

Student of Christ Church and Secretary to the Oxford Delegacy.

IN order to discharge the duty which has been laid upon me this morning, I shall attempt to describe to the conference the natural history of a typical University Extension centre. It often happens that it is a woman who first determines to establish University Extension in a new locality. She has attended Extension lectures elsewhere, or has heard from friends what they have gained from the system, or she has been to some summer school and there realized the advantage of stimulating guidance in higher studies, or she may have learned from magazines and newspapers the promises and the possibilities of University Extension, —come the inspiration whence it may, she sets to work to obtain for her fellow-citizens an opportunity of profiting by this new educational advantage. We in England have seen scores of centres begun or saved through the efforts of a few girls, who, first by interesting their immediate friends, next by securing the support of influential citizens, have aroused an interest in, and provided the means for, the successful introduction of University Extension teaching into a town where it had not been previously established. In University Extension work, it is the spirit that really matters. Be the course however short, be the teaching however intermittent, if it is introduced and carried on in a spirit of true democratic zeal for the widening of intellectual opportunity, if it is maintained by men and women who are determined that they for their part will not allow their own faculties to rust, or their own knowledge to grow dim, or smattering to take the place of thoroughness, or gossip and triviality to exhaust leisure that might have been rich in study,—if the spirit is right, organization may be trusted to follow in due season. The centre which fails is the centre which relies on arid organization alone, which thinks that printing an armful of circulars and posting a basketful of envelopes and advertising in the nearest newspaper are enough to insure the success of its work. Canvassing, publication, advertising, are all necessary and useful features in an educational campaign. We live in an age just learning how wisely to apply business methods to educational work. But, unless the organization is informed by the right kind of spirit, the spirit of self-sacrifice, of intellectual humility, of enthusiasm for learning, the work, however proudly it begins, can end only in costly disappointment, like the bare walls of some great house abandoned before it is inhabited.

It is unnecessary for me to describe the various methods which have been found useful in arousing in a locality public interest in University Extension. These methods are tersely and lucidly set out in the publications of the American Society for the Extension of University teaching. I must, however, in passing, dwell with emphasis, first, on the necessity of securing the co-operation of the conductors of the local press, an agency, to the constant efforts of which, on behalf of University Extension, I am happy to take this opportunity of publicly testifying; second, on the fact that it is essential that the Committees of Local Organizers should be representative of all denominations, of all shades of politics, of all sorts and conditions of men and women. The task in which we are engaged is a national (I had almost said an international) one; we must not let it be disfigured by any taint of partisanship or exclusiveness; third, on our experience that the only means by which the permanent success of a University Extension centre can be assured is by personal labor on the part of the local organizers. Personal canvassing, personal persuasion, personal sympathy, personal encouragement are the only methods by which in the long run you can get the people to take a strong interest in the higher discipline of the intellect. You may gather together for your opening lecture a large and miscellaneous audience, but it is the novelty of the thing that has brought many of them together; with most of the great crowd the local organizers will have no further chance of dealing. It is the small nucleus

The Organization and Function of Local Centres. 115

of sincere, serious students that is going to make the future of the centre. That nucleus may well be small. In a population of twenty thousand people there may not be more than ten or twenty who really will submit themselves to the tests of application and thoroughness which University Extension imposes on all who truly try to profit by it. But that little handful of ten or twenty people, young and poor as many of them will be, are just the very people whom it is both our duty and our interest to encourage in the higher kinds of mental self-improvement. They are the men and women who as they grow older will be the making of the town in which they live. They will be the salt of their community, and it is simply plain common-sense to save the salt from losing its savor.

But here comes in the characteristic difficulty of University Extension. Good teaching, like everything else that is good, costs money. But how can so small a group of students support the heavy charge which the arrangement of frequent and progressive courses will impose upon them? Financial help must come to them from the outside; they must partly rely on donations and subscriptions. Happily, however, for them, if there is one country in the whole world where a just appeal for educational benevolence will not pass unregarded, it is America.

The first problem, therefore, before the local organizers, after securing their nucleus of students, is to awaken educational interest in a sufficient number of the general public to such a point as to induce the necessary number of these outsiders to bear with the students the cost of the teaching. And here there enters into local organization that double element of interest which makes so much of University Extension work unstable. The tastes of the real students and of the general public, though they may run along the same road up to a certain point, are not always identical. The student yearns for sequence; the general public hankers after variety; the student wishes course to follow course in such a way as to build up a curriculum of ordered study; the general public is always crying out for literature as a relief from history, for science as a change from literature. And it is for this reason that the early labors of a local committee are generally labors which end in compromise, the students yielding in one session to the whims of the public, the public in the next grudgingly giving way to the needs of the students. It is, therefore, the duty of the Local Committee to neglect no means of gradually increasing the size of the student body,—and this is to be done by recruiting the corps of real students from the ranks of the general public. And it is the privilege of every lecturer to co-operate with the local organizers in this protracted effort to arouse in dull or flighty natures a perception of the noble beauty of earnest study, and to rescue promising but neglected talents from apathy or dilettanteism.

On the hidden rocks of intellectual unconcern the little ship of University Extension often founders. But I desire to speak from personal knowledge of a real case, as showing the permanently good results which sometimes follow from true University Extension work, even when hidden under apparent failure. To a little town in the north of England the University of Cambridge (which, it is both a pleasure and a duty for me to say, bore in Great Britain the labor of University Extension work long before any other university came forward to take its share in the task) sent nearly twenty years ago two lecturers on what was then the new University Extension scheme. Preparations had been made for their coming; the best people in the town had subscribed to the project; bills had been posted on every wall. But when the lectures began the audience was insignificant, and, as the course proceeded, dwindled down to eight people. There were five young women, there was a French dentist, a young engineer, and the local postmaster. Nothing could have seemed more disappointing, nothing more obscure. I remember going to one lecture as a boy from school when the lecturer was trying to illustrate his discourse by a magic lantern. He had brought his gas with him in a bag, and, through some difficulty of pressure, he found it necessary to retire behind the screen where the bag lay, and in this retreat concealed from the eyes of the audience and squatting on his india-rubber apparatus to continue his discourse. It was not thought that University Extension in that town had aroused sufficient interest to warrant its continuance.

And yet, had the promoters only known, had they only been able to divine the future, they would have seen that these eight people contained in their number just those whom it was worth while to stimulate by educational opportunities. And I can bear witness to the fact that the seed sown in those few courses of lectures which came to such an untimely end sprang up at last into a harvest of new intellectual interests, and that the influence of those first University Extension lecturers can be felt indirectly in a hundred ways in the present fortunes of that town. The local postmaster, who was a true poet, is dead years ago. The French dentist is a dentist still; the young engineer is near the top of one of the greatest firms in the country; of the five young women not one but is now in some way or other connected with some of the highest educational work in England, having derived from those Extension lectures saving stimulus, if not her first impulse, to the higher kinds of intellectual interests.

For some sessions the ordinary centre will naturally content itself with a moderate measure of university teaching. It is unwise to choke the smoking flax, to impose upon a town educational provision beyond its appetite. A new centre must be coaxed, not satiated. Gradual signs will not long be wanting of the consolidation of educational effort even in the most backward town. One of the earliest indications is the formation of a Students' Union, a society, that is, of persons combining themselves together for a common purpose in study, and agreeing to meet on one evening in each week or fortnight for discussion of assigned topics studied by the members privately during the intervening days. For the present success of the Students' Unions we owe in England a debt to the great initiative guidance of Mr. R. G. Moulton, the well-known Cambridge lecturer, of whom it is hardly too much to say that in its most critical days he saved the University Extension movement.

As the Students' Union becomes more influential, its wishes are considered with greater deference on the part of the Committee of Local Organizers, which should always include representatives of the Students' Union. The courses themselves are then arranged so as to cover a longer period of study, and subjects are chosen by the local committee in such a way as to promote sequence of interest, until at length either lecture or students' meeting takes place once or twice in every week from October to April. Each year, too, efforts will be made to prevent educational work from falling during the summer into its long abeyance. Field work for the naturalist, summer ramble for the botanist, mountain trip for the geologist, excursion to some distant art gallery or object of antiquarian interest for the student of history, will all serve as attractive items in a programme of summer; study, but, above all, attendance at the summer school provides the best opportunity for the student to carry on his work between the courses and this excellent institution, which we in England have adopted from your own famous American examples, has done more than anything else to provide a year-long continuity in Extension efforts.

Sooner or later the local centre will find itself drawn into co-operation with neighboring towns. Indeed, the sooner this happens the better. Concert of this kind facilitates organization, reduces railway expenses, economizes waste, lessens fatigue, and by degrees there will break on the minds of the local organizers the realization of the possibilities which lie in this co-operation of neighboring towns in educational effort. They can establish, as Dr. Roberts well put it, a floating university college. The federation of centres carries with it many incidental advantages. It welds local effort into an impressive unity; it calls public attention to the widely-diffused character of the effort which is carrying on University teaching in so many towns. It promotes the frequent and friendly interchange of experience between local organizers, who, though engaged in the same work and resident in the same district, are often strangely ignorant of one another's personalities, methods, and aims. But the chief purpose of federation in University Extension work is to enable contiguous centres to secure at the most economical rates and for convenient periods the services of an efficient staff of lecturers. Every lecturer does not suit every district. It would be wise therefore for the co-operating centres to find a young man to act as their

The Organization and Function of Local Centres. 119

organizing secretary, to put him on his mettle to make the educational work of the federation a success, and to pay him a stipend which would make it worth his while to give the federation his best thought and the necessary time. Such a step, though involving outlay at first, would be in the long run economical. For the newly-appointed secretary, after fully acquainting himself with the different natures of the different centres in the federation, would make it his duty to visit head-quarters in order to ascertain by personal inquiry and interview which of the lecturers would suit the federation best. Returning then to the centres he would visit the towns in turn and lay before them his suggestions as to the best course for them to arrange. With tact and consideration he would then draw the various wishes of the different centres to a focus, and would induce them all to agree to hire a small staff of lecturers for the ensuing year. He would then plan out the amount of time which each of the lecturers should give to each of the centres, the division of their services being made in accordance with the amount of each centre's contribution to the common purse. One of the lecturers would probably be a man who would worthily bear the duty of principal of this new kind of university college, and represent its interests on public occasions with dignity and judgment. The advantages of this plan lie in its elasticity. The co-operating towns would not be tied to any permanent obligation. They could change their staff of teachers, they could vary their curriculum, they could widen or contract their operations, in accordance with the dictates of prudence and the changing needs of recurring years. No town would find itself permanently encumbered with the services of a teacher who, however learned, was unable to commend his subject to the expectations of his hearers. We need scholars, but not pedants, for our work. No town would find itself compelled to raise large capital sums, or to erect costly buildings. For by using a peripatetic staff of teachers, by employing existing though possibly scattered accommodation, a town would get the substance of University teaching with economy and promptitude. It is men, not walls, that make a city, as the Greek poet said. The principal strength of University Extension teaching lies in the personalities of inspiring lecturers, not in the costliness of their material equipment.

In short, University Extension in a local centre will find its crowning development in the foundation of what I may call a University Extension institute. I mean by this a central institution which will bear witness in a city to the dignity and civic importance of higher education. Beginning with small efforts, never despising the day of small things, a local committee will gradually find itself enabled by the support of grateful students and the generosity of far-seeing benefactors to provide in orderly sequence stimulating courses of progressive study, so that in their city no man or woman, however poor, however busy, however far removed from other University influence, shall not find at last the chance of studying under trained and sympathetic teachers the lessons of history, the masterpieces of literature, the mysteries of science until at length we shall have removed for ever the aristocratic exclusiveness of learning and have equipped the democracy of the civilized world with such a measure of intelligent culture as will enable them not only to admire and appreciate as never before the researches and attainments of scholars and researchers, but more worthily to bear their part in the public duties which our advancing civilization is every year throwing more heavily on each of them.

REMARKS.

Professor Henry W. Rolfe, of the University of Pennsylvania, questioned Mr. Sadler in regard to the fees of lecturers in the English work. After some discussion on this point, the conclusion was reached that the fees of lecturers in England were relatively the same as those required by the American Society, being equivalent to about twenty dollars for each lecture, with the travelling expenses of the lecturer. Considerable diversity was apparent in the charges in different States of the Union. At many universities the charge is fixed at ten dollars, with expenses for each lecture. In few cases, however, does it seem possible to continue Extension teaching beyond the trial stage, at this rate.

President Charles DeGarmo, of Swarthmore College, questioned Mr. Sadler as to the use of fellows and graduate students as lecturers in Extension work. It appeared that the development of University Extension in England has been possible largely on account of the number of fellows and tutors at the great universities, who, being comparatively free from university duties, are able to devote themselves to outside work. The sense of the conference was, that a similar plan might be found practicable in the United States, as the number of resident graduates and fellows increases at the leading universities.

SOME EXTENSION EXPERIMENTS IN AMERICAN HISTORY.

BY JAMES ALBERT WOODBURN, PH.D.,

Professor of American History in the Indiana University.

THE purpose of this paper is to relate briefly some personal experience and observations in University Extension teaching in American History. The experience is chiefly confined to two Extension classes. The classes are still in operation, and as the end is required to crown the work, permanent conclusions from the experiments in many important respects may not yet be safely drawn.

The first extension of university teaching in Indiana was undertaken in Indianapolis one year ago under the auspices of the Indiana branch of the Association of Collegiate Alumnæ. This Association in Indiana, through its committee on University Extension,—Mrs. May Wright Sewall, President; Miss Amelia Waring Platter, Secretary,—engaged Prof. J. W. Jenks, then of Indiana University, now of Cornell, to give twelve lectures on political economy. The lectures were given on consecutive Friday nights during the winter months, with a small quiz class the following Saturday morning. This, like many first courses, was not self-supporting, but it was so satisfactory and successful in every other essential respect, and from the stand-point of public education it had paid in such positive returns, that the committee determined, at the risk of further financial loss, to continue, the following winter, the course in political and social science, and to add another in American history. For the second year in their Extension course in political science they engaged Dr. Edward A. Ross, the successor of Dr. Jenks in the Indiana University, who will begin in February a series of twelve lectures on social and economic reform.

In beginning the course in American history last October, by the invitation and under the auspices of this committee, the conception which we had in mind of the work to be done was published with the outline announcement of the course. The design embraced these points, included in all complete Extension teachings:

1. A series of lectures on connected topics as usual in the development of a continuous subject. For this course twelve lectures were chosen as the unit. As *lectures* they were to be distinguished from a popular course in that they were not to be on disconnected themes for general instruction and public entertainment, but on connected themes for special instruction and private study.

2. A syllabus of each lecture was to be printed.

3. The lectures were to be followed by a class exercise of equal length with the lecture, for review, tests, quiz, and inquiry on the part of the class.

4. An examination was to be held on the course, a certificate to be given of work done, which was to be made a matter of record and credit by the university.

As a general subject for study we chose American Political History from 1776 to 1832, dividing the term of study by the following twelve subjects:

1. The Causes of the American Revolution.

2. The Continental Congress: The Nature of Its Work and Its Constitutional Relation to the States.

3. The Old Confederation and Its Failure: "The Critical Period of American History."

4. The Northwest and the Ordinance of 1787.

5. The Constitutional Convention of 1787. Its Great Men, Its Great Questions, Its Great Compromises.

6. The Financial Measures of Hamilton.

7. Our Neutral Policy: Foreign Relations under Washington and Adams.

8. Early Political Parties: The Alien and Sedition Laws and the Fall of the Federalists, 1800.

9. Jefferson and Louisiana.

10. The continued Struggle for Neutral Rights in the War of 1812.

11. The Monroe Doctrine and its Applications in American History.

12. Jackson and the Bank Controversy.

The syllabus of the first lecture contained a statement of the required reading for the course, embracing Johnston's The United States: Its History and Constitution. Fiske's Critical Period of American History. Burke's Speech on American Taxation. Certain pages of Lecky's chapter on The Controversy with America. Certain papers in The Federalist. Assigned papers in Schouler's History of the United States, and the study of certain State papers like the Declaration of Independence, The Constitution, The Ordinance of 1787, The Virginia and Kentucky Resolutions of 1798, Washington's Neutrality Proclamation, and Jackson's veto against the Bank.

We took this method of getting before the class, in the beginning, the course *in extenso*.

During the seven lectures which have been given, the lecture audiences have varied from one hundred to one hundred and fifty in number. The quiz class, presumably doing the required work, numbers forty-seven. In addition to these forty-seven, eight have paid the additional fee for the quiz class, and have chosen to come in as *listeners*, but not as reciters and participants; and the Senior Class in the Indiana Blind Asylum with their teacher, numbering thirteen, are in regular attendance at the quiz. This gives us altogether in our conference and quiz a class of sixty-eight. The class meets on Friday evenings, one hour before the lecture, and considers the subject of the lecture given the week before. The syllabus, which the class has had in hand a week, besides containing a topical outline of the week's study, suggests questions for review which they are expected to be ready to answer, and a reference list of books, chapters, and monographs in the way of a bibliography. Special topics are assigned to individual members of the class for special reading and reports. And every member of the class who designs to complete the required work is expected to hand in a written summary of the previous lecture. This is part of the written work. The class have access to the public libraries of the city, which, it is reported, are already noticing the effect of the courses.

Only oral quizes have so far been held, though written ones may be expected, and the effort is made to use the first half-hour for the purpose of testing the class, the last half-hour for the purpose of conference, interchange of information and opinion, and questions on the part of the class. In the class of fifty-five, —not counting the class from the Blind Asylum,—fifty are women and five are men, and all but ten are teachers in the public schools. The most of the class are graduates from the Indianapolis High School, or the Sewall Classical School of Indianapolis. A number are graduates of colleges, some are very capable of doing advanced university work, and the majority of the class may be said to be generally well informed on American history. I am not able to say how many will complete the required work, or pass the final examination. I shall expect from ten to twenty out of the fifty. The examination will be held the middle of February, and Dr. H. B. Adams, of the Johns Hopkins University, has consented to set the topics on the basis of the series of syllabi.

The business managers have charged two dollars for the series of twelve lectures, and five dollars for attendance upon both the lecture and the quiz. It would seem to me much better to charge a higher fee for the lectures, with merely a nominal sum for the further privilege of attendance upon the quiz. This is the essential part of the work, where lies the test of success, and it should receive every possible encouragement. It does not require much exertion to absorb something—or to attempt to do so—from an evening lecture, but to undertake the reading and the tests, this only the most eager and the most capable will endure. The many who will consent to the former should be led to bear the expenses for the elect few who may be led to attempt the latter. The managers, however, are able to report that the course will cover its expenses, amounting in all to about four hundred dollars, and will realize a surplus of over one hundred dollars.

The Chicago experiment is from many points of view a more

interesting one. This course in Chicago is representative of the Extension work, both of the Indiana University and of the Chautauqua movement for college education, as the course is given there under the advice of President Harper of the Chicago University, who is also the Principal of the Chautauqua Colleges. The course is a repetition of the one being given at Indianapolis, and is, I understand, the first Extension course given in Chicago. Valuable college teaching has been carried on for two years by a volunteer corps at Hull House, West Side, under the direction of Misses Adams and Starr, but no University Extension courses have been attempted in Chicago before this winter. Our Chicago course will probably not pay its expenses in a mere financial sense. Between ninety-five and one hundred have bought tickets for the lectures. Of these forty-five are taking the class hour work, thirty-eight of whom have signified their readiness for the quiz by handing in their names. The ages of the class range from fourteen to sixty, and one-third of the class are men. Much of the interest of this class attaches to its miscellaneous character. There are three graduates of colleges; there is one physician, one dentist, twenty-one clerks, ranging from three boys at $3 per week to men receiving from $1200 to $2400 per year. Of these two have a high-school education, seventeen have a grammar-school education, and two are reported "fairly well read." There are five women clerks, one with a high-school education, the other four with grammar-school training. There are seventeen public school teachers, who have attained the grade of the ordinary normal school, some of whom are graduates of such schools. Five are classed as school girls, the youngest of whom is still in a grammar grade, the others in the high school. There are twenty-three wage-earners, comprising bricklayers, stone-masons, car-drivers, conductors, painters, carpenters, unskilled laborers, all with grammar school education or less.

This Chicago course is under the auspices of the Workers' Church, 3037 Butler Street, Dr. Doremus Scudder, pastor, a church which may be said to be established on very broad philanthropic and educational lines,—the outcome of the missionary efforts of Plymouth Church, in that city. The Workers'

Church has been described as "independent, undenominational, non-sectarian, and creedless, with a Christian aim." The church is located in the centre of a population of ninety thousand laborers and their families. The region seems to be one in which it is yet to be proved whether there is a sufficient popular demand for the extension of university and college study, or whether real university work can be sustained by a local constituency. But it is already evident, although so far only three lectures have been given on alternate Thursday nights, that much benefit may be derived in public education in such centres from such courses. The spread of intelligence, the cultivation of a taste for better reading, inciting young people to the further pursuance of their studies, giving direction to those who desire to read, and who thus may be helped to avoid idle and desultory reading without a purpose,—these and other considerations are great compensations for the expense, if those would pay for the cost of the course who could well afford to provide voluntarily a foundation for Extension enterprises. But if it be found, as I think very probable, that the Extension course, upon a second experiment, may be found self-supporting by the constituency in such a centre, it is certain that they may be so in scores of other centres now about to open in that great city.

The fact that such a constituency is demanding such instruction and is asking to be directed in such study, leads us to reflect upon the eager thirst for higher knowledge among scores and, I think I may say, hundreds and thousands of men and women who are by necessity denied the opportunities and privileges of higher studies.

The Chicago course of twelve lectures will cost altogether only about $250. More than $200 will be covered by those subscribing to the course. It has been to me a source of much encouragement—and such experiences will give all true university men a sense of responsibility to become helpers and missionaries of learning to their fellows—to see the anxiety and self-sacrifice at personal inconvenience, displayed by men and women, some of them in straitened circumstances, in their efforts to obtain University instruction. In this connection the words of Dr. Scudder written to me a few days ago are significant. He says, "If to our expenses there were required to be added hall rent and other ordinary expenses which we have escaped, I fear University Extension would prove too expensive a luxury for laboring men in Chicago."

We all understand that University instruction has never anywhere in all its history paid its own way, and, of course, it is not thought that these centres can in any sense compensate the lecturers for their services. The lecturers have to be supported and paid as they are supported for all students now resident in our universities, not by fees but by foundations, in other ways provided. If this cannot be done in Extension centres among a laboring population, it does not argue that provision should be withheld till a better standard of support is attained by these centres, but that provision should be increased, especially in view of the evidence already accumulated of the ability and willingness, yea, even the eagerness, of these centres to profit by their opportunities.

There is one other phase of experience which may be worth mentioning.

The movement for the Extension of University teaching is many-sided. However uncertain some of its phases may appear from the reports of various centres (although I think our American experiments point to ultimate and early success in complete university courses), yet there is one phase in this educational movement of which no doubt need be expressed. In education from the public platform, the lecture for instruction, if it does not supersede, will find a co-ordinate place by the lecture for entertainment; the course of lectures on connected themes, to be followed as one follows a course of selected reading, is to supersede the kaleidoscopic and pyrotechnic character of the miscellaneous courses of the Lyceum bureau, however valuable in a public way many of the Lyceum lectures may be. This improvement in public education is one of the results and characteristic features of University Extension. My experience convinces me that at least this feature of the movement can reach great masses of people for their instruction and inspiration. The quiz class with readings assigned and tasks performed may be important parts of university discipline; but university instruction may be given without these, though it may not be recognized as complete Extension work; for, after all, the lecture must form the backbone of the instruction. A good course with the substance of the university class-room, with the manner of presentation cleverly modified for popular uses, the course thoroughly studied by the lecturer, well prepared and well delivered, cannot fail to be of great educational benefit.

For the series of lectures on connected themes, with quiz, conference, and examination, but without concurrent reading and study,—for these features of the work the Chautauqua Assemblies in the summer stand, to my mind, as offering the best opportunity in America. These centres throughout the States, even the great centre of the Lake itself, are without adequate library facilities, and, of course, because of this, and because of the brief time spent in these resorts, students could do but little in the way of supplementary reading and study. But from observation of courses given at Chautauqua last summer by Dr. H. B. Adams, of the Johns Hopkins University, and Dr. Francis N. Thorpe, of the University of Pennsylvania, and of a course which I attempted myself, on all of which competitive examinations were held and quizes and conferences might have been held,—from this observation I feel justified in asserting without reservation that Chautauqua offers to this method of instruction by university lectures the widest and most profitable field of application. Thus, the forces which may create and control thousands of centres throughout the country may be, within a brief season, touched to vigorous life and endeavor, not to mention the benefits immediately derived from such courses in several weeks' residence at these summer centres.

HISTORY AS AN EXTENSION STUDY.

BY PROF. WILFRED H. MUNRO,

Brown University.

MR. PRESIDENT,—When I received your very courteous note inviting me to present an essay on some phase of University Extension work to this conference, I had before me on my desk such a huge pile of examination papers from my history class in Brown University as made the preparation of a paper quite impossible in the limited time at my disposal.

I am glad, however, that I have the opportunity to say a few words to this audience respecting "History as an Extension Study,"—first, because I am myself a teacher of history, and, second, because I can say a few words about one of my predecessors in the historical faculty of Brown University who was really the pioneer worker in the University Extension field in the United States.

More than twenty years ago that peerless teacher of history, Professor J. L. Diman, who—as every graduate of Brown University (and I see many alumni of Brown in this audience) will testify, and as every graduate of Johns Hopkins University who heard him in Baltimore deliver that matchless course of lectures upon the "Thirty Years' War" will testify—filled the chair of history in Brown University more fully and more completely than any historical chair in America ever was filled before—was doing in America, outside the walls of Brown, exactly the kind of work that James Stuart was doing in England. He was giving daily instruction in history to the senior class in Brown University. He was lecturing weekly to an association of ladies in Providence. He was delivering each year courses of lectures on constitutional history before the pupils of the Rhode Island State Normal School. He was also delivering successive courses of lectures to the students of Johns Hopkins University and of other universities. He was delighting the people of Rhode Island and Massachusetts by his graceful addresses on historical subjects of local interest in many towns and cities of those two States. More than this,—he was writing daily for the Providence *Journal* those masterly leading articles which gave to that paper a reputation that was national. As James Stuart has earned the title of "Father of University Extension" in England, so ought Jeremiah Lewis Diman to be called the Father of University Extension in America.

It is pleasing, also, to be able to tell something which shows the appreciation in which his Extension lectures were held.

When Professor Diman was stricken down in the very zenith of his powers and the hearts of all Brown men were throbbing with the bitter sense of their loss, it was proposed to raise for the college a "Diman Fund," which should commemorate his name. The income from this fund was to be used for the purchase of historical works for the University library. But it is easier to plan than to accomplish. After the first few months, interest in the project languished and finally died. Last year, however, it occurred to my colleague, Professor Jameson, that the ladies to whom Professor Diman had given these Extension lectures had never been asked to contribute toward this fund. They were asked. They contributed. What the alumni in ten years had failed to do this Extension class of ladies accomplished in less than six months. The "Diman Fund" now enables our librarian to place each year upon his shelves all the best new books upon mediæval and modern history.

So much must be said of the work done by the pioneer University Extension lecturer in the United States,—so much for the estimation in which his labors were held by Extension classes which he taught.

It seems to me, Mr. President, that we must have a scheme of work very carefully planned before we send our historical lecturers into the Extension field. It is most important that the work done should be uniform, in order that the Extension certificates may have value everywhere. This is, of course, true of all Extension work, but it is specially true of historical work.

The subject is too large to be handled in a satisfactory way by any one man, or by any one association. It should, I think, be placed in charge of a general executive committee, and that committee should recommend to all the Extension associations the work to be done by their lecturers. It is not for the welfare of the cause that every lecturer should be allowed to hurl any set of lectures he may happen to have ready at the heads of his audience. Regard should be had for the attainments of his hearers. The specialist should not be allowed to get in his work until good, broad foundations of general knowledge have been laid.

Here I must say that I do not place the same value upon the syllabus that most people set upon it. In many cases it hampers the lecturer instead of helping him. It is a most powerful weapon in the hands of a skilled teacher who knows his audience, but it is not always a good thing for inexperienced lecturers. It was first adopted as a lesson in note-taking (English audiences, as a rule, are not so much accustomed to note-taking as American audiences are), and it was not meant to take the place of note-taking. Moreover, it is not well at the beginning of our Extension work to have a Procrustean bed on which to stretch our audiences. It is better to have only a general plan outlined, and to leave the lecturer to fill out that plan *according to the needs of his audience*. What is one man's meat may be another man's poison. One of our lecturers last year was forced to throw away one set of lectures because he found that he was shooting over the heads of nine-tenths of his audience. If he had already sold a copy of his syllabus to each one of his class, every member of that class would have deemed himself swindled if the lecturer had not kept to his lines. But if the instructor had used his original notes the whole course would have been a failure. He changed his lectures to suit his hearers, and a most brilliant success was the result. Thus far we of Brown have printed no syllabus, and we shall not print any until the trial of a year has shown us how we can do the best work. (The syllabus is not necessary as a test of the lecturer's knowledge, because we know what kind of work each member of our faculty is capable of doing. We use no untried men.) In any case our syllabus will be a brief one, and we shall insist upon much note-taking. I much prefer in my own classes to dictate the heads only of a lecture, leaving the members of my audience to do all the filling-in for themselves. It seems to me that the other system encourages laziness, and is too much like text-book work. The most valuable part of a printed syllabus is the "bibliography." We always furnish full bibliographies.

Now, of what shall the first historical lectures treat?

Plainly of those subjects which form the basis of all historical knowledge. Of those subjects which scholars everywhere—in Germany, England, France, as well as in America—prescribe as the groundwork of historical study.

For a first course of twelve lectures I should say take some such course as this, covering the period from the Fall of Rome to the Reformation,—that is to say, a course on Mediæval History:

I. The dissolution of Rome.
(A general discussion of the beginnings of mediæval history.)
II. The Barbarian Invaders of Italy.
(The Visigoths, Huns, Vandals, Ostrogoths, and Lombards.)
III. The Germanic Element in European Civilization.
IV. The Early Christian Church.
V. Charlemagne.
VI. Hildebrand and his Times.
(The Contest between the Papacy and the Empire.)
VII. and VIII. The Feudal System.
IX. and X. The Crusades.
XI. The History of the Great Monastic Orders.
XII. The Rise of the New Nations.

A second course, equally broad in its scope, might give the groundwork of modern history:

I. The Beginnings of Modern History.
II. Plans of Reform within the Church.
III. The Renaissance—the New Birth of the World.
IV. The Protestant Revolution.

V. The Catholic Reaction.
VI. The Age of Elizabeth (England, 1558-1603).
VII. The Civil Wars in France (Charles IX—Nantes, 1562-1598).
VIII. The Policy of Richelieu (France, 1624-1642).
IX. Revolt of the Netherlands (1568-1648).
X. The Thirty Years War (Germany, 1618-1648).
XI. The Rise of Puritanism (England under the Stuarts).
XII. The English Revolution of 1688.

Then, the broad foundations having been carefully laid, such courses may be built upon them as the classes may call for. The fact, however, must always be borne in mind that the audiences are not made up of specialists, and that, consequently, the carefully minute treatment which may well be employed before a class of university students must not be used in lecturing to an Extension audience. The aim of this whole movement is not to cultivate specialists, but to diffuse general knowledge.

REMARKS.

President Fell, of St. John's College, Annapolis, Md., said:

I have been in particular interested by the opening remarks of Professor Munro, in which he stated as his opinion that it was necessary to secure uniformity of action among all institutions which might embark in the work of University Extension. This suggestion appears to me to be one of great weight. We have heard from Mr. Sadler of the amount of labor and thought bestowed by the University of Oxford upon the preparation of a syllabus or of a course of lectures which would be deemed attractive to the public. Now, outside the great centres of Philadelphia, Boston, and New York, there are a great number of Southern and Western institutions willing to take part in this movement, but which hesitate to do so, as they feel the need of a directing head. Is it assumed that such an institution must work out its own plans and its own methods, or should it not rather be guided by the direction of the American Society?

THE UNIVERSITY EXTENSION CLASS.

BY EDWARD T. DEVINE, M.A,,

Staff Lecturer of the American Society.

IN the theory of University Extension the class holds a preeminent place. In the practice of University Extension it is for the most part a failure. Let us assume that the lecture has been an entire success,—that it has attracted an audience, that it has exhibited literary finish, command of the material, skill in presentation, adaptation to the audience,—whatever other excellences you please, that when the hour for the class has arrived, the lecturer finds himself in a position to answer correctly, even brilliantly, all the questions asked, and that the invitation to ask questions meets with actual response. It will be objected that I am assuming too much. What anxiety is removed from the breast of the young lecturer if even most of these favorable conditions are found to be present at the crucial hour! These are the very ends, it will be said, to be attained. But I have thought that we can best get at the heart of the matter by assuming these favorable conditions and then putting the question as to why it is that even then the class fails for the most part to satisfy the teacher, as distinguished from the lecturer, from the born debater, and from the scientific specialist.

In the first place the student is never heard from in class. The woman or man, young or old, who readily enrolls in the unwritten list of real students, who grasps at the chance of doing the weekly exercises, searches the returned paper anxiously for the word of approval, or the criticism which shows, however kindly, that the answer is wrong, who ventures to express independent opinions only under cover of a *nom-de-plume*—this is not the one who is heard from in the class discussion. It requires greater courage to participate in the class discussion as a student, as a questioner, than to conduct that discussion as a regular lecturer. I cannot take time to set up any theory to account for this somewhat anomalous fact, but that there is this hesitation, more than that, this refusal to give expression to private opinion, and to ask for explanation is a psychological fact with which we must reckon, and which deserves more attention in our scheme than we have hitherto accorded it. For, under these circumstances, it is the experienced speaker, the professional talker, if there is one, who monopolizes the time which should belong to students. The school-teacher, particularly the school principal, the preacher, the lawyer, the labor agitator, any one but the student talks. Do not understand me to say that the student is never found in the ranks of the professions referred to, but it will be admitted that they seldom furnish the student class in our common and perfectly legitimate sense of the term. The argument which he whom I call the professional talker makes in reply to objectionable passages in the lecture may take the form of rhetorical questions, or a prolonged formal controversy may arise, the results are the same; the interests of the students are sacrificed, or rather students are not made to know that they have interests; in fact, they remain an undiscovered element.

I do not hesitate to say that the discussions as now actually held, the questions actually asked and answered, so far from constituting genuine class work, are an obstacle to it, simply render it impossible. The very size of the class is a chief cause of this difficulty. As University Extension is now organizing—practically without local endowment—no audience can consist of less than about two hundred persons, and it will generally be larger. If the course is regarded as a success by the members of the centre, most of them will stay for the second hour's work, if for no better reason, because they have paid as much as others, and wish to come as near getting their money's worth as they can. Normally, therefore, the class will consist of a hundred students and upward. No human being can teach at once a hundred persons. In the universities themselves, the overflowing lecture-rooms have made it necessary for us to adopt the German seminar system for that part of the professor's work which he is willing to call his real teaching, as distinguished from his knowledge-imparting lecture or his examination quiz. The Sunday-school teacher wisely limits his class to ten or fifteen pupils; even the Great Teacher, a reference to whose example makes further argument or illustration unnecessary, found that while He could instruct a multitude by parables and other features of the lecture system, He could really teach but twelve.

This is not of itself an argument for abandoning that which we call a class, but it is an argument for abandoning the delusion that it is a class, or a seminary, of which the chief aim is to benefit those who wish to know more and to get clearer ideas. There are some advantages in the present system, considering it simply as an appendix to the lecture, as an extension of the evening's entertainment. It is probable that many a one who does speak, voices the question which has suggested itself to many others, and that the answer will be awaited as eagerly by a dozen or by all as by him who puts the question. Sometimes a much-needed correction is made by some one in the class who is really in position to know that a statement made by the lecturer is incomplete or incorrect, and again a question reveals to the lecturer that he has inadvertently omitted a necessary qualification, which he had himself intended to introduce, and the omission of which leaves on the audience an entirely false impression of the lecturer's position. Then, finally, the criticism of a student frequently supplies just the stimulus needed to enable the lecturer to send a more telling shot to the centre of truth, to make doubly clear a position in which the lecturer was entirely correct, but which had been somewhat obscurely presented. It is, of course, true that the lecturer will find in the weekly exercises material for a certain amount of valuable class criticism, and that the timid student will sometimes add to a paper a query which can be answered in class, but this could all be done far better if the obstacles to which reference has been made were absent.

Two ways out of the difficulty present themselves. One is to say frankly at the close of the lecture hour that the entertainment is now over and that some business is about to begin in which most of them will not be interested. I am not sure that the class should necessarily be restricted absolutely to those who do the weekly exercises, though I fail to find any impropriety even in a measure so drastic as that. It would certainly be an effective winnowing-fan even if the minimum of work required were made so light that the preparation of the paper would consume no more time than the composition of an ordinary letter. If this change were made, some of the attractions inhering in the ordinary class would of course be sacrificed. Those brilliant tilts between skilled questioners and speakers, the interesting general discussion in which a half dozen or more are anxious to participate at once, those gratifying outward evidences that the course is making an impression in the community would be gone. If we must choose between them and the opportunity for accomplishing with a handful of students an educational result far greater, our choice must certainly be against the popular class. It cannot be too strongly insisted upon that some one feature of the Extension system must be for this nucleus of students to which Mr. Sadler has just referred. In some exceptional cases the Students' Association, meeting on another evening of the week, supplies this need; where it does, no objection against the present organization of the class will lie. But the necessary absence of the lecturer from the meetings of the Association and the difficulty of finding a leader who can do the particular work which the lecturer knows ought to be done, are objections too serious to be disregarded.

Better perhaps than the plans suggested is that of holding at a different hour a conference especially intended for the students who have sent in written exercises. It could be done either entirely informally, each one who had sent in a paper calling at the lecturer's rooms or at some appointed place, looking over the paper to note corrections in the presence of the lecturer, asking questions, and holding a short personal interview with the lecturer, or a regular hour could be appointed when all those who had sent papers could meet for a short seminar discussion. The lecturer would call their attention to points of common interest and could put some questions to each member of what would then be in reality a class. Certainly much greater progress could be made if this plan were adopted. It will be replied that it will be better for the few but not so good for the centre as a whole. But I maintain that the gain to the class under these circumstances would not be offset by any loss in the general economy. We must work through the few in any community. When we wish to get a great furnace of coal on fire we do not apply a lighted match immediately to the large masses of coal. We light first the shavings and the kindling wood and let the fire grow naturally. And note that I am not advocating a measure which will benefit a particular set. The members of the conference, or class, would not be selected by others, but the class would be the outcome of a very natural self-selection, or would embrace all who chose to become students.

The real difficulties are two in number. 1. The fixing of an hour for the conference which will make it possible for the students to attend, and which will not interfere with the lecturer's preparation for the evening's work. While the half-hour immediately preceding the lecture is in many respects an ideal time for a conference of the kind under discussion, it would, if held at that time, leave the lecturer in a less satisfactory condition for his lecture; and if held at another hour it might become too great an additional tax on the student's time. It might tend to discourage some from undertaking the exercises at all if it were expected that they must attend an additional meeting.

2. It might add eventually to the cost of Extension teaching if the lecturer were to undertake this additional work, though I consider that doubtful, at least in the case of staff lecturers. The latter are in position to do certain things of this kind, which, if we would maintain our standard, it will be necessary for us to do. In short, I do not believe that the difficulties to a higher grade of class work are insuperable. We must choose, I take it, between changing our class into a smaller body of students properly so termed, and adding the special conference for students, either of which plans would work beneficial results. The latter plan has the special advantage that it would enable us to retain the so-called class of the present organization with all its advantages.

I have not thought it necessary in this short paper to dwell exclusively on the necessity of doing in Extension teaching that work for which as distinguished from the lecturing the class itself stands. We should probably all agree that the lecturer who spends but one hour in the lecture-room, and in the neighborhood, however valuable and interesting his lecture may have been, has not done his full duty by the centre with which he has made his engagement. In view of the general announcement, by Extension societies, of the class as an essential feature of the Extension method, it is doubtful if a committee is justified in making an engagement with any lecturer who is too busy to undertake the class work, without providing that it shall be done by some one who shall act as the lecturer's deputy. There may be special reasons for engaging a lecturer whose time is thus in demand, but there can scarcely be a justification for sacrificing this feature which we hold up as the most valuable for the sake of getting a brilliant series of lectures, which we have repeatedly in circulars and from the platform declared to be no essential feature of our system.

The class is valuable because it gives the best opportunity for that personal contact without which there can be no teaching; because it reveals the teacher, and reveals the student, and strips the mask from the pretender in either position. Every tendency away from this strict Extension ideal of class organization should be checked,—every change which brings us nearer its realization should be welcomed. It will be objected, perhaps, that I have been discussing the form rather than the substance of this matter. It is, of course, the kernel, not the shell we are after, but University Extension, if it is anything, is a mechanism for accomplishing certain ends. Here, as in the case of a wagon-wheel, very much depends upon the form. I have suggested some changes in form which merit at least discussion and experiment. If a profession of faith on the main question is needed, I willingly subscribe myself again a firm believer in the Extension class, as the most important discovery of the age, in the line of popular education, as a discovery too valuable and a weapon too efficient for us to allow it to become anything else than it was meant to be, a bringing together of students and teacher.

REMARKS.

Rev. Benjamin J. Douglas, of Philadelphia, said:
With the aim of the writer to give the class its proper place and function in University Extension methods, I am in hearty sympathy. With his resolute determination not to allow sham work to pass as real, but to insist upon the written exercise and the examination as well as the lecture and the class I fully sympathize. The object of the writer is no doubt to get at greater thoroughness in class-work, and this is a point constantly to be kept in view, and one which, if I am correctly informed, the experience of each successive course of study at the local centres is gradually accomplishing.

What brought me to my feet was the perception of what I thought was a too great eagerness to restrict the class in the beginning only to those who had time to prepare the written exercises, and this in view of the statement that those who did the real work, those who took the pains to study and write out their thoughts at home, were not the ones to ask questions in the class. The time devoted to class-work was for the most part monopolized by others than the real students, by "professional talkers" and the like. I put in a word by way of apology for these "professional talkers," in view of the patent fact that if those who prepare the papers will not ask questions in the class, the class becomes a useless appendage. If those who do the same work in paper exercises will not do their part in the class, what is the use of the class?

Right here comes in the need of this outside help, not to supersede, but to start the discussion. The farmer, when he wants to start his fire, goes to his wood-pile and collects all kinds of chips. If the solid wood won't burn at once, he gets light wood to kindle it. Or, to vary the illustration: here is a pump which will not work at once; you pour in a little water and the stream is started. I really believe there are very few who use the class simply as an occasion to air their own opinions. In nine cases out of ten, people are there to gain information, to profit by what they hear, and, if they venture "to speak out in meeting," it is generally after a pause sufficiently long to show that their superiors will not.

A class after a University Extension lecture is not a class in a University recitation-room. It is an indiscriminate crowd, composed of all sorts of men and women, eager to learn, or they would not be there. And what if some one does put an irrelevant question, or a question which only displays his or her ignorance or crankiness? It is the crank that starts the machinery of the locomotive and the steamship. Not much harm will be done. The individual who has had the laugh turned against him suffers most. For the rest, the ice is broken, and the timid encouraged to speak out.

The truth is, that a lecturer, if he is worth anything, has things in his own hands and is backed by the good sense and the respect for decorum on the part of the class itself. As a man of affairs, as well as a student, he is equal to the occasion and can, with a little tact, turn even an unfriendly criticism to good account. Unless there is a flagrant breach of order or an utter want of respect for the ordinary proprieties of social intercourse, we would have the greatest freedom of discussion,—at least to start with. Professional talkers, as a profession, scarcely exist, but professional men occasionally do a little talking by way of help, and often for the purpose of acquiring information on points on which they are a little rusty, or a little behind the age. They wish, if it is possible, to keep abreast of the times, to keep in touch with the best thought of the age. And hence you will find them sitting in the place of the learners, especially when they have "one who knows" to expound a subject.

Now, I contend that the most of these have not the time to prepare the written exercises. Their time is taken up, as a general rule, with their professional duties. Still, like the old warhorse, they scent the battle from afar, and love to take a hand in the pursuits which once engaged their youthful energies. They are, for the most part, liberally educated : some are specialists in certain branches, and some without a liberal education are recognized leaders, and worthily so, in certain movements. Are these to be shut out?

I pointed out in the course of my remarks, and I cannot go into further detail as a proof of my position, how much we owe in this Conference, in seeking a solution of the problems involved, to the presence of a distinguished representative of the labor interests in this country, who met with us as a fellow-citizen and student, whose heart was aflame with sympathy with all that belonged to the uplifting of his fellow-men in the scale of social and mental and moral improvement. We need such in the classroom, even if their pressing duties will not allow them time to enter into the severe work of preparing papers.

But I must close. I have no manner of intention of traversing the main drift of the excellent paper of Mr. Devine. It is the standard towards which University Extension methods must ever be approximating. But as things actually are, I am only pleading for certain additional conditions which enter into the account, as in adapting a machine for actual use we must sometimes make allowance for friction and other existing elements.

The Conference just closing has been a wonderful success. The reports from all parts of the United States are in no small degree encouraging. May the year just opening and all coming years add to the efficiency of the University Extension movement.

UNIVERSITY EXTENSION IN CINCINNATI.

BY W. O. SPROULL, PH.D., LL.D.,

Professor of Latin and Arabic in the University of Cincinnati.

THE Cincinnati idea of University Extension is to extend the University. The first steps taken in this direction were in 1889, when a course of seven lectures was given on Saturday mornings in the University building. In 1890 three courses were given: one at the same time and place, a second in the Newport High School, and a third in the Bellevue High School, both in the evening. These lectures were a close and careful treatment of some subject in each lecturer's line of work. They were exceedingly well attended, especially by teachers.

Towards the close of the last academic year, a committee of principals and teachers requested the faculty of the University of Cincinnati to provide college courses of instruction on Saturdays. The faculty did not deem it wise to undertake this officially, but left the matter to individual professors.

Accordingly the following courses were offered, each to consist of *thirty* lectures or recitations:

"Lectures on Experimental Chemistry," by Professor Norton; "Mediæval and Modern History," by Professor Myers; "A Critical and Exegetical Study of Horace," by Professor Sproull.

"Analytics," by Professor Hyde.

"Mechanics," by Professor Baldwin.

The teaching staff organized by electing Professor Sproull, president, and Professor Norton, secretary and treasurer.

Although there was but little time for the necessary publicity, and besides the fact that different teachers' institutes hold their meetings on Saturdays, *seventy-two* persons, mostly principals and teachers, were enrolled. In addition are those who attend single lectures on visitors' tickets. At the end of the courses, voluntary examinations will be held and certificates given signed by the examiners.

The direct benefit of these classes is very decided, both to those taught and to the instructors. The work of teachers in our schools is so varied and consists of so many details, in addition to the strain of exercising discipline, that they have neither the time nor are they in the proper mental condition to specialize. No text-book, moreover, and this is markedly true in science, can be abreast with the times. The Germans recognize this, for a text-book has scarcely made its appearance before the author is at work on a new and revised edition. With us it too often happens the book is stereotyped, as if further progress for years were impossible, and published until the plates are worn out. Discoveries recorded in journals and periodicals quickly put the best text-books into the background, and these discoveries can be watched and noted only by the specialist. Even excellent editions of the classics fail before long to meet the demands of the scholar. The finding of a manuscript, the critical examinations of texts, the discussions of grammatical and lexical questions, the flood of light thrown upon Greek and Latin authors by archæological investigations are contributions to our knowledge of the many phases of Greek and Roman life, and they can be recorded only in the current literature.

What teachers can keep up with this? Supposing they had the time, what schools,—even high schools,—are there where journals and periodicals of any specialty are at their command? By means of Saturday classes, teachers come into contact with specialists, whose duty and endeavor it is not only to know what each day brings forth in their departments, but also to contribute thereto.

The writer now speaks of his own experience. In Latin a course in Horace had been offered, but, by request, this is now preceded by a course in the Æneid. The book is discussed exegetically and critically by the aid of palæographic fac-similes. Collateral reading on Latin Literature, Classical Mythology, Roman Antiquities and especially on the author read, is marked out and commented upon. Every opportunity is given for asking questions. The effect is magical. Some of these teachers have gone over the first six books of the Æneid frequently, but, as one expressed it, they are reading Vergil for the first time. The book had become dry and ceased to have any interest for them, but now it has all the freshness of a new author.

What is the effect upon the lecturer? What effect must it have upon any professor devoted to his calling, to have before him a body of teachers who give up their Saturday mornings to the class-room, their spare time during the week to preparation? Nothing could awaken more enthusiasm in him, and a desire to do his utmost, than so many adults before him eager to learn and ever on the alert. It acts as a mental stimulant with only good effects. The writer's colleagues bear similar testimony.

How great is the indirect benefit? Of these *seventy* and more students, *fifty* are teachers. Each teacher comes into daily contact with at least *thirty* scholars. Thus a class of *thirty* teachers is representative of *fifteen hundred* scholars. College faculties, moreover, complain, oftentimes unjustly, of the instruction in the preparatory schools. These teachers' classes give them the means of remedying this, in a great measure. The community is alive to the importance of this movement. The Union Board of High Schools of Cincinnati appointed a committee of conference to have additional courses established. The following extract is taken from an article that appeared in the Cincinnati *Times-Star* of October 22, 1891:

"Every Saturday between sixty and seventy earnest workers gather at the University for these classes. As yet the work is only in its beginning. This movement promises to be a telling force in educational affairs. Next year, with further experience, the work done will be an improvement upon that of this year. In this way the influence of the University will go radiating out through the community. The professors engaged in this work combine enthusiasm, zeal, tenacity of purpose, sound judgment, and more devoted and determined students cannot be found. Cincinnati may not be aware of the fact, but it is nevertheless true, that since the organization of the school system, this University Extension work is the most important step taken in the interests of higher education. It broadens the field of work and offers the opportunity of a liberal education to hundreds of those to whom fate in youth has denied it."

It may be added, the whole tendency will be to systematize and unify the entire plan of education and to bring all the teachers into sympathetic and helpful relations.

The good accomplished by University Extension throughout the country in organizing centres with unit courses of lectures is very great. More credit is due this movement, however, for showing how little relatively the colleges and universities are doing, and so forcing them to inquire wherein they have been derelict. Consider the wealth and facilities of these institutions, and then look at the vast array of those whom University Extension has brought together, longing for these advantages, but cannot enjoy them on account of restrictions and conditions. According to the report of the Bureau of Education for 1888–89,* the Colleges of Liberal Art have an invested capital of $122,638,-681 (not including the value of 3,716,625 volumes), with an income of $8,293,444. The number of graduates was about 7500. This does not convey an accurate idea of how many were benefited, but since the object of a college is to map out lines of work that can be completed only by those who reach the time for graduation, the number of graduates must be taken as a test of efficiency.

The question as to how colleges and universities situated in the cities can do more for the community has been in part answered. Separate classes should be formed, especially for teachers, to meet on Saturdays. The instruction should be of a high order along the lines of college work. This should be only the first stage. Every applicant for admission to college must comply with at least three conditions: First is the condition of preliminary education. Second is the condition of place. Instruction is given only within the college walls. The third is the time-condition; that is, the student must attend during the day.

---

* The writer wishes to express his thanks to Dr. W. T. Harris for advance sheets of the Report for 1888-89, also to Professor Coy, Principal of Hughes High School, Professor Harper, Principal of Woodward High School, and Professor Weaver, Principal of Bellevue (Ky.) High School, for statistics and suggestions.

It is the third condition that should be modified or done away with, if possible, in certain cases.

A great advance has been made by President Harper in his announcement that the University of Chicago will be open the year round. This adds one-fourth more time, in which the University can carry on its work and extend its facilities to the large number of persons who cannot attend during the other nine months. The writer proposes another innovation, that colleges and universities in cities offer full college courses leading to degrees, to be carried on in the evening during the year.* There is an element of justice in making this as a demand on those institutions so situated and receiving State or municipal aid. In 1888–89, the Colleges of Liberal Arts received such aid to the amount of $1,326,395, and, as far as the writer knows, there is not one where he who must work by day can prosecute college work by night.

These evening classes would be recruited from the following sources:

First.—Of the high schools of Cincinnati (and the same is no doubt true elsewhere) there are every year many graduates both qualified and desirous to engage in college work, but circumstances compel them to earn their living.† Professor Coy, Principal of the Hughes high school, thinks this would include from *twenty* to *thirty* per cent of each graduating class, which last year numbered in both schools *one hundred and sixty-six*. There are also those who had time, opportunity, and perhaps every encouragement to go to college, but no inclination, and who would now like to rectify their mistake. Many college graduates, moreover, would continue their studies if they could perform the class-work in the evening.

Second.—There is a large number of students pursuing their professional studies in the cities, who never went to college; or,

---

* This was advocated by the writer first in the Cincinnati *Courier*, June, 1890. It is urged strenuously by J. Spencer Hill, Hon. Treas. of the Chelsea University Extension Centre, in the London Academy, December 26, 1891.

† The high schools of Cincinnati prepare students to enter without conditions the B.A., B.S., or B.L. course of any institution.

it may be, for a year or two. Oftentimes the reason is that their professional training, if deferred until after graduation, would make their start in life too late. Here again financial straits may come into play. By such students some collegiate studies could be carried on in the evening, and after they had entered upon their vocation, ample time would be at their service during a few years for such work. Those students who had gone to college for a year or two might be able to complete their course by the time they had finished their professional studies. In 1888–89 there were enrolled in the college department of the Colleges of Liberal Arts 57,121 names, and not one-seventh of this number graduated.

Third.—The principal source would be from the body of teachers, chiefly of the common schools. There are within reach of such classes at the University of Cincinnati *fifteen hundred* teachers. Most of these have graduated from the high school, for this is one condition of appointment in the common schools. Judging from the success of the Saturday classes, and according to the opinion of teachers who have studied the subject, *two hundred* of these teachers would matriculate in evening classes. There are more than a dozen cities, each of which has a collegiate institution, where the average prospect for such classes would be as good as in Cincinnati. One important fact is that these classes would be made up of students attending of their own volition, and thus by their presence under such circumstances showing their appreciation of a higher education.

Educators have failed to set a proper value upon the influence of the common-school teacher in shaping the course of the youth in after-life. Her personal influence (for they are mostly women) is far greater than the subject-matter of her instruction. Her dictum has with the child often the force of an oracle. She meets the boy at that age when he is eager to give up all higher aims for a chance to make money. In elementary education the personal element of the teacher has greater weight than at any other period. The relative effect of the subject-matter and the teacher's personal influence approach each other as the child grows older, until they occupy reversed positions. The personal element of the professor usually makes little impression upon the student in comparison with the subject taught. The common-school teacher is consequently not the least, but the most important, factor in deciding the child's future. She should, therefore, have the greatest intellectual breadth. It would not do to demand of her a college education as one condition of appointment. The salary is so small that it would not be fair to require four additional years of preparation without additional compensation. By means of evening classes teachers would have an opportunity to acquire that knowledge, breadth of intellect, and mental discipline they so much need. Besides this, teachers transferred from the common schools to the high schools cannot have, under our present system, qualified themselves for their new position. As a rule, they have not only not advanced, but have forgotten much they learned during the high school curriculum. On the other hand, a few years' experience in teaching, combined with the training of a college education, will admirably prepare them for their new duties.*

The additional expense connected with these evening classes, except for the increase in the teaching force, would be comparatively little. The same buildings, grounds, apparatus, and libraries could be used both for day and evening classes. It would be, without doubt, necessary to enlarge correspondingly the faculty of any institution that engaged in this work, but that new outlay would be far more than offset by the much greater use that would be made of the immense capital invested in buildings, grounds, libraries, and apparatus.

These evening classes could not go over the whole ground in four years, but let graduation depend upon the quantity and quality of the work done without any time-limit.

Can these questions be answered affirmatively? Do those high schools taught by college graduates send the largest num-

---

* The Union Board of High Schools of Cincinnati will probably at its next meeting make a rule, that hereafter only graduates of reputable colleges will be appointed teachers in the high schools. This rule will not apply to the present teachers.

ber of students to college? Do those common schools in which are teachers, graduates of high schools or colleges, send the largest number of pupils to the high schools? If these questions can be affirmed, then give the teachers in the schools a college education by giving them opportunities to secure it, and do this by abolishing in their cases, as well as in those of the other classes mentioned, the present condition of time, both as to when and how long they must study to secure the end. If colleges and universities in cities provide for these classes also, University Extension can meet the wants of those who cannot comply with the conditions of preliminary education and place. The most ardent friends of University Extension belong to the faculties of city institutions. They can hasten or retard the introduction of this innovation. At all events, the time will come when the doors of many such institutions will be open to students, not only the year round by day, but also the year round by night.

THE STATE AND UNIVERSITY EXTENSION.

BY RALPH W. THOMAS,

Chief Examiner, University of the State of New York.

NOTHING in the University Extension movement is more significant than its progress towards government recognition.

The title of the first edition of the book published by Halford J. Mackinder and Michael E. Sadler was "University Extension, has it a Future?" The last edition is entitled "University Extension, Past, Present, and Future." Among the facts which have caused this change none is more important than the action of the British government in giving official support to the movement.

Of the States of our country, New York is the first officially to recognize University Extension. When our system of higher education is considered this seems natural. All the interests of higher education in New York are committed to the State University. It has the power to grant, amend, or repeal charters of higher educational institutions. It has the duty of inspection and visitation. It has a great system of examinations by which to test the work of the schools; and it is commissioned by the legislature annually to distribute $106,000 to high schools and academies. The State Library and the State Museum are departments of the university, and their interests are closely allied to the general educational work of the State. The natural agent, therefore, to carry forward the work of University Extension in New York was the University of the State of New York.

As the appropriation of last year was the first of its kind in this country, it will doubtless be of value as a precedent, and, therefore, it may be proper to submit a brief statement of the manner in which the merits of the Extension movement were presented to the legislature.

When the regents of the university had satisfied themselves

that this movement was of real worth, they communicated with the faculties of all the colleges in the State to ascertain whether or not the colleges would favor such a project. Without a dissenting voice the colleges heartily favored the plan, and urged the regents to appeal to the legislature for the appropriation necessary to carry on the executive work.

The bill introduced in both houses of the legislature provided "that no part of the appropriation should be expended in paying for the services or expenses of persons designated or appointed as lecturers or instructors." It was intended that all such expenses should be borne by the localities benefited. A joint hearing was given to the advocates of the measure by the Finance Committee of the Senate and the Committee of Ways and Means of the Assembly. At that hearing every college in the State was represented either by a delegate or by a letter. As the secretary of the university called the roll, the representatives of the various institutions urged upon the members of the committee the importance of the measure under consideration. The great fact which the hearing developed was the unity of the educators of the State in favor of the proposed measure.

A former Senator remarked that it was the most impressive hearing that he had ever seen. Wonder has been expressed that a measure of such importance should have passed the legislature with so little opposition. The explanation seems to be that the educators of the State were a unit in asking for its passage, and this unity of sentiment was the strongest argument in favor of the bill.

The present position of the movement in New York differs from that in England in these respects:

1. The expenditure of the fund is in charge of one central authority.

2. The appropriation is not restricted to the advancement of technical education, but can be used for the purposes of organization without reference to the studies which are to be taught.

The lesson of the New York movement is that the most valuable ally of University Extension is the unqualified, enthusiastic, and united support of the educational forces of the State.

REPORTS.

REPORTS OF PROGRESS.

MAINE.

Professor Leslie A. Lee, of Bowdoin College, reported to the Conference the action of the faculty of that institution in favor of University Extension. Courses are offered by many of the professors on different subjects, and some have already been arranged for several towns in the State.

VERMONT.

President M. H. Buckham represented the University of Vermont at the National Conference, and reported great interest in the work. The attitude of the University of Vermont is cordial toward the movement, and there is prospect of earnest effort being made at an early date to introduce the system in towns throughout the State.

NEW HAMPSHIRE.

No courses have so far been established in New Hampshire, but many of the leading newspapers of the State have shown their interest in the work by publishing articles descriptive of the movement and by advocating its introduction.

MASSACHUSETTS.

Centres have been established in Massachusetts in Attleboro', and North Attleboro', under the general direction of Brown University. President Merrill E. Gates, of Amherst College, has been from the first an earnest advocate of University Extension, and the interest of that institution is being exerted in behalf of it. The Prospect Progressive Union, of Cambridge, founded and carried on by students of Harvard College, is offering now to workingmen many of the advantages of University Extension. Courses are arranged for evening work, and instruction is being given by not less than forty students out of the entire membership of two hundred. For this year twenty courses have been offered in history, languages, mathematics, and political science. The meetings are on every week-day evening from seven to nine o'clock. At Westfield, Professor Williston Walker, Ph.D., of Hartford, Conn., is to deliver a course of Extension lectures on "The History of Modern Italy" before the History Club. Professor Graham Taylor, D.D., of Hartford, has an Extension course of eight lectures on "Sociological Conditions of Christian Work" before the Y. M. C. A. Training-school, at Springfield.

RHODE ISLAND.

Professor Wilfred H. Munro, Director of the University Extension for Brown University, read the following report:

In the academic year 1890–91, University Extension work, as such, was begun experimentally in Providence and in Pawtucket, Rhode Island, by Professors Bailey, Bumpus, Upton, and Williams, of Brown University. Lecture courses were given by these gentlemen in Botany, Biology, Astronomy, and German Literature. The audiences were as large as could well be handled, and the interest they manifested was most gratifying.

As a result of these experimental courses, the Corporation of Brown University, at its meeting in June, 1891, voted to make Extension teaching a part of its scheme of work, appointed one of its faculty Director of the University Extension, and granted permission to all the members of the faculty to engage in Extension teaching wherever they could do so without detriment to their regular college work.

The peculiar situation of Providence, in the midst of a large and compact population, and its excellent railway facilities, enable the University to accomplish more in this line than is possible for most colleges. In order to reach the largest number (and because the lecturers feel that they ought to do, at least at the outset, much missionary work), the lecturer's fee has been placed at one hundred dollars ($100) for a course of twelve lectures,— a much lower price than is charged anywhere else, in America or in England. No half-courses are given. This low charge makes it possible for centres to be organized in small towns, and for the most part results in small classes of from thirty to fifty persons; that is, in classes having about the number of students which the best schools ordinarily assign to one teacher. The element we make most prominent is the teaching element. Our object is not to amuse, but to instruct. We wish to do away entirely with the motive which governed the old lyceum. Smaller classes do better work than larger ones, in the Extension not less than in the regular University work, and the personality of the instructor counts for much more.

With one exception, all our lecturers are members of our own faculty. There is no raw material in the force, and the work done is more systematic and thorough than is usually the case with early Extension teaching. The Director knows personally the capabilities of his men, and can place them to the best advantage.

Not so much importance is given to the syllabus as is usually assigned to it, and, except in a very few instances, no syllabi have thus far been printed. The lectures have been prepared with special reference to the needs of the particular audience before which they were to be delivered, and the lecturers have not hesitated to vary them wherever it seemed wise to do so. This has required more labor on the part of the instructor, but the benefit to the class has been great. Not infrequently written lectures prove to be beyond the comprehension of those who listen to them, and if in such a case a cast-iron syllabus has to be used, much harm results. All the lecturers have prepared full analyses, which have most frequently been dictated to the class, and all furnish full bibliographies. All give special prominence to the class-work.

All ages and conditions of life are found in our classes. The larger proportion of the members are women, but two classes are composed entirely of men. One of these latter—in Practical Physics—is made up almost entirely of skilled mechanics from the famous factory of the Browne & Sharpe Manufacturing Company. The other numbers upon its roll only members of the Young Men's Debating Society, in whose rooms it meets. The place of meeting is almost always a school-house. The use of these buildings has been given by the school authorities.

Twenty-one (21) courses of lectures are now being delivered, by thirteen (13) lecturers, in nine (9) cities and towns of Rhode Island and Massachusetts.

Five courses in Constitutional History.
One " " Mediæval History.
One " " Botany.
Two " " Zoölogy.
One " " Physiology.
One " " Political Economy.
Six " " English Literature
Two " " Physics.
One " " Astronomy.
One " " Art and Architecture.

CONNECTICUT.

University Extension work has been undertaken in Connecticut actively by professors of Trinity College and Hartford Theological Seminary. Pioneer work of an excellent kind has been done by teachers of the Norwich Free Academy. More recently, the professors of Yale and Wesleyan University have become interested in the movement and are arranging courses for the coming year. President Dwight, of Yale, has always been one of the warm friends and advocates of University Extension, and President S. P. Raymond, who represented Wesleyan University at the National Conference, is equally favorable to it.

Mr. H. E. Bourne, of the Norwich Free Academy, read at the Conference the following forecasting of University Extension in Eastern Connecticut:

Connecticut.

"The work I have been asked to describe is not an example of University Extension. It is an effort to do something in a modest way for those who live in the small mill villages in the neighborhood of Norwich, in Eastern Connecticut. You will remember that there are in that part of the State a large number of such villages. As many of them are off the railroad and poorly furnished with means of intellectual development, such as libraries, reading-rooms, and the like, the life of the people is necessarily quiet, not to say dull. It is almost an unending routine of mill work, lasting from seven o'clock in the morning till six at night, with nothing in the evening except an occasional prayer-meeting or travelling variety theatre to stir up the mind. In such villages as these some of us on the faculty of the Norwich Free Academy thought we might profitably give courses of lectures on subjects in which we were especially interested. The first lecture, which had for its subject the plainer facts of astronomy, has been given during the month of December in four villages, to audiences numbering from seventy-five to one hundred and fifty, and composed of employers as well as employees, but, of course, largely of the latter. The listeners have seemed to pay excellent attention, although little training in the act of attention can be presupposed in their case. No doubt the views of different astronomical objects cast upon a screen by the stereopticon greatly assisted them in giving attention. This lecture is to be followed by others, some of which are of a more practical nature. They do not, in any sense of the word, constitute what we hope will be the permanent work of the Academy for these villages. They will serve, we think, however, to make us acquainted with the people and them acquainted with us, and to establish sympathetic relations between us, so that a permanent work may be successfully organized for such villages, constituting what we may call an outside academy. The permanent instruction would concern itself chiefly with the more useful facts of natural science, American history, and American ways of governing. Thus far we have made no charge for admission to these lectures, because we did not wish our purpose to be misunderstood. We wished the people to feel that the whole enterprise arose out of a brotherly spirit of interest in them. The slight incidental expenses have been borne in each case by the owners of the mills. Perhaps later it will be possible to have the people themselves assume the incidental expenses, or part of them, without any danger that our motives may be misconstrued, and our enterprise be stigmatized as a money-making affair.

"I wish to add one or two remarks upon another subject suggested by this meeting. Why is it not possible for the educated men of this country to establish courses of instruction in the essentials of good citizenship, including a knowledge of American history and our national, State, and local governments, and of the elementary principles of political economy especially adapted to attract those who have come to our shores from foreign countries, and who are almost totally unacquainted with our national aims and political methods? It seems to me that such courses of instruction, planned in a sympathetic spirit and patiently conducted, will do more to solve our problem of immigration than any amount of cheap lamentation over the startling inroads of undesirable foreigners."

Rev. F. B. Hartranft, of the Hartford Theological Seminary, read the following account of University Extension in Hartford:

"The most notable enterprise in which the Seminary has this year embarked outside its routine work is the system of lectures and classes organized under the general caption of University Extension.

"With the spirit and purpose of this movement, Harvard Seminary has long been sympathetic. In actual accomplishment it has considerably anticipated the wide-spread organization of the matter throughout the country. The first definite step was taken eleven years ago in the establishment of the Choral Union, which has ever since served as a most significant extension of Seminary resources for the benefit of the people of Hartford and vicinity. The Union has already been a source of musical knowledge and inspiration to at least fifteen hundred different singers, has given thirty-four public concerts at which a long list of choral masterpieces has been presented to some thousands of auditors, has stimulated the formation of a score or more of choral societies throughout the State, and is now a most flourishing institution, with two choruses, an enthusiastic constituency, and a bright future.

"The attitude of the Seminary toward this kind of work was emphatically set forth in the inaugural address of President Hartranft in May, 1888. As an immediate fruit of the policy then promulgated, the experiment was tried three years ago of occasional public lectures by members of the faculty. This plan was continued until this year. The list of lecturers has included Professors Hartranft, Bissell, Pratt, Beardslee, Richardson, Gillett, and Walker. In 1889-90, also, a system of 'Popular Classes' was set up, including the following subjects:

1. *Prof. Zenos.* Introduction to the Literature of the New Testament.
2. *Prof. Zenos.* Elements of New Testament Greek.
3. *Prof. Bissell.* Introduction to the Literature of the Old Testament.
4. *Prof. Bissell.* Elements of Hebrew.
5. *Prof. Hartranft.* The Post-Apostolic Church.
6. *Prof. Walker.* The Reformation.
7. *Prof. Richardson.* History of Philosophy.
8. *Prof. Beardslee.* The International Sunday-school Lesson.
9. *Prof. Gillett.* Studies in Psychology.
10. *Prof. Taylor.* Training in the Methods of Practical Christian Work.
11. *Prof. Pratt.* Musical Sight-Reading.

"The enrolment for that year included over four hundred and fifty students in the various courses, most of which consisted of about fifteen lectures.

"In 1890-91 this system was continued, with the following list of subjects:

1. *Prof. Bissell.* Literature of the Old Testament.
2. *Mr. Wright.* Elements of Hebrew.
3. *Prof. Zenos.* The Bible and the Monuments.
4. *Prof. Zenos.* Elements of New Testament Greek.
5. *Prof. Hartranft.* Christian Literature from Hadrian to Septimius Severus.

6. *Prof. Walker.* Europe and America from the Rise of Frederick the Great to the Fall of Napoleon.

7. *Prof. Beardslee.* The International Sunday-school Lessons.

8. *Prof. Gillett.* History of Philosophy.

9. *Prof. Taylor.* Training in Methods of Christian Work.

10. *Mr. F. B. Hartranft.* The Thiersage and Fabel in German Literature.

"The enrolment that year included about three hundred and fifty students.

"At the beginning of the present year it was felt that some extension of the system was desirable, with some modifications of its details. Hitherto only Seminary professors had served as teachers, and no fees whatever were exacted. This year the effort was made to consolidate the many disconnected instructional undertakings of a popular character in Hartford, to give them a common centre and name, and to maintain more or less nominal fees to cover expenses of administration, and, in some cases, to remunerate the lecturer. The initial inquiries revealed a remarkable readiness on the part of about twenty teachers to join in this enterprise, so that with very little effort a list of subjects was announced by means of a general circular, which was widely distributed over the city and suburbs. The administration of the whole undertaking was lodged in the hands of a committee of the faculty, consisting of Professors Hartranft, Taylor, and Gillett, with Mr. F. B. Hartranft as secretary.

"The subjects announced in the circular are as follows:

LANGUAGE AND LITERATURE.

1. *Miss Margaret Blythe.* Carlyle.

2. *Richard E. Burton, Ph.D.* English, as it is written and spoken. Twelve lectures.

3. *Mr. Frederick B. Hartranft.* German Poetical Literature from Opitz to Gottsched (1624–1750). Six lectures.

4. *Prof. Charles F. Johnson, M.A.* English Poetical Forms. Six lectures.

5. *Prof. W. E. Martin, LL.B., Ph.D.* Outlines of the Rig-Veda.

Connecticut.

HISTORY (inclusive of History of Culture).

6. *Mr. Frederick H. Chapin.* 1. History of Exploration in the Southwest (New Mexico and Arizona). 2. Cliff-dwellings of Mancos Cañon, Colorado. With stereopticon views.

7. *Prof. Henry Ferguson, M.A.* Europe before the Crusades. Six lectures.

8. *Mr. Otto B. Schlutter.* Old-Time German and English Beliefs and Customs, and their Meaning. These lectures are delivered in the German language. Six lectures.

ETHICS.

9. *Prof. Stephen G. Barnes, Ph.D., Litt.D.* Principles and Practice of Morality; on the Basis of Robinson. Twelve lectures.

SOCIOLOGY.

10. *Prof. John F. McCook, M.A.* The Alms Question—Past and Present. Six lectures.

THEOLOGY.

11. *Samuel F. Andrews, D.D.* Life of Christ. Twelve lectures.

12. *Prof. Clarks S. Beardslee, M.A.* The International Sunday-school Lesson.

13. *Edwin P. Parker, D.D.* On the Tendency to Materialize Religion.

MEDICINE.

14. *Melancthon Storrs, M.D.* Physiology. Twelve lectures.

LAW.

15. *Hon. Nathaniel Shipman, LL.D.* The Development of the Constitution by Judicial Decisions.

ART.

16. *Hartford Art Association.* Under its auspices six lectures will be given. Lecturers, dates, and terms will be announced later.

17. *Edward D. Hale, M.A.* Piano recitals, with lectures on the Romantic Composers.

18. *Mr. William C. Hammond.* Two Organ Recitals, at dates to be announced later.

19. *Edwin P. Parker, D.D.* 1. Hymnody. 2. Church Music.

20. *Prof. Waldo S. Pratt, M.A.* Some Curious Things in Musical History.

NATURAL SCIENCE.

21. *Prof. Flavel S. Luther, M.A.* Tycho, Brahe, Kepler, Galileo, Descartes, Newton, in their Several Positions as Factors in the Development of Modern Physical Science.

"To the list is appended the announcement of the following free lectures.

"*Prof. Charles C. Stearns, M.A.* Six lectures on the Carew Foundation, to be given early in 1892. The Hittites. New Lights from Old Records of a Forgotten People.

"*Rev. Alpheus C. Hodges, M.A.* Religious Leaders of New England. 1. The Founders and Opponents of the Theocracy. 2. Edwards and His Friends and Foes. 3. Later Developments.

"*Rev. Edward H. Knight, M.A.* 1. Critical Examination of certain Books of the Old Testament Apocrypha. 2. The Relation of certain Parts of the Old Testament Apocrypha to the Inspiration of the Bible.

"*Rev. Charles S. Lane, M.A.* The Septuagint. 1. Its Text. 2. The Septuagint in the New Testament.

"It is too soon to pronounce upon the success of this undertaking as a whole. But it is evident that the fraternal co-operation in it of so many instructors, from Trinity College and from the city, as well as from the Seminary, is a significant and delightful fact. It is evident, also, that the response on the part of auditors has been ample and enthusiastic enough to make the enterprise from the start a decided popular success. Doubtless after this season's experience the plan will be carried to a still greater perfection another year. In particular, it is probable that lectures will be more generally supplemented by recitations and examinations."

For other Extension work in Connecticut, see "The First Annual Report of the American Society."

NEW YORK.

In New York excellent work was done for several years by the New York University and School Extension, the secretary of which was Seth T. Stewart, of Brooklyn. By his earnest and whole-souled devotion much was accomplished for this movement both in New York and throughout the country. Under the auspices of the society of which he was secretary, many lectures were given in New York City, Brooklyn, and other places by such eminent men as Professor Boyesen, of Columbia; Professors Marquand and Frothingham, of Princeton; Professor Kittredge, of Harvard, and Professor Ladd, of Yale.

The appropriation by the New York Legislature of ten thousand dollars, to be expended in the line of University Extension under the direction of the University of the State of New York, has given a great impulse to the work in the entire State. Secretary Dewey has entered actively on the work of establishing centres, and with his able assistance much progress will doubtless be made in the coming year. (See also the addresses by Secretary Dewey and Mr. Thomas, and Appendix A. in this volume.)

NEW JERSEY.

President F. L. Patton, of Princeton, has been one of the earliest advocates of University Extension, and has been strongly supported by the faculty of the College of New Jersey, many of whose members are lecturing under the auspices of the American Society. More recently, Rutgers College has taken official action in reference to University Extension and established it as a department of the College, with Professor Louis Bevier, Jr., as secretary. At the meeting of the American Society on November 10, President Austin Scott gave an account of the starting of the work under the impulse of the success gained at Philadelphia and other places. On November 16, Rutgers College issued a circular calling the attention of the people of the State to the Extension lectures offered under its auspices. These include courses on Agriculture, by Professor Edward B.

Voorhees; The English Language, by Professor Louis Bevier, Jr.; Physics, by Professor Frank C. VanDyke; Chemistry, by Professor Peter T. Austin; Botany, by Professor Byron D. Halstead; Entomology, by Professor J. T. Smith; Biology, by Professor Julius Nelson; Astronomy, by Professor Robert W. Prentiss; and Practical Questions on Political Economy, by Professor Edward L. Stevenson. The full course consists of twelve weekly lectures, the cost of which, including lecturer's fee, travelling expenses, printing and incidentals, is about four hundred dollars. Professor Bevier submitted this as his report to the National Conference, laying especial emphasis on the character of Rutgers as a "State College for the benefit of Agriculture and Mechanic Arts," and calling attention to the special scientific nature of the courses offered.

For other Extension work in New Jersey, see "The First Annual Report of the American Society."

DELAWARE.

University Extension work in Delaware has been under the direct supervision of the American Society, and a report of it will be found under the heading—"The First Annual Report of the American Society."

PENNSYLVANIA.

The work of University Extension in Pennsylvania has been part of the general object lesson of the American Society and is reported under "The First Annual Report of the American Society."

MARYLAND.

Much work of a pioneer nature has been done for University Extension by men connected with Johns Hopkins University. Professor H. B. Adams is one of the earliest and most vigorous champions of the system. In connection with Johns Hopkins, courses of public lectures have been given in Baltimore for several years, and, although these have not been characterized by a full application of the system, they have been of great help in leading gradually to it. Extension centres are being now organized in several towns by the American Society.

VIRGINIA.

From Virginia, President H. McDiarmid, of Bethany College, and President W. W. Smith, of Randolph-Macon College, were present at the National Conference to show their interest in the work and their earnest desire for its advance. The first centre established in the State was that at Winchester, from which the secretary, W. Roy Stephenson, sends the following account: .

"In October, 1891, Mr. W. Roy Stephenson, of the Winchester, Va., bar, set to work to organize and put in operation a branch of the University Extension Society, and wrote first to Professor H. B. Adams, of the Johns Hopkins University, and afterwards called upon Professor Adams in Baltimore to obtain his advice as to the best plan for a society in Winchester to adopt, and to secure Professor Adams or some other member of the Johns Hopkins University to deliver the first course of lectures. Professor Adams gave all encouragement, but was unable to deliver a course himself, or suggest any one for the purpose. Members of the faculty of the University of Virginia were also written to by Mr. Stephenson to the same end, and with the same result. He then wrote to Mr. Walter C. Douglas, of Philadelphia, and to Professor W. D. Cabell, and Professor J. H. Gore, of Washington, D. C., on the subject.

"Mr. Douglas promptly replied and referred the matter to the Secretary of the American Society, Mr. George Henderson, and in a short time the correspondence between Mr. Henderson and Mr. Stephenson led to the engagement of a lecturer from Philadelphia.

"On November 24, 1891, a meeting called by several gentlemen by publication of a notice in the town papers of such persons as might take an interest in the subject of education was held at the Y. M. C. A. rooms in Winchester, Va., and Professor J. H. Gore, who is the secretary of the Washington, D. C., Society for the Extension of University Teaching, was kindly present, by the request of Mr. Stephenson, and delivered a well-considered and most interesting exposition to the audience.

"The Executive Committee then invited voluntary subscriptions to a guarantee fund of two hundred dollars to cover the expense of the first course of lectures, to be paid, in whole, or part, in case the public did not buy tickets enough to defray the cost thereof, and twenty gentlemen promptly responded, and more would doubtless have done so, if desired. The Executive Committee thereupon directed the secretary to arrange for a course of lectures to begin at once, and accordingly Professor Henry W. Rolfe, of the University of Pennsylvania, was engaged to give a course on English literature. The tickets for the course have been sold for one dollar, and tickets for a single lecture for twenty-five cents. The audience has been largely composed of school-girls, there being three large female seminaries in Winchester, the Principals of which gladly embraced the opportunity to give their pupils the unusual advantages of the course; in addition, a number of tickets to this first course was given by the Executive Committee to persons scarcely able to buy them, but who were considered apt to appreciate and take an interest in the society, but these gifts were judiciously distributed.

"The class-work after each lecture has called forth from members of the audience some excellent discourses upon the subject of the lecture. It is fair to say that the Winchester Society is a success, and its outlook promises much useful work and large benefits resulting therefrom to the community. An effort has been made by the gentlemen managing the Winchester Society to arrange for the organization of a circuit of centres to include Frederick and Hagerstown in Maryland, Martinsburg and Charlestown in West Virginia, Carlisle, Pa., and Winchester, Va. Such an arrangement would be very advantageous to all, because of the easy access and proximity of these towns to each other."

WEST VIRGINIA.

Professor Howard N. Ogden, of the University of West Virginia, presented to the Conference a report of the founding of the West Virginia Society.

West Virginia.

"In West Virginia, we have the State University at Morgantown, Bethany College at Bethany, six State Normal Schools, in which the chief instructors are graduates of the University, and some twenty or more academies, seminaries, colleges, and town high schools, doing satisfactory preparatory and secondary work.

"The members of the faculty of the State University interested in Extension teaching thought it best for the cause to organize a voluntary society, which should embrace in its membership instructors from all the institutions for higher and secondary education in the State, and others taking a general interest in the movement.

"With this view the West Virginia Society for Extension Teaching was organized, chiefly by the professors of the State University, some six weeks ago.

"Members of the faculties of Bethany College and of a large number of other schools have signified their intention to join with us in the work locally and some as lecturers.

"Some three weeks ago the Society published a preliminary statement of the lecturers and courses offered, which has been widely distributed and favorably received. This circular contains the names of twelve lecturers, who offer an aggregate of thirty-five different courses.

"As yet, we have not formally organized local centres, preferring that such organizations shall come as the spontaneous aftergrowth of a healthy local interest. The plan of operations adopted by the Society for the next half-year is briefly this: to send one or more of its teaching staff to some ten or twelve of the most favorable points for the establishment of local centres, and there give experimental courses of six lectures each, conforming as closely as possible to the best methods of Extension teaching, as object-lessons, illustrating the results and purposes of the movement. This work will begin early in January.

"Another feature of our work in West Virginia requires special mention. The members of the staff of the Agricultural Experimental Station, which is connected with the University, have been lecturing to the farmers of the State for some two years past and organizing what they call local Farmers' Institute Societies. The State Board of Agriculture has also recently undertaken similar work. Now, it is a fortunate coincidence, that the members of the Station staff and the President of the State Board of Agriculture are also members of the University Extension Society, and they are now seriously considering the policy of reorganizing these Farmers' Institute Societies into local University Extension centres, and conforming their lecture system, as far as possible, to Extension methods. It will be seen, therefore, that, in addition to the educational influences of Extension teaching upon those who attend the lectures, we have some collateral objects in view which we regard as of very great importance. The West Virginia Society for the Extension of University Teaching hopes (1) to become the means of harmonizing and unifying the methods, standards, and interests of higher education in the State; (2) to connect more closely the public free schools with the institutions for higher learning, and (3) to disseminate correct notions of the methods of true University teaching for adults, and to arouse an abiding popular interest in the subject-matters of University education.

"We have entered upon the work seriously and deliberately. We desire to accomplish permanent and not merely temporary results. It will require several years to bring all the towns of the State under the influence of the movement. Our first purpose is fully to explain and exemplify Extension teaching by experimental courses, and thereby stimulate the local community to take the initiative in the organization and endowment of a permanent local centre. We are also seeking to adapt our courses as closely as possible, both in method and subject-matter, to the preferences and peculiar needs of our people.

"Upon these lines we are assured of a measurable degree of success, and we may look for substantial recognition of the merit of Extension teaching by the University and local colleges. The inauguration of a system of State examinations under the direction of the University faculty, or other State authority, is contemplated, and ultimately we may obtain State aid, and thereby incorporate University Extension teaching as a permanent feature of the educational system of the State."

GEORGIA.

The first step in the introduction of University Extension into the State of Georgia was taken on December 7, at Atlanta, where a preliminary meeting was addressed by Professor H. C. White, of the University of Georgia. As a result of this meeting, a series of courses was arranged by the directors of the Young Men's Library Association in Atlanta. The faculty of the State University has cordially co-operated with the Library Association, and has agreed to provide the lecturers and teachers, and to arrange for the subjects and dates of the lectures. These matters have therefore been placed in charge of the University faculty, who will provide that the courses shall be genuinely educative, and as exhaustive of the special topics selected as the time allowed will permit. The members of the faculty have generously declined to receive any compensation for their services, being animated solely by the desire to popularize higher education, and to extend its benefits as widely as possible.

The business arrangements are in charge of a special committee of the Young Men's Library Association, made up of the following gentlemen : W. G. Cooper, Will Haight, F. H. Richardson, A. V. Gude, W. M. Slaton, I. S. Hopkins. Certain necessary expenses will be incurred in the payment of travelling expenses, in printing syllabuses of the lectures, etc., and it is proposed to meet these by a small charge for attendance upon the lectures.

For the present season six courses of six lectures each have been arranged, as detailed below. The class for each course will be regularly enrolled. There will be no recitations, but at the conclusion of each lecture the lecturer will hold an informal conference with the class for elucidation of any points that may be desired. The books of reference which it may be proper to consult in connection with the lectures will, for the most part, be found on the shelves of the Young Men's Library.

The lectures will be given in the halls of the library building. The fee for each course of six lectures has been fixed for the present at one dollar, or five dollars for the whole series of thirty-six.

SCHEDULE OF LECTURES.

MENTAL SCIENCE.

1. Friday evenings, December 11, 18; January 8, 15, 22, and 29. Six lectures on Mental Science, by Rev. William E. Boggs, D.D., LL.D., Chancellor of the University of Georgia.

These lectures will give some account of the science and its subjects, the human mind or soul, together with an outline of the great powers of self-consciousness, sense-perception, and memory, together with a brief view of the imagination, if time can be found for this faculty.

COURSE ON BIOLOGY.

2. Monday evenings, December 14, 21; January 4, 11, 18, 25. Six lectures on Biology, by John P. Campbell, A.B., Ph.D., Professor of Biology, University of Georgia.

This course is designed to present in detail a sufficient number of living things to give broader conceptions of the terms plant and animal, than those generally held. The types chosen will be mainly microscopic forms, because in these life is exhibited without any of the complications found in higher and more familiar plants and animals. From these the attempt will be made to proceed inductively to some of the fundamental properties of living things, and show as far as possible the exact basis upon which rests some of the now accepted theories of biology.

ROMAN LAW AND JURISPRUDENCE.

3. Monday evenings, February 1, 8, 15, 22, 29; March 7. Six lectures on the History of Roman Law and Jurisprudence, by J. H. T. MacPherson, Ph.D., Professor of History and Political Science, University of Georgia.

This course will open with a description of the nature of the primitive Roman state and early legal institutions, and will trace the progress and development of the Roman law through all its stages down to the codification of Justinian. Special attention will be paid to the sources of Roman law, and to the gradual development and continuity of Roman legal and political institutions. The influence of Roman codes during the middle ages will be briefly sketched, and the influence of Roman law as the basis and goal of modern continental systems emphasized.

THE GREEK DRAMA.

4. Friday evenings, February 5, 12, 19, 26; March 4, 11. Six lectures on the Greek Drama, with readings from the "Alcestis" of Euripides, by Willis H. Bocock, A.M., Professor of Ancient Languages, University of Georgia.

Some account will be given of the probable origin of tragedy, of its development into drama, and of its perfection in the hands of Æschylus, Sophocles, and Euripides. The Greek theatre will be described, and the methods of producing plays will be explained. The lecturer will sketch the career of Euripides, give the story of "Alcestis" in outline, explain the peculiar character of the play, and will read the play in English with comments, using mainly Browning's "Balaustion's Adventure" with his own translation of selected parts.

BUILDING MATERIAL.

5. Monday evenings, March 14, 21, 28; April 4, 11, 18. Six lectures on Building Materials, by Charles M. Strahan, C.E. and M.E., Professor of Engineering, University of Georgia.

This course will be addressed primarily to workingmen and to others interested directly or indirectly in the building arts. Its aim will be to present the properties of the principal building materials, and to discuss the conditions connected with their economic employment and preservation from decay.

ENGLISH LANGUAGE AND LITERATURE.

6. Friday evenings, March 18, 25; April 1, 8, 15, 22. Six lectures on the English Language and its Literature, by Charles Morris, M.A., Professor of English, University of Georgia.

The aim of these lectures will be, from an examination of the language, its sources, and history, its matter, forms and structure to ascertain its rank among literary tongues, and to show its power and adaptability to the highest forms of literary art as witnessed in its literature.

It will be observed that two lectures are given each week, thereby carrying forward two courses at once. The first two are on mental science and biology.

LOUISIANA.

In Louisiana, President William Preston Johnston, of Tulane University, has been an earnest writer and eloquent speaker in behalf of University Extension.*

In many special lines Tulane University has offered its advantages to the people of New Orleans; public courses have been given on various subjects, and special opportunities afforded in technical instruction. Through the influence of President Johnston much has been accomplished, and this work has been reorganized into Extension teaching, properly so called. The University has issued an announcement of Extension courses, the list including English Language and Literature, by Professor Robert Sharp; English History, by Professor John R. Ficklen; Le Drame en France, by Professor Alcée Fortier; Psychology, by Professor Brandt V. B. Dixon; Chemistry, by Professor John M. Ordway; Electricity and Magnetism, by Professor Brown Ayers; Mathematics, by Professor J. L. Cross.

TENNESSEE.

Professor Edward W. Bemis, of Vanderbilt University, one of the earliest Extension lecturers of America, and the one who gave the first course ever given in New York State, at Buffalo, and the first one ever given in Missouri, at St. Louis, submitted to the National Conference a sketch of University Extension in Tennessee. "Because of the lack of public libraries and of many public-spirited men of wealth, the University Extension movement will have a far slower growth in the South than in the

---

* See his article in *University Extension*, September, 1891, on "University Extension in the South."

North. For these reasons I have found it hard to do very much Extension work here. The institutions of learning also have insufficient endowment for travelling libraries and aid by lecturers. A few cities, however, in Tennessee and in the Gulf States will, I think, be led in a year or two to take hold of the movement in co-operation with Vanderbilt University and other Southern institutions.

"I am nearly through a very successful course of Economic lectures at Evansville, Ind., where the full system, including syllabus, class-work and exercises, has been in operation. A succeeding course, for which two hundred have already taken course tickets, is to be given by President Coulter, of the University of Indiana, on Botany. I shall give the same course in Louisville, Ky., and Nashville, Tenn., at an early date.

"Until some money can be secured for good travelling libraries, however, I do not look forward to much solid study on the part of the people who attend Extension courses. In the South good public libraries are very few in number, and it is accordingly much more difficult to obtain the necessary reference-books for students. I have the greatest interest in the work, an interest which is shared by the most progressive and influential of the college men in the South."

KENTUCKY.

In Kentucky, the beginning of University Extension was due to the Teachers' Association in Louisville, which, in May, 1891, appointed a committee, of which W. O. Cross was chairman, and E. H. Mark, Hiram Roberts, and W. H. Bartholomew were members. In accordance with recommendations of this committee, President J. M. Coulter, of Indiana University, was secured to open the work in September, 1891. President Coulter lectured on botany, while Professor O. B. Clark, of the same University, was engaged to lecture on literature. The larger part of the audience was composed of teachers, but all persons who desired to follow the course were heartily welcomed. From the first the following classes were noticed in the audience: those who helped forward the cause by their contributions and occasional presence; those who attended regularly, but had no time for further work; and lastly, those who followed the work closely as outlined in the syllabus, and prepared the exercises therein contained with a view to passing the final examination.

For nearly twenty years the lectures that have been given by the Polytechnic Society have been somewhat on the University Extension plan. About a year ago Dr. James Lewis Howe decided to modify the work, so as to bring it within the regular line of University Extension. After passing the summer of 1891 in the study of the system as developed in the East, he entered with the approval of the American Society actively upon the work, giving courses of lectures on chemistry in the Polytechnic lecture-room on Friday afternoons. The lectures were illustrated by experiments and have interested many in the study of science. On February 11, the opening lecture of a course on economics will be given by Dr. Edward W. Bemis, of Vanderbilt University. The lectures are to be given at Hampton College under the auspices of the local centre of University Extension. Dr. Bemis is under engagement to deliver the same course at Frankfort and Lexington.

Much interest has been manifested in University Extension in various parts of the State, and centres will doubtless be established in several places during the current year. The development of the work in Kentucky is impeded not only by the absence of good public libraries, but also by inadequate railway facilities and the lack of men fitted to do the work. At present the latter difficulty is overcome by calling distinguished men from the higher institutions of neighboring States. The question of lecturers, fundamental everywhere, is especially difficult under such conditions, and the future of the movement will depend largely on the possibility of training good lecturers from the excellent material which certainly exists among the educators of the State.

OHIO.

The University of Cincinnati was the first to undertake systematic Extension teaching in Ohio.* The interest of other

---

* See W. O. Sproull, University Extension in Cincinnati, page 144.

universities has been rapidly attracted to this subject. An important meeting was held in Columbus, on January 21, 1892, looking toward the organization of a State Extension Society. There were present: President Stubbs, of Baldwin; Professor Scott, of Ohio State; President Zollers, of Hiram; President Sanders, of Otterbein; President Marsh, of Mt. Union; Professor W. A. Merrill, of Miami; and Professor C. B. Austin, of Ohio Wesleyan. Communications were read from the Presidents of Oberlin, Adelbert, Buchtel Colleges, and Ohio and Denison Universities, all favorable to the movement. After a careful discussion of the relation of the college to this movement, and of the best methods of organization, it was resolved to form the Ohio Society for the Extension of University Teaching. The membership is to comprise the faculties of the various Ohio colleges and such other persons as they may deem proper to elect. The management is to be in the hands of a Board of Councillors, of which there will be one member for each college. Friends of University Extension look forward with confidence to the establishment of such a society in each State of the Union. At the annual meeting of the Ohio State Teachers' Association, and the Ohio College Association during the Christmas holidays, the movement of University Extension was thoroughly discussed and received the hearty endorsement of the leaders, both in primary, secondary, and higher education.

President D. B. Puriton, of Denison University, reported at the National Conference the establishment by that institution of a University Extension centre at Newark, Ohio, a manufacturing town of some eighteen or twenty thousand inhabitants. Superintendent Hartzler, of the City Schools, is president of the local organization, and Principal Swartz, of the High School, is secretary and treasurer. The class numbers more than two hundred; of this number fifty are city teachers, about twenty are pupils of the High School, and the remainder are ministers, lawyers, physicians, business-men, mechanics, and laborers. Courses are given in economics, electricity, literature, and psychology. The lecturers are R. S. Colwell, D.D., J. D. S. Riggs, Ph.D., A. D. Cole, A.M., and D. B. Purinton, LL.D.,—all members of the faculty of Denison University. The courses are not yet completed. Thus far they are eminently successful. The interest is universal and well sustained in psychology, as well as the more practical subjects. The notes, taken with great care and accuracy considering the varied elements in the class, and the general quiz, are features of value and importance. Already the local centre is looking forward to the second course in the winter of 1892–93. The work as a whole is very gratifying and encouraging. Other centres will be established in the near future.

President Charles W. Super represented the Ohio University at the National Conference. Many courses have been arranged by the professors of that faculty, and some have been given with entire success in different parts of the State.

Professor W. A. Merrill, who was the delegate of Miami University at the Conference, expressed the hearty sympathy of that faculty with the University Extension movement, and spoke of the careful thought that is being given to the inauguration of the work in his section

At Toledo one of the strongest Extension societies of the country was established on December 15, 1891. The movement owes its inception there to the energy and influence of Superintendent W. W. Compton, who was chosen president of the society; the secretary is Miss Mary Smead, one of the teachers of the city; the treasurer is Colonel D. Isaac Smead. The Executive Committee is composed of Superintendent Compton, Miss Emily Bouton, Professor H. C. Adams, Rev. Dr. J. A. McGaw, and Mr. W. S. Daly. The following courses of six lectures each have been arranged, to be given in succession: "Economics," by Professor H. C. Adams, of the University of Michigan; "English Literature," by Professor Isaac N. Demmon, of the University of Michigan; "Geology," by Professor G. Frederick Wright, of Oberlin University. The first course by Professor Adams was begun on January 12. Additional courses in chemistry and physics have also been announced.

At Cleveland the first step toward the establishment of a University Extension society was due to the influence of President

Charles F. Thwing, of Adelbert College, one of the Advisory Committee of the American Society. A meeting was held early in December at the rooms of the Broadway Branch of the Young Men's Christian Association to consider the subject. Miss Emma Perkins read a paper setting forth clearly the aims and methods of the American Society, and describing the development of the movement in England and America. On December 14, the Cleveland Society for University Extension was incorporated. The officers of the society are: President, Hon. Samuel E. Williamson; Vice-President, General M. D. Leggett; Chairman of the Board of Trustees, Charles F. Thwing, President of Adelbert College and of Western Reserve University; Secretary, Emerson O. Stevens; Treasurer, Charles J. Dockstader. The office of the society is at Adelbert College. The membership numbers now about one hundred and twenty-five of the foremost educational, professional, and business men of the city. The society offers twenty-three courses of study, and has issued a neat pamphlet giving a full description of the following courses:

I. Architecture.—President Cady Staley, Case School of Applied Science. *Ten lectures.*

II. Theories of the Drama in France.—Professor Frederick M. Warner, Adelbert College.

III.—Experimental Mechanics.—Professor Charles H. Benjamin, Case School of Applied Science.

IV. American History.—Professor Edward G. Bourne, Adelbert College.

V. Physics: 1. Terrestrial Physics; 2. Electricity and Magnetism. — Professor Harry F. Reid, Case School of Applied Science.

VI. Greek Antiquities.—Professor Abraham L. Fuller, College for Women of Western Reserve University. *Eight lectures.*

VII. Astronomy· 1. Descriptive Astronomy; 2. Study of the Constellations.—Professor Charles S. Howe, Case School of Applied Science.

VIII. Biology.—Francis H. Herrick, Adelbert College. *Five lectures.*

IX. Sound.—Professor Frank P. Whitman, Adelbert College. Seven lectures.

X. Roman Archæology.—Professor Samuel B. Platner, Adelbert College.

XI. English Literature: 1. Shakespeare and his Contemporaries; 2. English Literature of the Eighteenth Century; 3. English Prose Literature of the Nineteenth Century; 4. Carlyle.—Mr. Curtis H. Page, College for Women of Western Reserve University.

XII. French.—Mr. Curtis H. Page, College for Women of Western Reserve University.

XIII. Chemistry. — Two courses by Professor Edward W. Morley, of Adelbert College, and Professor Albert W. Smith, of the Case School of Applied Science.

Eleven courses have been formed in different parts of the city, and there are already over six hundred students. Other classes are being formed as rapidly as possible.

INDIANA.

Professor James A. Woodburn, Ph.D., of the University of Indiana, read the following report:

The Indiana Branch of Association of Collegiate Alumnæ formed the first centre for the Extension of University teaching in Indiana. The members of this association in Indiana organized a committee on University Extension in the winter of 1890, with Mrs. May Wright Sewall chairman, and Miss Amelia W. Platter secretary. Miss Harriet Noble, Miss Julia Moore, Miss Rose Baldwin, all of Indianapolis, were the other members of the committee. This committee, in the winter of 1890, wrote both to the Johns Hopkins University and the Michigan University, making application for a lecturer in political economy. By recommendation from these institutions, and from other sources, the committee learned that their prophet for economic teaching was in their own country, at their own doors. Following the suggestions of these recommendations, the committee invited Dr. Jeremiah W. Jenks, Professor of Social and

Economic Science in Indiana University, to give a course of twelve lectures in the elements of political economy. The course was a decided success. The Alumnæ committee determined to continue the study of political economy and social science the following year, and to add a course on American history.

As a result of this evidence of a present demand within the State, and of a growing public interest in the cause of Extension teaching, the faculty of Indiana University, at a meeting in June, 1891, called especially to consider the subject, appointed a committee on University Extension. This standing committee consists of Professor Ernest W. Huffcut, chairman, Professor Orrin B. Clark, and Professor E. A. Ross. The work of the committee has consisted chiefly in circulating information, answering correspondence, collecting and publishing literature on the subject of University Extension.

Soon after its organization, the committee issued Extension Circular No. 1, setting forth the purpose and methods of Extension work, and announcing the University departments from which Extension instruction might be obtained. Two months later the University issued, under the direction of this committee, "Circular No. 2," setting forth the offer of the following lectures and courses:

LECTURES AND COURSES FOR 1891-92.

I. BOTANY. President J. M. Coulter.
General morphology and physiology of plants. *Twelve lectures.*

II. ECONOMICS AND SOCIAL SCIENCE. Professor E. A. Ross.
1. Social and Economic Reforms. A study of co-operation, profit-sharing, the eight-hour day, factory legislation, State arbitration, postal telegraphy, railway control, bi-metalism, tax reform, municipalism, and socialism. *Twelve lectures.*

2. Live Economic Questions. A discussion of problems relating to money, railroads, taxation, rent, labor, monopolies, interest, and immigration. *Eight lectures.*

3. Elements of Political Economy. A presentation of the main features of modern industrial life. *Eight to twelve lectures.*

III. ENGLISH LITERATURE.
  A. Professor O. B. Clark.
    1. The Development of Shakespeare's Mind and Art. *Six lectures.*
    2. Chaucer and his Contemporaries. *Six lectures.*
    3. Robert Browning. *Six lectures.*
  B. Mr. W. E. Henry.
    1. The Development of English Literature. *Twelve lectures.*
    2. Elizabethan Literature. *Twelve lectures.*
    3. American Literature. *Twelve lectures.*
    4. Emerson and Lowell. *Twelve lectures.*

IV. FRENCH LANGUAGE AND LITERATURE. Professor Edouard Baillot.
    1. The Pronunciation of the French Language. Principles and laws of pronunciation with special reference to the needs of teachers. *Twelve lectures.*
    2. French literature. Including mediæval literature; the writers of the seventeenth century and their methods; the Romantic School; and modern literature. *Twelve lectures.*

V. GERMANIC LANGUAGE AND LITERATURE AND PHILOLOGY.
  A. Professor Gustaf Karsten.
    1. The Origin and Change of Language. *Six lectures.*
    2. Fritz Reuter. *Three lectures.*
  B. Associate Professor Carl Osthaus.
    1. Modern German Literature since Goethe. *Six lectures.*

VI. GREEK. Professor H. A. Hoffman.
    1. The Greek Land and People. *Six lectures*, illustrated with the stereopticon.

VII. HISTORY, AMERICAN. Professor J. A. Woodburn.
    1. American Political History, 1776–1832. *Twelve lectures.*

VIII. HISTORY, EUROPEAN. Professor G. E. Fellows.
    1. France under the Bourbon Monarchy; from Henry IV. to the Revolution. *Six to ten lectures.*

2. France under three Monarchies and three Republics—
1789-1889. Including the causes of the Revolution.
Six lectures.
3. Important Periods in English History since the Norman Invasion. *Six lectures.*

IX. LAW. Professor E. W. Huffcut.
1. Equity Jurisprudence. *Twelve lectures.*
2. American Constitutional Law. *Ten lectures.*
3. American International Relations and Diplomacy. *Six to ten lectures.*

X. MATHEMATICS. Professor R. L. Green.
1. Helmholtz's Theory of Arithmetic. *Six lectures.*

XI. PEDAGOGICS. Professor R. G. Boone.
1. The Science of Education. *Ten lectures.*

XII. PHYSICS. Associate Professor A. L. Foley.
1. Electricity and its Applications. *Eight to ten lectures.*

XIII. RHETORIC AND ORATORY. Professor G. W. Saunderson.
1. Oratorical Delivery: Its Practical and Scientific Basis. *Six to ten lectures.*
2. The Principles of English Composition. *Six to ten lectures.*

It was stated that the courses in Chemistry and Physics could not well be given away from the University, owing to the difficulty of transporting the necessary apparatus, but that these departments would receive special students at any time for laboratory work in brief courses. The lectures were to be given on Friday evenings, or at some hour on Saturday, which would permit the lecturer's returning to the University the same day.

The expense of a course of lectures was placed at ten dollars per lecture, and the necessary expenses of the lecturer, the centre to meet all the local expenses of rent, printing, etc.

As a result of these announcements and in consequence of the preceding years' experience in Indianapolis, the University has received applications from, and has provided courses in, the following centres:

I. In INDIANAPOLIS, under the auspices of the Indiana Branch of the Association of Collegiate Alumnæ, two courses:

1. In *American Political History from 1776 to 1832*, by Professor James Albert Woodburn.*

2. In *Social and Economic Reform*, by Professor Edward A. Ross. This course, like the one by Professor Woodburn in American history, is to include twelve lectures and is to be conducted on the same general plan. The course is to begin February 19, and is to continue thereafter for twelve successive weeks. The subjects of Professor Ross's lectures are as follows:

1. Reform.
2. Monetary Reform.
3. Railway Reform.
4. Tax Reform.
5. Agrarian Reform.
6. Labor Reform—Self Help.
7. Labor Reform—State Help.
8. Municipal Reform.
9. Socialism—Its History.
10. Socialism—Its Nature.
11. Socialism—Its Strength.
12. Socialism—Its Weakness.

II. In LOUISVILLE, under the auspices of the Louisville Teachers' Association. This Association has been used to holding bi-weekly sessions in the Girls' High School, and it has a membership of over four hundred. In the Louisville centre two courses are given:

1. In *Elementary Botany*, by President John M. Coulter.

This course comprises twelve lectures, and embraces such instruction as is given in the University to a beginning class in botany. The subject under development in the course is "The Evolution of the Plant Kingdom," considering this evolution from the lowest form up. The course is designed as merely an outline course in general morphology.

There are one hundred and twenty-five enrolled in this class. The class meets for an hour's quiz before the lecture, one-half of which hour is occupied in questions from the class which are

---

* For an account of this course, see the paper on "Some Extension Experiments in American History," p. 122.

reported as "coming full and eager," and the other half the hour is devoted to the questioning of the class by the lecturer. Most of the latter questions are on the reading which has been assigned to the class, endeavoring to group the salient facts on the week's study. For practical work in botany the class is in possession of sixty microscopes and is divided into squads for practical botanical analysis. Mr. Marks, Instructor in the Boys' High School of Louisville, is the leader of the class, who directs its study and reports its progress and its needs to Professor Coulter.

2. The second course in Louisville is given by Professor O. B. Clark, of the Department of English, on "Lowell and his Work." This course consists of six lectures, and is under the same auspices with Professor Coulter's course. This class was given the choice of subjects from "Shakespeare," "Chaucer," "Lowell," and, by a very large vote, "Lowell" was preferred. The class numbers one hundred and forty, and is aided and directed, under Professor Clark, by Mr. W. O. Cross, Principal of the Fourth Ward Schools in Louisville.

Both these courses are conducted on Saturday morning from nine to eleven o'clock, and of the two hundred and sixty-five members of the classes, mostly teachers, very few are taking both courses; the duplicated names do not number more than twelve.

The business managers have charged one dollar and fifty cents for a course of six lectures, or twenty-five cents per lecture, and they report on hand a comfortable surplus above all expenses.

III. EVANSVILLE.—In this city a class numbering over one hundred has been organized for the study of botany, and Professor Coulter has been invited to direct the course. He will repeat the course which he is giving in Louisville. The Evansville centre is under the direction and leadership of Mr. Samuel G. Evans, a private citizen of that city, who may be enrolled as an efficient co-worker in the Society for the Encouragement of Study at Home. Professor Coulter's Extension course in Evansville will begin in January, 1892.

IV. In CHICAGO, in the Workers' Church, Dr. Doremus Scudder, pastor.

In this Chicago centre Professor Woodburn is repeating the course which he is giving at Indianapolis.*

V. In NEW ALBANY, President Coulter is engaged in lecturing to a vigorous and growing centre, now numbering one hundred and sixty-five students, enthusiastic in the study of botany. The calls on President Coulter for instruction are more than he can supply. He is now addressing three Extension centres aggregating about five hundred students.

The summary of the Extension of Indiana University may best be seen in the brief statement by Professor E. W. Huffcutt, chairman of the Extension Committee of the Faculty:

(1) We offer 29 courses
    in 13 departments
    by 15 lecturers.

(2) We have actually under way 5 courses
    in 3 departments
    by 3 lecturers.

(3) We have arranged, in addition, 3 courses
    in 2 departments
    by 2 lecturers.

(4) Total, 8 courses
    in 4 departments
    by 4 lecturers.

(5) Registrations for the 8 courses,
    1115 students.

(6) Number of lectures in each course:
    Botany, 3 courses, 6 each.
    Literature, 1 course, 6.
    American Political History, 2 courses, 12 each.
    Economics, 2 courses, 12 each.

These courses, which are now in practical operation, are conducted by the heads of the departments in which the courses are given. The professors themselves go to the centres, give the lectures, and instruct the classes. The work is looked upon as being the most responsible now in hand, and President Coulter's

---

*See Professor Woodburn's "Some Extension Experiments," p. 122.

interest in, and personal attention to, the Extension course signifies the importance in which the work is held by the administration. The Board of Trustees of the University have formally expressed its approval of the work, and appropriations of money have been made to meet the necessary expenses. Further encouragement and financial aid will be given by the University authorities as the demands increase and the scope of the work extends. The policy of the University may be expressed by saying that it is the intention to push the work with energy, and to make provision for new demands as they arise.

Additional teaching force will be provided if calls for the Extension of the University increase, as present demands seem to indicate will be the case. Our experience would indicate that a professor can well manage a single course on Friday evenings without loss of efficiency in his regular work at the University, unless his present work is already too heavy. But to conduct two courses at the same time can only result in disparagement of the work he is attempting with the University classes in residence. If the University professors themselves, who are, as a rule, already overburdened with classes, should attempt to continue and develop Extension teaching, they can do so only by being relieved of some of their present labors. The Indiana University is considering the feasibility of providing, in the contingency of enlarged demands, a special body of Extension lecturers, or of releasing certain members of its Faculty during portions of the week or the college term, for exclusive attention to Extension classes. But future problems are deferred to future time.

It has not been the policy of the University to "work up" centres. The initiative is left with the community which may desire a course. Information, instruction, encouragement, sometimes financial help to the extent of furnishing the printed syllabus, —these the University stands ready to supply. But no centre is encouraged to attempt a course under any artificial pressure or demand. The University expects from every centre applying for instruction that the business success of the enterprise be guaranteed from the beginning, that the application represents a positive and genuine demand for University teaching, not for mere entertainment, and that the centre be under some organization or management which may be held, in a sense, responsible to the University. The University, as the institution of the State for higher education, desires to serve the Commonwealth of Indiana in every possible way, and it holds itself in readiness to carry its instruction at all the times it can, in all the ways it can, to all the people it can. This it conceives to be the spirit of true University Extension.

MICHIGAN.

The aim of the University Extension movement is to bring the masses close to the higher institutions of learning. Under no circumstances should this be more easily or thoroughly accomplished than in the case of the State universities. The University of Michigan is typical of these institutions. It stands at the head of a great public-school system whose various divisions reach by easy gradations to the door of the University. The system exemplifies well the idea of a natural sequence in the elementary schools, the secondary, and the University. The State University at the head of such a system is in a position to mould greatly the general education of the commonwealth, and through that the masses of the people. These institutions depend, further, on public sentiment for their support, and anything that increases the estimation of education in the minds of the people tends directly to their advantage. In the Extension system, then, is an element of strength which has naturally not passed unnoticed by the State universities, and of all these the University of Michigan was one of the earliest to take steps towards securing for itself and for the people of the State the opportunities which the movement offers.

In lieu of personal representation at the National Conference, the following letter was received from the head of the English department of the University of Michigan, who is, at the same time, the first Extension lecturer from its faculty.

"ANN ARBOR, December 26, 1892.
"PRESIDENT EDMUND J. JAMES, Philadelphia:
"DEAR SIR,—It now seems that other engagements will prevent

our being represented at the National Conference on University Extension next week. I accordingly forward to you herewith the official record of the action of our faculty, and of our board with reference to Extension teaching. We had a late start, and thus far few courses have been called for. There have been many inquiries, and doubtless other courses will be called for after the holidays. The Detroit people moved in advance of us, and I began work there before our faculty took definite action. I understand that the friends of the movement in Detroit feel much encouraged by the interest taken in the first course. I refer you to the Rev. C. R. Henderson, of Detroit, who has been active in the matter.

"Very sincerely yours,
"ISAAC N. DEMMON.'

The official record of the action of Michigan University is dated November 18, 1891. To the Board of Regents was presented at that time the report of the special committee appointed by the faculty of the University to consider the question of University Extension teaching. As a result of its thought, the committee, including Professors Isaac N. Demmon, Martin L. D'Ooge, and Volney M. Spaulding, made the following recommendations:

1. That the President be authorized to announce the willingness of the faculty to undertake University Extension work.

2. That the members of the faculty be requested to prepare, before December 1, a statement of the course each is willing to give during the current year.

3. That the Board of Regents be requested to give their approval to this plan, and to authorize officers of instruction to accept invitations for such regulations as the Board may deem wise.

In accordance with the action of the Regents on this recommendation, the University of Michigan made the following announcement: "The University, desiring to assist local bodies in the work of University Extension, has arranged the following courses of instruction. The general plan of the work will be that adopted by the American Society for the Extension of Uni-

versity Teaching. The University cannot undertake the local organization of classes, but will await the instruction of clubs, societies, or classes who may desire to enter upon the work. The entire expense will be borne by the local organization in each case. This may be done by lecture-tickets, class fees, or general subscriptions."

The courses announced by Michigan University on December 1, 1891, embrace nearly sixty courses in twenty-three branches of instruction, to be given by thirty of the University faculty. A special emphasis was laid on the educational nature of the work, and the intention that the courses should be not merely interesting and popular, but characterized by earnest and persistent study.

The first Extension centre in the State of Michigan was established in Detroit. In the early part of October, Rev. C. R. Henderson commenced the agitation of the subject, and made several earnest addresses in behalf of the movement. On October 27, President James B. Angell, of the University of Michigan, discussed the subject before the Congregational Club of Eastern Michigan. He was followed by Profesor M. L. D'Ooge, who gave an account in detail of the development of the system in England. The Detroit Institute of University Extension was organized on October 11, 1891. The following officers were chosen: Hon. Thos. W. Palmer, President; Mrs. John J. Bagley, Vice-President; Henry A. Ford, Secretary; George W. Duncan, Treasurer; R. L. Courtney, Financial Secretary. The Board of Directors is composed of the following: Hon. T. W. Palmer, Chairman, ex-officio; Charles E. Warner, Vice-Chairman; Henry A. Ford, Clerk; Mrs. S. C. O. Parsons, Mrs. H. J. Boutell, Rev. C. R. Henderson, D.D.; Professor S. Emory Whitney, Alanson J. Fox, Albert L. Olds, Henry Maslen, and M. Frederick Martin. Circulars were immediately issued in reference to the work and great interest aroused among all classes of the community. The price of a single-course ticket was fixed at fifty cents, and single admission, to the extent of seating capacity, for each of the six lectures in the average course, at fifteen cents. The price of the syllabus for each course was fixed at ten cents. An extra charge of fifty cents was made to the members of the classes who handed in written exercises, and an additional charge of the same amount for the final examination papers and certificates.*

From Secretary Henry A. Ford the following report was received at the National Conference:

"I regret that our Institute for University Extension cannot be represented at the coming Conference. Our first course closed on the 15th instant, and proved a great success, self-sustaining, with a good balance in treasury. Four hundred and seventy-four course tickets were sold; there were regularly full houses, despite unfavorable weather. About one hundred followed the class, though most of the audience remained to its exercises. The course was a thoroughly popular and instructive one on 'Masterpieces of English Literature,' by Professor Demmon of the State University. We announce next a course in political economy, and shall have probably two classes of twenty to twenty-five each in elementary chemistry. A petition of two hundred for a Shakespeare course cannot be satisfied until our next season. We have promoted the work elsewhere, and are happy to report organizations at Grand Rapids and Hillsdale, and at Toledo, Ohio, with hopeful movements in progress at Kalamazoo, Jackson, Saginaw, Pontiac, and elsewhere."†

ILLINOIS.

In Illinois much interest has been shown in University Extension, both by the college men and the common-school teachers, principals, and superintendents. Hon. Henry Raab, State Super-

---

* The usual price in the United States of a ticket for a single course of six lectures has been one dollar, with no extra charges for those writing exercises or taking the examination. Such an arrangement seems certainly preferable, since the object of the lecture is to induce as many as possible to enter upon systematic and earnest study. It has even been the custom in some places in England to remit part of the regular fee to those who follow the work as students and prepare the weekly exercises and pass the final examination.

† More recently Extension centres have been formed at Kalamazoo and Bay City.

intendent of Public Instruction, Superintendent A. G. Lane, of Chicago, and many others have actively associated themselves in the work. President William R. Harper, of the Chicago University, and President Henry Wade Rogers, of the Northwestern University, discussed the movement before the State Teachers' Association of Illinois at Springfield at the time of the National Conference, and thus were prevented from attending the latter. Professor A. V. E. Young, of Northwestern, and President Carl Johann, of Eureka College, represented the higher education of the State and presented reports of Extension work in Northern and Central Illinois.

The first meeting in reference to University Extension in Chicago was held on May 22, 1891. President Edmund J. James, of the American Society, presented the subject on that occasion to many of the leading citizens of Chicago, explaining clearly the important place which University Extension can fill in public education. He spoke in detail of the origin and development of the movement and of the system of teaching which embodies its fundamental idea. The first centre was organized in November, 1891, through the instrumentality of Dr. Doremus Scudder, Pastor of the Workers' Church. To this centre was called Professor James A. Woodburn, of the University of Indiana, to give a course of lectures on American political history. On November 28, the Chicago Society for University Extension was formed by representatives of the Northwestern, Chicago, Lake Forest, Indiana, Wisconsin, and Illinois Universities, and Beloit and Wabash Colleges. The society is controlled by two representative bodies: the joint university board, consisting of the president and two professors from each college, and an advisory council of Chicago citizens. At a subsequent meeting, Mr. Franklin H. Head was elected president, Mrs. Charles Henrotin, vice-president; Mr. Franklin MacVeagh, treasurer; and Mr. Charles Zeublin, secretary. On the list of the advisory council appear the names of the leading clergymen, lawyers, business men, and educators of the city. Eighty-five courses of lectures on history, literature, economics, philosophy, the mathematical and natural sciences and law, are offered by the society. The first centre organized by the society was that at Oak Park, a suburb of Chicago, where Professor Butler, of the University of Illinois, is giving a course on English literature to an audience of one hundred and seventy-five subscribers. Professor Butler is to open his centre at the Newberry Library on February 19. At the Workers' Church, Professor Woodburn is to be succeeded by Professor Ross, of the University of Indiana, who lectures on economics. The Union Church of Hyde Park, and the Wesley Church on the north side have Extension classes. A number of additional centres will be founded in the near future.

The University of Illinois has entered vigorously on Extension work under the direction of the acting Regent, T. J. Burrill, and a standing committee of the faculty, including Professors S. A. Forbes, N. C. Ricker, and C. M. Moss. The standard of an Extension course is fixed at six lectures, for which there is a charge of ten dollars and travelling expenses for each lecture. The official list includes the following courses: "Botany," by Professor T. J. Burrill; "English Constitutional History," by Professor J. D. Crawford; "Agriculture," by Professor G. E. Morrow; "Civil Engineering," by Professor I. O. Baker; "Physical Astronomy," by Professor I. O. Baker; "English Composition and Oratory," by Professor J. H. Brownlee; "English Language and Literature," by Professor N. Butler, Jr.; "Municipal Engineering," by Professor A. N. Talbot; "Political Economy," by Professor H. J. Barton; "Psychology," by Professor C. M. Moss.

As a special feature of the Extension work of the University, the faculty offers to county superintendents of schools, lecture courses to be delivered at the County Teachers' Institutes during the vacation months.*

The subjects have been selected with special reference to the needs of the more advanced teachers, and also with a view to attracting the interest and attendance of the citizens of the

---

* The development of University Extension in the form of summer courses at County Institutes, Summer Chautauquas, mountain and seaside resorts, both for teachers and general audiences, will be studied as a phase of the movement with great interest by all friends of the work.

towns in which the institutes are held. While this instruction is in substance and in aim essentially the same as that given at the University, it is adapted in method to the character of the classes and audiences receiving it.*

WISCONSIN.

President T. C. Chamberlin has been one of the foremost champions of University Extension in America, and a careful student of the development of the movement in its various phases in the United States and abroad. The University of Wisconsin, of which he is president, has been active, largely through his influence, in establishing this system in that State. Without exception, the University of Wisconsin has so far established more centres than any other institution in the United States. Besides having the advantage of heading the educational system of the State, it has in its location at the capital a special means of influencing the thought of educators throughout the commonwealth. The favorable attitude of the State government may be noted in the offering free of charge of the Assembly Hall of the Legislature for the purpose of the work. The University is further fortunate in having in its faculty a number of men whom experience has shown to be especially qualified both in scholarly attainments and personal gifts for Extension teaching. The list of Extension lecturers includes Professor F. J. Turner, on American History; Professor J. C. Freeman, on English Literature; Professor Julius E. Olson, on Scandinavian Literature; Professor L. F. Van Cleef, on Greek Literature; Professor J. B. Parkinson, on Economics; Dr. H. C. Tolman, on the Antiquities of India and Iran; Professor E. A. Birge, on Bacteriology; Professor C. R. Barnes, on The Physiology of Plants; Professor H. B. Loomis, on Electricity; Professor R. D. Salisbury, on Landscape Geology. The cost of a course is ten dollars per lecture and travelling expenses.

The following report was sent to the National Conference by

---

* Extension courses are being given at Urbana and Quincy, and organizations for the promotion of this work effected at Rock Island and Jacksonville.

Wisconsin. 197

Professor Edward A. Birge, Dean of the College Faculty of the University of Wisconsin:

"MADISON, December 26, 1891.
"PRESIDENT EDMUND J. JAMES, Philadelphia:

"DEAR SIR,—In the absence of President Chamberlain, I reply to your invitation of December 19. I greatly regret that it is impossible for any member of our faculty to be present at the National Conference on University Extension. We are engaging somewhat actively in this work, and should be very glad to have the aid and counsel which would come from being present at such a meeting as that which you have called. The distance, however, is so great that it is impossible for any member of our faculty to be present.

"During the spring of 1891 the subject of University Extension was considered by the faculty of the University of Wisconsin, and they recommended to the Board of Regents, at its meeting in June, 1891, that courses of University Extension lectures be offered for the coming collegiate year. The report was adopted by the Regents, and early in the fall term the faculty determined upon detailed plans for the work and issued a preliminary circular, a copy of which is enclosed. From the circular you will see the scope of our work and its general plan.

"In some of the departments which are advertised in the circular the work has not yet begun, and only a few of the courses of six lectures have been completed, so that at present it is impossible to speak in detail of results reached. In general it may be said that the movement has met with a very warm response on the part of the people of the State. In most of the departments applications have been made for lecture courses beyond the capacity of the lecturer. Under the rules of the Board of Regents, the Extension work is to be done by the professors without interference with their ordinary college duties. This necessarily limits the lectures to Friday and Saturday evenings, or to such places as can be reached by train in such a way as to return for duty on the following morning.

"So far as I can report at present, there are forty-three courses of lectures finished, in progress, or definitely engaged for the future, while there are a large number of other applications which have not yet been acted upon, and which will undoubtedly increase the number of courses given during the current year to more than fifty. The greatest number of applications has come in the department of English literature, in which thirteen courses are now in progress. Most of these lectures are given in connection with a reading circle in the town, and are, therefore, given at intervals greater than once a week; some once in two weeks, others once a month. The number in the audiences has ranged from ninety to two hundred and seventy-five, averaging, perhaps, one hundred and fifty. Each lecture is followed by a conversation in which, as a rule, the entire audience has taken part. The reading circles have ranged in number from twenty-five to eighty.

"In history two courses have been completed, with audiences respectively five hundred and one hundred and fifty, with quiz classes following each lecture, attended by from forty to seventy-five persons. In these courses eight persons have taken the examination indicated in the circular. Five other courses in history are engaged.

"In geology only one course has been completed, but several others are in progress, with audiences and classes ranging about as in the department of English literature. Altogether eight courses are in progress or engaged in this department.

"In bacteriology six courses have been engaged, but none have been as yet entered upon.

"In economics one course has been completed at Milwaukee, with audiences from one hundred and fifty to two hundred; a class of thirty-three was organized for special work. The examinations in this course have not yet been held.

"In Scandinavian literature two courses are under engagement.

"In electricity two courses; and in antiquities of India and Iran one course is engaged. In plant physiology and Greek literature no courses have as yet been reported as engaged.

"I enclose a list of the towns at which courses of lectures are being given or are under engagement, and also a map of the

State on which the same places are indicated. From this you will see that in spite of the limitations which distance imposes upon us, we are covering the area of the State pretty thoroughly. I enclose also synopses of the lecture courses in economics, history, and English literature, and synopsis of part of the course in geology.

"We have entered into arrangements for mutual work with the Chicago Society for University Extension, and with the Chautauqua organization for the same purpose. Our plan is to work from our own institution as a centre, and also to work in co-operation with any other societies which may be formed for the furtherance of University Extension. As yet no work has been done by the University in connection with these societies.

"Our general plan embraces courses of six lectures, each lecture followed by quiz or conversation class; an examination is held at the end of the course. The cost of each course is sixty dollars and the expenses of the lecturer. In several cities the expenses have been born by some citizen, so that the course has been made free to the public. The correspondence work indicated in the circular has not as yet been called for.

"The places at which courses are in progress or engaged are in English Literature: Ashland, Baraboo, Beaver Dam, Clinton, Fond du Lac, Fox Lake, Janesville, Milwaukee (two courses), Reedsburg, Sheboygan, Spring Green, Superior, Washburn.

"In History: Brodhead, Fond du Lac, Madison, Milwaukee, Monroe, Poynette, Oshkosh.

"In Economics: Milwaukee (two courses), La Crosse, Ashland.

"In Bacteriology: Eau Claire, La Crosse, Madison, Milwaukee (two courses), Whitewater.

"In Electricity: Milwaukee, Watertown.

"In Scandinavian Literature: Stoughton, Milwaukee.

"In Geology: Oconomowoc (two courses), Green Bay, Fort Howard, Oconto, Platteville, Watertown.

"In the Antiquities of India and Iran: Milwaukee."

From Milwaukee, President R. C. Spencer, of the People's

Institute, submitted the following report to the National Conference:

"Milwaukee nas taken the course in American History, the Colonization of North America, by Professor F. J. Turner, of the University of Wisconsin. It was delivered under the auspices of the Chautauqua Club, in the Entertainment Hall of Plymouth Congregational Church, and has been successful, both in attendance, character of the audience, and interest manifested. The expense of the course was guaranteed by Hon. John L. Mitchell, member of Congress for this district. Tickets for the course of six lectures were fifty cents. The course in English Literature, by Professor J. E. Freeman, is in progress at the State Normal School, under the auspices of the faculty of that institution. It is also being given in the Guild Hall of St. Paul's Church, under the auspices of the Young People's Society. In both places the attendance is large and comprises our most intelligent and cultured people. The tickets for this course are seventy-five cents for six lectures. The course in Scandinavian Literature, by Professor Julius E. Olson, will be given after the holidays, under the auspices of a society auxiliary to the People's Institute. The expense of this course is guaranteed by Mr. John Johnston, cashier of the Wisconsin Marine Insurance Company Bank, tickets for which are fifty cents for six lectures. The course in Economics, by Professor J. B. Parkinson, has just been concluded, and was given on successive Saturday mornings at half-past ten o'clock. It was attended principally by students from the various schools and institutions of the city and by teachers. It was given under the auspices of the People's Institute, and the expense was defrayed by the Spencerian Business College. It will be repeated after the holidays, Friday evenings, for the convenience of business-men. The course in Bacteriology, by Professor E. A. Birge, will begin after the holidays in the Science Department of the Public High School. The expense is defrayed by Mrs. E. P. Allis, for the benefit of students of this branch of science. This course will also be given before the Medical Society. The course in Electricity, by Dr. H. B. Loomis, will be given under the auspices of the Wisconsin Electric Club, of which Professor A. J. Rogers, of the Public High School, is President. Judge George H. Noyes, of the Board of University Regents, is chairman of the University Extension committee of the People's Institute, which has fostered and encouraged, without attempting to manage or direct. Regarding University Extension as experimental in Milwaukee, it was deemed best to let it shape itself. The result is better than expected. Little has been attempted through the press or otherwise to create special interest in the movement, and it has, therefore, been spontaneous. If we may judge from our limited experience, Milwaukee will be counted as an auspicious field for University Extension work. Before the close of the season a meeting will be held of the societies, persons, and professors interested in the several courses of University Extension lectures given in Milwaukee, for the purpose of comparing notes and arranging plans for the coming year."

Aside from the State University, Beloit College is the most important institution of Wisconsin. The faculty has, after careful consideration, taken up the work of University Extension and arranged an excellent list of Extension courses. The price of each of the six lectures in the typical course is ten dollars and travelling expenses. Special emphasis is laid, by the lecturers of Beloit College, on the class-work connected with the system. The following courses are offered: Ethics, by Professor J. J. Blaisdell; English Literature, by Professor. H. M. Whitney; Electricity, by Professor T. A. Smith; Chemistry, by Professor E. G. Smith; The New Astronomy, by Professor Chas. A. Bacon; German Literature, by Professor C. W. Pearson; The Physiology of Plants, by Professor H. D. Densmore.

MINNESOTA.

Professor Harry P. Judson, of the University of Minnesota, submitted the following report, read by Professor M. L. Sanford.

The Extension movement in the North Star State dates from the winter of 1889-90, and began in the city of St. Paul. A group of gentlemen who were interested in educational work, and who had kept watch of what had been done in England and in the East, determined to see what could be accomplished at home. They accordingly prevailed on the St. Paul Academy of Science, of which they were active members, to undertake the management, and under its auspices proceeded to set on foot a local centre.

General interest was easily aroused, and arrangements were soon made for a variety of courses. The Board of Education granted the free use of the High-School building for one evening in the week. Course tickets were sold, the proceeds of which went to compensate the lecturers. Other incidental expenses were provided by private subscription.

In the spring of 1890, a beginning was made, with classes in English Literature, History, Botany, Electricity, Geology, and Mathematics. Instruction in the last two subjects was given by members of the faculty of Carleton and Macalester Colleges respectively. The remaining instructors were from the State University. Each course comprised twelve weekly exercises.

During the year 1890–91, the work in St. Paul was continued, courses being given in English Literature, American Literature, International Law, and History.

In Minneapolis the work was begun in the fall of 1890, under the direction of the public library board. Courses in English Literature and International Law were given by professors from the State University. These were followed in the second term by a course in History.

For the present year the management is in the hands of the Collegiate Alumnæ Association. A short course in Astronomy has already been given by a Carleton professor, and other subjects will be studied after the holiday recess.

The example of the twin cities has proved contagious, and during the fall just past a beginning has been made in other places. Members of the State University faculty are giving work in Political Economy to a class of about three hundred in Duluth, and in History to about two hundred and fifty in Faribault. Arrangements are also on foot in other towns of the State.

From this hasty sketch of what has been done, several things will appear.

In the first place, the movement in Minnesota has been quite spontaneous. It has not been "worked up," but has apparently been a natural growth.

As to the subjects of study, the necessity of self-support has made them rather limited. That must be the case until public or private munificence is ready to supplement the efforts of local centres. The higher education is not self-supporting anywhere, and it must not be expected that it will prove so in this more than in other forms.

Until recently, the Regents of the State University have refrained from any official connection with the Extension movement. They have not felt warranted, in the absence of a special appropriation, in incurring expense. And it has seemed better, on the whole, to wait until it should appear plain that there is an actual call for authoritative direction.

But at the annual meeting of the Board at St. Paul, on December 22, it was voted to undertake the experiment of conducting Extension work in the State for the current academic year. Definite plans will be formulated at once. Of course, the expense must still be borne by local centres. But if the experiment shows that there is promise of permanence, the Legislature will undoubtedly be asked at its next session for a moderate appropriation.

And this leads at once to the question whether the movement in America is a real and permanent one. Enthusiasts, of course, have but one answer. The success of nearly twenty years in England seems conclusive evidence. The crowded lecture courses last winter in Eastern centres and the rapid spread throughout the country would appear to be unanswerable corroboration.

Many cool observers, however, are of the opinion that all this must be taken with a large allowance of salt. To begin with, we must not infer too much from the popularity of certain lecturers. And then the English experience really counts for little, so far as we are concerned. The conditions in the two countries are radically different. A vast deal that passes in England under the head of "University Extension" is nothing but the work of the Chautauqua Circles here. A vast deal more is merely the ordinary work of our American high schools, and is "University Extension" only in the sense that all study leading to the University is an extension of the University downward. It must be remembered that the free public high school does not exist in England. When we have eliminated these two elements, the volume of the English work shrinks materially.

In saying this, of course, it will be understood that there is no intention of depreciating what our English friends have done. But there is danger in indiscriminating imitation.

An interesting outcome of the experience in Minnesota relates to one of the points to which attention has been called above.

It early became apparent in St. Paul that there was a very eager desire for instruction among certain classes of busy people, but that the instruction they needed was in subjects regularly taught in the city high schools. Accordingly, as an immediate result of the first Extension courses, in the school year 1890-91, evening classes were organized in the city manual-training school. These classes were attended through the year by an average of one hundred and fifty, mostly young mechanics.

The success of this experiment led the public-school authorities in the fall of 1891, on the recommendation of Principal G. N. Carman, to open the Central High School for an evening session two nights in the week. The evening classes in the manual training-school were continued for the benefit of mechanics, and classes in the high school were formed in such subjects as the demand seemed to show desirable. The attendants on these proved to be mostly teachers and employees in various kinds of business, whom we may perhaps group under the name of clerks. Whether mechanics, teachers, or clerks, all the students are occupied during the day in some form of self-support. The entire attendance in these evening classes has averaged about four hundred and fifty for the three months of October, November, and December. The total registration has reached nearly eight hundred, but the average attendance is a much safer criterion of the actual extent of real work.

These evening classes in the high school are something tangible and practical. They afford an immediate outlet to a demand for instruction that ought to be met, but which is in no proper sense a part of University Extension.

It needs no argument, however, to point out the great significance of such an arrangement to real University Extension in the future. As a result of this high-school work, there will soon be a considerable number of people well fitted to take up work of University grade in evening classes. Thus, entirely aside from its general value, the evening high school at once becomes a preparatory school to feed the Extension side of the University.

In fact, to the writer, the evening high school seems the element of greatest promise bearing on a permanent Extension of University Teaching. It is true, undoubtedly, that in all our communities there is a certain number of busy adults whose maturity and experience in life fit them to do work of University grade in some lines, but these lines are limited. If there is to be any breadth to Extension work, there must be provided a sufficient foundation. And only when the high school and the academy join in the task will the plan be complete.

IOWA.

The State University of Iowa entered upon Extension work in the fall of 1891, in accordance with the recommendation of Henry Sabin, State Superintendent of Instruction, and member of the Board of Regents. A circular was issued, explaining the design of University Extension, giving its history and the plans proposed by the State University of Iowa, with the list of lecturers and subjects. The latter includes: President Schaeffer, Public Education; Professor Courier, Latin Language, Literature, and Antiquities; Professor Calvin, Geology and Physiology; Professor McBride, Botany; Professor Andrews, Chemistry; Professor Perkins, History; Professor Patrick, Psychology and Ethics; Professor Jamison, Hygiene; Professor Wilson, German

Language and Literature; Professor Veblen, Physics; Professor Weld, Mathematics and Astronomy; Professor Nutting, Zoology; Professor Loos, Political Economy; Professor McConnell, Pedagogy; Assistant Professor Call, Greek Life and Literature; Assistant Professor Neff, French Language and Literature. The first course was commenced at Davenport on January 9. The course is of twelve lectures, four each being given by Professors Calvin, McBride, and Nutting. The general topic is "The Making of the World," and the respective divisions are entitled "The Formation of the Earth," "The Vegetable Kingdom," and "Animal Life." The course was arranged by a committee of citizens, of which Regent Richardson, of the State University, is Chairman. Tickets for the entire course were sold at two dollars and fifty cents. The influence of the University of Iowa in Extension work is felt beyond the limits of the State. Professor Loos, of the Chair of Political Science, began a course on subjects related to his own department, at Quincy, Ill., in the latter part of December.

KANSAS AND MISSOURI.

The Southwest was represented at the National Conference by President W. H. Black, of Missouri Valley College. He gave a most encouraging account of the interest in University Extension on the part of the people and willingness on the part of the university and college authorities and faculties to give their efforts as far as possible to the spreading of University advantages beyond the walls of the various institutions. President Black read a letter from Chancellor Snow, of the University of Kansas, regretting his inability to be present at the Conference, and submitting reports of the work in that State. The University of Missouri has formulated and published a plan of Extension teaching under the direction of its new head, President R. H. Jesse. Extension teaching has so far been carried on in Kansas and Missouri jointly by the faculties of the institutions in both States. For convenience' sake, it seems preferable to unite the reports of the two States, and give the following summary of

"University Extension in the Southwest," submitted by Professor Frank W. Blackmar, of the University of Kansas, and one of the most successful lecturers in that field.

The State Universities of the West have from their foundation held a very close relation to the people. Created by State authority, they have endeavored to supply the peculiar wants of young, growing commonwealths. Composing a part of the great public school system, they have sought to be in every sense the schools of the people. But while they have entered into the sympathies of the people and endeavored to supply the kind and quality of education suited to their peculiar needs, on the other hand they have assumed the leadership in thought and learning of the State and country in which they have been located.

The modern State University has had occasion to feel in a special way that it is truly the servant of the people and the commonwealth, and has therefore been more in sympathetic touch with the life of the people than perhaps many older institutions of different foundation. Consequently, while we find in Western institutions the instructors endeavoring to give full and complete instruction in the branches of the University curriculum, and to develop individual students as far as possible in the way of higher learning, many of the instructors have been called from time to time to lecture to the people and to mingle with the public affairs of the State. Thus their influence has extended beyond the University walls to the community at large.

Institutions of this nature take kindly to the University Extension movement. It is only necessary to enlarge and systematize the work of the casual lecturer, and University Extension is accomplished. The recent Extension movement, which spread so rapidly over the United States, reached Kansas just in time to take immediate and permanent effect. It began in Topeka,* Kansas, and Kansas City, Mo., about the same time. The initiative of actual work was made by Mr. Beers, the librarian of the city library at Topeka, who was instrumental in organiz-

---

* Topeka is a beautiful city of about forty thousand people, and, being the capital of the State, is essentially a centre of learning and educational enterprises.

ing a local association at that place. Professor Blake, of the University of Kansas, was invited to deliver a course of twelve lectures on Electricity and Magnetism. A class of one hundred and twenty-five pupils was composed of many of the best people of Topeka. Electricity was conducted into the hall, and apparatus for experiments furnished from the department of Electrical Engineering of the University of Kansas.
The lectures are given in an attractive manner, and each one amply illustrated with the best modern experiments. One lecture is delivered every two weeks, on Friday nights. A short syllabus of each lecture is printed one week in advance and distributed among the members of the class for suggestive reading and study. These are arranged in a small book prepared for use, which also contains the list of authors and books to be studied. As the class is not completed, it is impossible to tell how many will take the examination and try for grades at the University. The topics discussed were: The Scientific Conception of Energy, The Electric Current, The Electro-Magnet, Electro-Dynamics of Current, Ampère's theory of Measuring Instruments of Electric Current, Theory of Electro-Magnetic Potentials, Electro-Magnetic Induction, Alternating Current, Electro-Chemics, Static Induction, Electrical Radiation.

Almost simultaneously with the movement in Topeka began that of Kansas City, Mo. It may not be inappropriate to state that Kansas City is a thriving city of about one hundred and forty thousand inhabitants, and that it is the metropolis of Western Missouri and Eastern Kansas. There are consequently many people in Kansas City who formerly lived in Kansas, and still retain pleasant memories of their former home. Indeed, the city is so closely connected with the State whose boundary it joins, as to be logically named Kansas City. Although a Western city, full of business enterprise, the people are wide-awake to all kinds of available intellectual culture. Here are found graduates of Kansas and Missouri universities, as well as graduates of Columbia, Yale, Harvard, Michigan, and other institutions of the United States, who are still interested in higher education. Desiring to form a University Extension society, they naturally looked to the nearest State institution for assistance,—the University of Kansas. The writer was invited to address a meeting called for the purpose of organizing a local Extension association. The association was permanently organized with Mr. E. H. Allen, President of the Board of Trade, as President of the association, and Mr. John Sullivan as Secretary. Later on a preliminary meeting was addressed by Prof. W. H. Carruth, of the University of Kansas, and the writer. Spalding's Hall, a large and centrally located auditorium, was obtained for the meetings of the association and classes, and the secretary immediately wrote to all of the institutions in the vicinity, asking them to submit a list of Extension lectures in courses which they were willing to deliver in Kansas City. The following is a partial list of lectures submitted. It is to be regretted that a complete list is not at hand, but those offered by the William Jewell and Park Colleges are not to be found at present. Constitutional Law, Alexander Martin, LL.D.; Semitic Languages, J. S. Blackwell, Ph.D.; History of the English Language, E. A. Allen, Litt.D.; History of Education, J. P. Blanton, A.M.; History of Mathematics, W. B. Smith, Ph.D.; Greek Life, W. G. Manly, A.M.; Roman Religion, J. C. Jones, Ph.D.; Roman Constitutional Law, J. M. Burnham, Ph.D.; Homer and Homeric Antiquities, Walter Miller, M.A.; The Electro-Magnet, William Shrader, Ph.D.; Botany, G. D. Purinton, Ph.D.; Astronomy, Milton Updegraf, B.C.E. The above courses were offered by the instructors of the University of Missouri, located at Columbia.

The following courses were offered by the University of Kansas: The Chemistry of Every-Day Life, E. H. S. Bailey, Ph.D.; Political Economy, Economic Problems and Sociology, F. W. Blackmar, Ph.D.; The German Empire, E. D. Adams, Ph.D. Electricity and its Modern Applications, L. I. Blake, Ph.D.; The Romantic School in France, and the Development of the Novel in France, A. G. Canfield, A.M.; English Literature of the Nineteenth Century, C. G. Dunlap, A.B.; History and Philosophy of American Literature, E. M. Hopkins, A.M.; German Literature, First Classic Period, and German Literature, Modern Period, W. H. Carruth, A.M.; Municipal and Domestic

Sanitation, F. O. Marvin, A.M.; Astronomy, E. Miller, A.M.; The Art of Piano-Forte Playing, G. B. Penny, B.S.; Roman Poetry, D. H. Robinson, Ph.D.; Botany, W. C. Stevens, B.S.; Medical Chemistry and Sanitary Science, L. E. Sayre, Ph.G.; Psychology, Olin Templin, A.M.; Classical Greek Literature, A. M. Wilcox, Ph.D.; Physical Geology, S. W. Williston, Ph.D.

It was decided by the Kansas City Society to take the course offered above on Economic Problems as introductory to the work. The preference in courses was determined by replies to circulars freely distributed by the association among the prominent people of the city and vicinity. A class of one hundred was formed for the first course, ninety-two of whom registered for examination and credits. The aim of this course was to discuss in a scientific manner the principal topics of the day, especially those in which the people are most interested in the West.

In the lectures it was intended to apply all of the principal laws and principles of political economy, so that during the twelve weeks students might observe the workings of political economy and discover its laws through its applications to present industrial life.

The following is a list of the subjects of the lectures given: Money and its Circulation, How a Nation Grows Wealthy (Production), The Division of Wealth Products, Monopolies, Socialism and Communism, Immigration, Taxation and Tax Reforms, Irrigation of Arid Lands, Transportation, Social and Economic Reforms (two lectures), The Scope. Method and Services of Political Economy.

A great deal of interest was shown on the part of the students, and permanent good resulted from the course. At the time of writing, it is not known how many will take the examinations, consequently certain results may not be estimated. In the two classes referred to, one in Topeka and one in Kansas City, the membership was largely composed of teachers, lawyers, judges, business-men, and artisans.*

---

*In Professor Blake's class there were twenty-one lawyers, twelve teachers, twelve students, four engineers, physicians, electricians, operators, clerks, public officers, etc.

A syllabus of each lecture was printed in the leading papers prior to the time of delivering the lectures. These outlines were quite full, for the purpose of assisting students in their daily studies and of giving them a well-rounded idea of the subject. One lecture was delivered each week on Thursday evening. The first hour was devoted to the formal presentation of the subject of the evening, and the second to the informal discussions and questions. Arrangements were made with the librarian of the city library to collect the books relating to the subjects of the lectures in a private reading-room for the consultation of those who were taking the course. Some studious ones availed themselves of this privilege.

While this work was being inaugurated, the Kansas State University, and the University of Missouri, were not idle. They each organized for the work, sent a prospectus of the conditions on which the Extension would be made, and established a system of credits for students in the prescribed courses. To meet the immediate demands of students in these courses, the University of Kansas adopted the following regulations: " Persons who hold the degree of Bachelor of Arts from the University of Kansas, or from other institutions of equal rank with it, may receive the degree of Master of Arts upon the satisfactory completion of nine University Extension courses of twelve lectures each. These courses shall be accompanied by such study, reading, and examination as shall be prescribed by the professors in charge."

" Persons not holding the bachelor's degree upon the satisfactory completion of nine University Extension courses of twelve lectures each, shall receive a University Extension diploma."

" Work done under instructors from other institutions than the University of Kansas will be accepted upon examination for not more than four of the nine courses necessary for a degree or a diploma. This work will also be accepted as undergraduate work, a full course in the University Extension being reckoned as a two-thirds term in the University. Nine twelve-lecture courses will be accepted as equivalent to a full year's work at the University."

In making these rules the faculty of the University realized that only a comparatively small number out of the large classes receiving University Extension lectures would care to avail themselves of these provisions. But it was thought best to make it possible for all who desired, to receive such credit extended by the University. All such persons are duly registered as students of the University of Kansas. The University of Missouri formulated similar provisions respecting credits in that institution.

The second course, begun under the direction of the Kansas City Society, was that of English Literature of the Nineteenth Century. This was also a large and interesting class, and was successfully carried on by Professor C. G. Dunlap, of the University of Kansas. The following list of subjects will indicate the scope of the work: Literature at the Close of the Eighteenth Century, William Wordsworth, Samuel T. Coleridge, Percy Bysshe Shelley, John Keats, Lord Byron, John Henry Newman, The Novel (Thackeray and Dickens), Tennyson, George Eliot, Robert Browning.

The association arranged for four other courses: One on Constitutional Law, by Professor Alexander Martin, of the University of Missouri, and one on the Semitic Languages, by Professor J. S. Blackwell, of the same institution. Although classes were about completed for these gentlemen, owing to the unfortunate occurrence of the burning of the main building of the Missouri University, they found it necessary to give all of their attention to home work. These courses of lectures will probably be given next year. The other two courses arranged for are by Professors Blake and Carruth, of the Kansas University, the former on Electricity and its Modern Applications, and the latter on German Literature. Professor Blake's course is similar to that given in Topeka in many respects. The class has already been formed and numbers over three hundred,—the largest class yet formed. The course in German Literature will begin soon. The following subjects indicate the scope of the work: Martin Luther, From Luther to Lessing, Lessing (two lectures), The Storm and Stress Period, Goethe (four lectures), Schiller (three lectures).

A new course has been formed in Topeka under the auspices of the Trades and Labor Assembly. This will be carried on by the writer, after the course in Kansas City is completed. The subject is Political Economy, and the course is especially arranged for intelligent working-men.

Professor E. H. S. Bailey, of the Kansas University, is conducting a very interesting course in the Chemistry of Every-Day Life at Olathe, Kansas. The class is large and enthusiastic. The following outline will suggest the nature of the course: The Atmosphere, Combustion, Artificial Lighting, Water, Cleansing and Bleaching Materials, Foods, Sugars, Nitrogenous Foods, Fruits, Non-Alcoholic Beverages, Digestion and Assimilation of Food.

A course of eight lectures is being given at Abilene, Kan., by various instructors of the University of Kansas. The lectures are all literary, but are given by different individuals. Among those who have already been selected are E. M. Hopkins, A. G. Canfield, W. H. Carruth, O. Templin, A. M. Wilcox, and C. G. Dunlap. Over ninety persons have entered the class. This course is a little different from other courses, but is worthy of mention as a genuine extension of university instruction. The people of Abilene are so well pleased with the success of the enterprise that they have already begun to plan for other courses during the next academic year. This may also be said of the people of other towns. They say, "Next year we will know how to carry on this work in a more acceptable manner."

Two courses of lectures will be given in Wichita, on Astronomy and Geology. The former will be given by Prof. E. Miller, and the latter by Prof. S. W. Willston, both of Kansas State University. Each course will consist of six lectures only. This promises to be an excellent field for University Extension.

While these lectures are being given to those who desire them, the single-lecture system is kept up by the instructors of the University. They are called here and there over different parts of the State to give a single lecture for the benefit of some association, college, or high school. Thus we have an account of the inauguration of University Extension in the Southwest. It will be seen by the foregoing statement that the movement is taking a permanent place in Western education. Many lessons have already been learned, but the enterprise is still in an experimental stage, and one cannot predict what will be the future outcome. It would seem that as the work has sprung up of itself, unaided by any systematic urging, it has a fair prospect of becoming permanent. The University of Kansas has not urged the movement in any degree. It has endeavored to supply the demands, and to give such information as has been sought for in the formation of local associations. The instructors take up the work somewhat reluctantly, owing to the fact that they have plenty of work at home, yet they feel it a duty to respond to such calls when they can do so without interfering seriously with their regular work. It will be found that a reasonable amount of such work, bringing the instructor, as it does, in contact with the world outside of the University, is a great advantage to him, for it tends to quicken him and prepare him for more vital instruction.

The preceding brief review of actual work done has been for the purpose of indicating the amount and quality of instruction that has been given in this line, and for the purpose of designating the general plan of operation. From the foregoing history, and from the record of similar work done in other parts of the West, it will be seen that the general plan of the work is well defined. Each prominent institution will be the centre for the propagation of Extension ideas and for furnishing lectures. Around these centres local associations are being formed, which will take the responsibility of arranging courses for the people, of forming classes, and attending to the financial part of the enterprise. Immediately connected with the people whose wants and whose ways it fully understands, a strong local institution is best prepared to carry on University Extension within the radius of its influence. This is its natural field and its legitimate service. It is a natural centre of educational influence, and the people look upon it with pride and are willing to be instructed by its professors. If such an institution be a living one, strong and vigorous, it is within sympathetic touch with the people and close to their lives and thoughts. While it may administer to their educational needs, it will, on the other hand, lead them to enter the realm of higher learning, or to complete the course which they have abandoned long ago. It will be seen by the foregoing outline that much of the work is of an advanced nature, and some of it is prepared for classes who have made considerable progress. There has been an honest, and I may say successful, endeavor on the part of the lecturers to suit their instruction to the needs of the classes under their charge. A great improvement might be made in some instances in the preparation of outlines of the lecture, which are to be placed in the hands of the members of the class. These outlines might be more complete, and be composed of full statements of facts and principles laid down, instead of the suggested heading. These principles and facts might be illustrated fully, so that the student could carry in his mind a living syllabus rather than a dead one. Also, it may be seen that the process of classification of the students must be entered into more fully than has been done, if the Extension movement is to grow in thoroughness and efficiency. The registry for examination and for grades is a step towards this, and in due time the problem will gradually solve itself.

The writer would not have it appear that the University of Kansas is the only institution in the Southwest engaged in Extension work. Such institutions as the University of Missouri, William Jewell, Park, Baker University, Manhattan Agricultural College, Washburn College, and the Emporia Normal School, have furnished many lectures to the people, but the University of Kansas has taken the most complete and radical departure in this respect of all the institutions of the Southwest. Already nine full courses, of twelve lectures each, have been commenced, or are arranged for since last October, and the regular system of single lectures has been maintained. The limit for work of this nature, without interfering seriously with routine work, is in the neighborhood of about twenty courses each year of twelve lectures each.

COLORADO.

The Denver Society for University Extension was organized on May 24, 1891. Secretary George Henderson, of the American Society, gave on that evening an address before the trustees and friends of the University of Denver. After his address a temporary organization was effected, which was afterwards made permanent, and Chancellor William F. McDowell, of the University of Denver, was chosen president of the Society. On its executive committee appear the names of State Superintendent N. B. Coy; Superintendent Aaron Gove, of Denver; Professor J. H. Barker, Dr. James C. Shattuck, Rev. Dr. A. A. Cameron, Bishop H. W. Warren, and Hon. H. B. Chamberlin.

During the current year much interest has been shown in Extension teaching throughout the State. In addition to the work in Denver, where the Colorado State College and the University of Colorado are co-operating with the University of Denver, a centre has been established in Greeley, where Chancellor McDowell is delivering a course of six lectures on the French Revolution.

WYOMING.

The Wyoming University Extension Association was organized at Laramie, Wyoming, October 24, 1891, with sixteen charter members. The president of the Association is A. A. Johnson, President of the University of Wyoming; Vice-President, J. D. Conley; Secretary, G. R. Hebard; Treasurer, J. F. Soule. In addition to these gentlemen, the following are members of the council: C. M. McDonald, H. Merz, and F. J. Niswander, of Laramie; J. O. Churchill, of Cheyenne, and J. B. Logue, of Evanston. The University of Wyoming is organizing the system of Extension teaching throughout the State, and under the able guidance of President A. A. Johnson, the founder and late President of the Fort Worth University, Texas, is making itself strongly felt in all parts of the commonwealth.

CALIFORNIA.

Under date of September 23, 1891, the Academic Council of the University of California announced that Extension courses would be given in San Francisco during the current year, on history, literature, and mathematics. The course on history by Professor Bacon is being delivered at present in the rooms of the Unitarian Church, on Thursday evenings, the special subject being "The Transition from Mediæval to Modern History." At the Academy of Sciences, Professor Charles M. Gayley, of the University of California, is delivering an afternoon course on Shakespeare. Professor Stringham is lecturing on algebra to audiences of nearly one hundred at the College of Pharmacy. The number of students in attendance on the lectures in history and literature is about four hundred. These courses extend over a full college term of fourteen weeks, and are entirely free to the public. Full credit for corresponding courses at the Universities is given to those passing satisfactory examinations. It is to be noted that these courses have tended directly to the advantage of the University in increasing public interest in their work. A special proof is the action of those attending the lectures in English Literature. The class, which numbers about four hundred, has generously contributed two hundred dollars towards a Shakespearian library for the University. It is proposed to give courses in ethics and political economy later in the year.

A University Extension Club has been organized at San José, Cal., with the following officers: H. Melville Tenney, President; Miss Mary Hazelton, Secretary, and Professor Manzer, Treasurer. The membership fee for the first year was fixed at two dollars, and transferable tickets for the first course of lectures was at one dollar and a quarter for those not members of the club. Two courses of six lectures each have been arranged for the current year. The first on Evolution, by President David Starr Jordan, of the Leland Stanford University, is to begin in the latter part of January, and is to be followed by a second course on Astronomy, by Professor E. E. Barnard, of the Lick Observatory.

At Oakland, an Extension centre has been established, and Professor George H. Howison, of the State University, has been engaged to lecture on Ethics during February and March. A fourth Extension centre is organized at San Diego, the President of which is Mr. B. F. McDaniel.

CANADA.

On November 5 and 6, 1891, a conference, under the auspices of the Ministry of Education, was held in Toronto to discuss the subject of University Extension. The evening address on October 5 was by President Edmund J. James, of the American Society, who pointed out the place of University Extension in a general scheme of public education, and emphasized the importance of the movement as supplementing the primary and secondary schools, and as extending greatly the influence of the higher institutions of learning. The account he gave of the American Society, and of what had been accomplished in the United States, was the moving impulse towards the organization on the succeeding day of the Canadian Society for the Extension of University Teaching, the constitution of which was modelled on that of the American Society. The following gentlemen were chosen officers: Presidents, Sir Daniel Wilson, Chancellor of McGill University; Hon. G. W. Allan, Chancellor of Trinity University; Hon. Edward Blake, of Toronto; Sandford Fleming, Chancellor of Queen's University; Professor Goldwin Smith; and Abbe Laflame, of Laval University; Treasurer, B. E. Walker, of the Bank of Commerce; Secretary, William Houston, M. A., the distinguished economist. Under the general direction of the Canadian Society many centres have been established, and courses, principally on history, literature, and science, delivered in Toronto, London, Ottawa, and Hamilton. Among the most successful lecturers have been Professors Clark, Huntingford, Schofield, Pitman, and Rigby, on literature; Professor G. J. Hume, on ethics, and Professor J. T. Crawford, on electricity.

The University of New Brunswick, in connection with the New Brunswick Natural History Society, has organized University Extension in and around St. John, N. B. The following courses, of eight lectures each, were begun on Monday, November 23, and continued during the succeeding weeks: Monday, "Physics," Professor Duff; Tuesday, "History of England, 1640-1659," Rev. J. DeSoyres; Wednesday, "Botany," Mr. G. U. Hay: Thursday, "Philosophy," Dr. D. Macrae; Friday, "Zoölogy," Dr. Bailey. On the completion of these courses, about the end of January, the following will succeed them: "English Literature," Professor Stockley; "Geology," Mr. G. F. Matthew; "Chemistry," Mr. A. E. Macintyre; "Political Economy," Professor Murray; "Law," Dr. I. A. Jack and Dr. A. A. Stockton.

THE REPORT

OF THE

AMERICAN SOCIETY

FOR THE

EXTENSION OF UNIVERSITY TEACHING,

NOVEMBER 3, 1890,—DECEMBER 31, 1891.

BY GEORGE HENDERSON,
General Secretary.

In the first months of 1890, there was in the United States not only no particular interest in the definite work of University Extension, but no clear idea as to what the movement really is or what the methods are which it employs. Attempts had indeed been made to introduce here and there some particular idea or phase of the work. These, however, had excited little attention, and even when measurably successful had hardly tended to make the details of the system known or its results appreciated.

This condition of things has greatly changed. It is no longer necessary to appeal to transatlantic experience when a question is asked as to the purposes, methods, and results of Extension Teaching. The objection cannot now be made that this system may be good for England or for Austria, but is not adapted to American conditions. The success of the great object-lesson carried on by the American Society and reaching now into six States, and the experiments conducted by various other societies and institutions have made it henceforth easier to introduce the work throughout the country.

In February, 1890, a number of the leading educators of Philadelphia met, by the invitation of Provost Pepper, to discuss the movement and the advisability of organizing it. It seemed to all that the work offered great opportunities for the whole country, and it was proposed to make the first trial in that city. The plan met the approval of those present and of all who were consulted during the succeeding months, and the co-operation of the neighboring higher institutions was pledged. In order to commence the work with the advantage of an intimate acquaintance with English methods, the secretary was sent to study the system as organized in Oxford, Cambridge, and London. On his return in the fall, he drew up a "Report on the University Extension Movement in England," which was published by the Society. In the mean time a communication had been sent to libraries, institutes, and associations of every character, describing the work about to be undertaken and inviting their co-operation in the formation of local centres. A descriptive brochure was also issued to the general public explaining the nature and scope of the new movement.

General interest was easily aroused. It was determined to organize at least six local centres, and it was at first thought that much stimulation would be necessary. This, it was soon seen, was unnecessary, as a stream of applications came pouring in from every section, and instead of six centres within a radius of fifty miles of Philadelphia, during the first year of work, there were formed twenty-three. The work to a large extent was spontaneous, and great caution had to be observed in restraining the local organizations from attempting too many courses.

At every point where lectures and classes are held we have formed an organization called a local centre, governed by a local committee, which takes entire charge of every detail connected with the work at that point. Of these organizations there are many types. One is formed by a library, Young Men's Christian Association, or institute; another by the establishment of an entirely new organization composed of the influential people of the place; still another, by using the local institution as a nucleus around which to rally a representative committee. On the whole we believe the last type of centre to be the most successful. But as the centre develops so must its organization. Generally the centre starts out with the definite aim of successfully carrying through a course of six or twelve lectures. The one thing before the mind of the organization during that stage of the work is the securing of sufficient funds to make it financially safe. After the first course is finished, too many of the centres endeavor to go on floating a second or a third course on the same basis. They have overlooked the fact that the first course was organized spontaneously, that they have not yet become a permanent factor in the life of the community, and that they have really no nucleus around which to rally. True it is that they have a nucleus of organizers, but this is not enough; they must have a nucleus in a student body. Indeed, it should be the effort of the organization at this stage not so much to secure subscriptions as to secure students. This has been the rock upon which a great many of our local centres have been thrown, and upon which, I am sorry to say, two or three have foundered.

Association Local Centre was organized in the building of the Central Branch of the Young Men's Christian Association, which is located in the heart of Philadelphia, at Fifteenth and Chestnut Streets. That Association did not abandon its educational work, which was of an elementary character, but practically gave over the more advanced work to the local centre. While the local committee is presided over by a man who is one of the Board of Managers of the Central Branch of the Young Men's Christian Association, the latter organization has no voice whatsoever in its deliberations. The committee was formed, numbering about thirty, broadly representative of the section of the city in which the centre is located. There are upon it physicians, lawyers, bankers, teachers, business-men, and a large percentage of ladies. Owing to its peculiar position this centre has been compelled to carry on work of a more or less popular character. However, it has this year been successful in securing a sequence of courses; the first one being on the "Study of

Political Economy;" second, "Socialism;" third, "The Change in Political Economy;" fourth, "Some Economic Questions;" and fifth, "Revolutions in Commerce."

The local committee at the West Philadelphia Centre was formed without the usual nucleus. A number of the influential people living in that neighborhood were invited to attend an informal meeting, which was held in the library of the University of Pennsylvania. The secretary of the society was present to explain the aim of the work about to be undertaken and the plan of procedure. After securing an informal organization, the use of the University Chapel was granted to them, and, as several members of the committee were actively interested in the West Philadelphia Institute, the co-operation of that institution was secured. At first the local committee was composed very largely of men, but when it was found that ladies could lend a very material assistance, a number were invited to serve on the committee, and as a consequence great stimulus was given to the work. A public meeting was arranged, at which the leading educators of the city spoke and a formal organization effected. The general local committee appointed a number of sub-committees, which are held responsible for certain definite parts of the work.

The Wagner Institute Centre was organized at the Wagner Free Institute of Science, located in the northwestern part of Philadelphia. The managers of the Institute were instrumental in calling into existence the local committee, their actuary becoming the local secretary, and their splendid hall being granted for the use of the centre. The section of the city in which this centre is located is one of the most favorable for work of this character. For ten or fifteen years the Wagner Free Institute has been giving, annually, courses in special branches of science which have been free to the public. This fact has proved only slightly to the disadvantage of the Extension courses for which a charge is made. The organization at this place was formally announced by a public meeting at which many leading educators spoke.

Germantown, one of the flourishing suburbs of Philadelphia,

with a population of fifty thousand, is one of the points most favorable for organizing this work, but was one of the last to take hold of it. The matter was first taken up and discussed at one of the Monday morning meetings of the ministers, and they held that, as several of the leading Evangelists had failed to secure any considerable audiences, it was in their opinion very doubtful if the work could be made a success. In the mean time, however, a number of gentlemen connected with the Workingmen's Club, took up the discussion of the question and decided to make an attempt to organize the work. As a preliminary step they arranged for an illustrated lecture by Dr. Henry Leffmann on Bacteria, and announced that at the close of the same there would be an address on University Extension by Provost Pepper of the University of Pennsylvania, and that an organization would be effected. As the Koch discoveries had just been announced, an overflowing house was obtained and much interest evinced in the work about to be started. A committee representative of the different interests was formed, and the carrying out of the details was delegated to two or three subcommittees. During the first year a Students' Association was organized for the study of Tennyson. Its meetings were continued far into the summer, the average attendance being forty-seven.

Frankford was one of the first sections of the city to take hold of the new movement and organize a local centre, the Board of Trustees of Wright's Institute taking the initiative. The Institute placed its hall at the command of the local centre, and its facilities, in the way of library and reading-room, were thrown open to the students. In organizing the work the local committee arranged for two popular illustrated lectures on Napoleon, by Mr. Charles H. Adams, and announced that at the close of these there would be an address explaining University Extension. A large audience was secured, and, as a result, an enthusiastic centre which has increased in usefulness and strength. It should be added that at this centre a large part of the work has devolved on the very energetic local secretary. The school-teachers living in that vicinity took a very active interest in the work. A strong

Students' Association was formed, which has ever been anxious to secure a sequence of courses. In one instance, their number pledged the necessary funds to do this.

The first local centre to be formed was at Roxborough, a suburb of Philadelphia, in connection with St. Timothy's Institute and Workingmen's Club. Through the influence of several members of the Institute, a large representation was secured at an informal meeting, from the workingmen of the Pencoyd Iron-Works and other shops in that vicinity. The secretary explained the work about to be undertaken, and, before the meeting adjourned, a committee was appointed to look into the plans. They arranged for two lectures on Napoleon, by Mr. Charles H. Adams, at which a large audience was secured and an opportunity given to explain the objects of the new movement. A local committee was selected, with the foreman of the Pencoyd Iron Works as chairman. The difficulties attendant upon the work at this place are great. This section of the city is composed almost entirely of the working classes, and, while there are a number who could aid them, they do not seem so disposed. It being a mill district, strikes and fires have several times interfered with the progress of courses.

At Holmesburg, one of the older portions of Philadelphia, a local centre was organized in connection with those interested in the Holme Library. In previous years there had been a lyceum committee, which was abandoned. The local committee took hold of the work with great vigor, thoroughly canvassing the town and securing a large number of subscribers within forty-eight hours.

Lansdowne is located but a few miles from the city; it has a total population of but eight hundred people. For several years they had had an entertainment committee, which was reorganized for the new purpose. As a preliminary step, the two lectures on Napoleon, by Mr. Charles H. Adams, were given. The work was explained and a centre organized. The centre has been remarkably successful and the attendance most encouraging, the average being over a hundred.

At Norristown, the secretary met with the preliminary committee a number of times before they finally decided to take hold of the work. They held that the people did not take an interest in the work and that Norristown had no place for it. It was, however, decided to make an effort to see what could be done, and a public meeting was called in the Court-House, and Provost Pepper, of the University of Pennsylvania, announced as the speaker of the evening. The result was that a large audience was secured and an organization effected. It can be added that this is one of our most successful centres.

For a number of years in Camden there has existed a Fortnightly Club, the officers of which came to the Society to secure lecturers. They wanted them, however, for their own meetings, and did not at first care to organize a local centre. The Society took the ground that as nearly all the influential people of Camden were connected with the Fortnightly Club, and as it seemed unlikely that a local centre would be formed without their aid, that University Extension should not be made so exclusive an affair. The Fortnightly Club then agreed to organize a local committee and open the courses to the general public. The work has gone on with increasing success from the outset.

In the early days of the organization of a centre, there is a tendency to over-confidence, and it is not until the real struggle for the continuation of the work commences that the local committees will make an effort to acquaint themselves with the general history of the movement. The centres which have been most successful are the ones that have emphasized the work of the students. University Extension must be more than a substitute for the Lyceum, and this can only be accomplished through the students whose interests should be properly cared for.

In connection with every course, immediately after or before the lecture, a class is held at which the students and the lecturer meet for an informal discussion of the subject. Also in connection with each course there has been published a syllabus, giving among other things an abstract of the course, suggested works for collateral reading, and questions upon which is based the weekly-paper work, which is mailed to the lecturer and returned at the following class. In the publication of these syllabi we have made it a constant aim that they shall be more than an abstract of the course,—a guide to the study of that portion of the subject. This fact will be more clearly recognized when it is understood that the average size of the syllabi thus far published is sixteen pages.

After giving two courses at Association Local Centre and Wagner Institute in Philadelphia, Mr. Moulton said in his report that the quality of the work done by the students had decidedly improved in the second courses at each of these places, adding: "The audiences are magnificent; they have had the effect of making the whole course a demonstration in favor of University Extension." In speaking of his course on "Astronomy," also given at Association Local Centre, Professor Charles A. Young, of Princeton, compared the work received from one of the students as equal to that of his best seniors. It was a gratifying surprise to Professor George S. Fullerton, of the University of Pennsylvania, to find that his somewhat difficult subject, "Psychology," should be so readily popularized. In his report on the course he says, "I never had more attentive audiences, nor I believe more intelligent on the whole."

Last year forty-three courses were given, with an average attendance of 9160, whose aggregate attendances numbered 60,573. (See table of results at close of report.) There were nineteen courses on literature, eight on history, one on descriptive astronomy, four on chemistry, one on psychology, one on biology, two on botany, two on electricity, one on mathematics with applications to mechanics, one on algebra, and one on zoölogy. The most of these were six lectures in length; the average for the forty-three courses being 7.6. The average attendance at the courses was two hundred and fifty. The number of those taking the examination, while not very large, was encouraging; two hundred and thirty-one passed successfully. Four of these were in geology, eleven in mathematics, twenty in algebra, one hundred and eight in literature, seven in physics, fourteen in history, fifty-one in botany, and eleven in psychology.

Twenty-four of the students received two certificates, nine three, four four, one five, and one six. Sixty-three per cent. of those attending the lectures remained to the class exercises; five and one-half per cent. of the class wrote weekly papers; seventy-two per cent. of those writing weekly papers took the examination, and ninety-three per cent. of these passed successfully.

The work thus far developed in this country differs very materially from that in England in these respects,—the audiences are larger and seem to possess, as described by an English lecturer, more intellectual curiosity; the proportion of the audience which remains for the class is also larger. This, indeed, has very clearly shown that the English methods must be materially modified. It may be necessary to develop what might be called a second class for the real student nucleus, or, possibly, as an alternate way out of the difficulty, we must look forward to well-organized Students' Associations, presided over perhaps by assistant lecturers.

In reaching those towns more or less isolated from our general offices, we have employed the plan of circuits with encouraging success. To form these, from four to six towns within easy reach by railroad unite and decide upon a common lecturer and subject, selecting successive nights in the week. The lecturer then repairs to that section and remains there during the progress of the course.

Thus far this season, dating from October 1, there have been delivered in all fifty-one courses: twelve on American history, four on English history, four on American literature, seventeen on English literature, nine on political economy, two on electricity, one on geology, one on mathematics, one on psychology, and two on physics.

It will be observed that in the last three months there have been given more courses than were delivered during the whole of last year. The number of centres has been more than doubled. This year's work is characterized by the organization of Students' Associations at most of the centres; some are already strong enough to pledge the necessary expense to the local committee in order to secure a sequence of courses. The audiences show a wide variety of occupation. The afternoon courses are, however, attended mostly by ladies, while at the evening courses can be found workingmen in small groups, teachers, lawyers, and university graduates.

The class in mathematics, to which a course of twelve lectures was delivered, is perhaps the most striking and unique illustration of the development of the work in this country. Last November a year, an artisan from one of the shops in this city called at the office of the Society to ascertain if a course in Mathematics, with its application to mechanics, would be delivered. He volunteered to organize the class, providing the Society would secure the lecturer. Every shop in the city and suburbs was visited, and the names of some forty of his fellow-workers who were willing to pledge themselves to payment of a fee of five dollars for the privilege of attending such a course, were secured. The Society then undertook it, and when the night of the first lecture arrived was surprised to find one hundred and sixty in attendance. The result was that the fee was immediately reduced to three dollars, and the course was successfully organized. The usual attendance was seventy-two. The average number of those writing weekly papers was twenty-three, or thirty per cent. of the audience; fourteen, or twenty per cent., presented themselves for examination; and eleven, or sixteen per cent., passed successfully.

For those who may be interested in this course, the syllabus of Lecture XI. is appended.

LECTURE XI.

MOMENTS.

The *moments* of a force with respect to a point is the product of the force into the perpendicular distance of the line of action of the force from the point. This distance is called the *arm* of the force. That is, the moment of a force is the measure of the tendency of the force to cause the body upon which it acts to revolve about the point with respect to which the moment is taken. The moment of a force as here defined is sometimes called, more specifically, the *statical moment*.

If two forces tend to cause a body upon which they act to revolve in opposite directions about the point with respect to which moments are taken, the moments of the forces are distinguished by the signs $+$ and $-$.

The moment of the resultant of a system of forces acting in one plane upon a body is equal to the algebraic sum of the moments of the individual forces composing the system.

If a body which can turn only in one plane about one point is acted upon by a system of forces, the algebraic sum of the moments of which, about that point, is zero, then the system will be in equilibrium, so far as revolution about that point is concerned. Should the algebraic sum of the moments of the forces not vanish, motion will ensue. If it is required then to establish equilibrium a new force must be applied, whose moment added (algebraically) to the sum of the others produces zero.

The above is a generalization of the well-known principle of the lever.

[See Todhunter's *Mechanics for Beginners*, Chaps. V., VI., XI., and XIII.]

PARALLEL FORCES.

If in a system of parallel forces all the forces act in the same direction, the resultant of the system acts in the same direction and is equal to the sum of the forces. If some of the forces act in one direction and some in the other, the resultant is equal to the difference between the sum of those acting in one way and the sum of those acting in the other, and it acts in the direction of the greater of these two sums. To find the point of application of the resultant we take moments about any point in the plane of the forces. Thus,— let $P_1, P_2, P_3 \ldots$ be a system of parallel forces, and $a_1, a_2, a_3 \ldots$ the perpendicular distances of their lines of action from any point in their plane. Let R be the resultant and x its arm. Then, first:

$$R = (P_1 + P_2 + P_3 \ldots .)$$
And: $Rx = (P_1 a_1 + P_2 a_2 + P_3 a_3 + \ldots)$
from which x and R can be computed. Great care must be taken to give each of the forces and each of the moments in these equations its proper sign. The $+$ sign used in them indicates the *algebraic* sum.

The point of application of the resultant of a system of parallel forces is called the centre of the system.

If two equal forces are parallel, and act in opposite directions, they have no resultant, and their tendency in acting upon a body is simply to produce revolution in their own plane. Such a system is called a *couple*. The moment of a couple is the same about every point in its plane, and is equal to the product of one of the forces into the perpendicular between them.

[See Todhunter's *Mechanics for Beginners*, Chaps. IV. and VIII.]

CENTRE OF GRAVITY.

The centre of gravity is defined thus (Todhunter's *Mechanics for Beginners*, p. 72): " The *centre of gravity* of a body or system of bodies is a point on which the body or system of bodies will balance in all positions, supposing the point to be supported, the body or system to be acted on only by gravity, and the parts of the body or system to be rigidly connected with the point."

To determine the position of the centre of gravity of a system of heavy particles, we regard the weights of the several particles as parallel forces and then determine the line of action of the resultant of the forces. We do this with the particles in two different positions with respect to the horizon. The intersection of the lines of action of the resultants will be the centre of gravity.

By the centre of gravity of a plane area is meant the centre of gravity of a thin uniform sheet of some substance in the shape of the area.

The centre of gravity of a uniform rod is its middle point.

The centre of gravity of a triangle is the intersection of the medial lines.

The centre of gravity of any plane figure symmetrical about a point is the centre of symmetry of the figure.

[See Todhunter's *Mechanics for Beginners*, Chap. X.]

It gives me pleasure to report that this course has been repeated this year with results even more surprising than last. Immediately after the holidays a supplementary course will be given by Professor H. W. Spangler, of the University of Pennsylvania, on "The Strength of Materials."

It is unfortunate that so many are inclined to look upon this as a class movement, and endeavor, after a fashion of their own, to reach workingmen in large numbers. Our experience is that they can best be reached through one of their own number. If they are patronized, and if courses are organized for them and for them alone, with these they have little or no sympathy. Indeed, a number of them in this city very frankly told us that if we should deal with them as workingmen, they would have nothing to do with the movement; but that if we were prepared to deal with them as citizens, then they would be glad to come in and take part in the work.

To show the range of courses given in this first year of Extension teaching the following list is appended.

American Literature.
Euripides for English Audiences.
Four Studies in Shakespeare.
General Survey of English Literature.
Milton's Poetic Art.

The Report of the American Society. 233

Modern Essayists.
Shakespeare Tempest with Companion Studies.
Stories as a Mode of Thinking.
Story of Faust.

Algebra.
Animal Life considered as a part of Universal Energy.
Applied Electricity.
Botany.
Chemistry.
Descriptive Astronomy.
Geology and Paleontology.
Mathematics with applications to Mechanics.
Practical Analytical Botany.
Psychology.
Zoölogy.

American History and Government.
Civil Development of the United States.
Constitution of the United States.
Epochs in American History.
Political History of Europe during the present Century.

The following are outlines of typical courses :
Six lectures by Edward T. Devine, A.M., Fellow in the Wharton School of the University of Pennsylvania, on *Political Economy*.

 I.—Development of Industry and Rise of Economic Science.
  Primitive Man.
  The Middle Ages.
  Modern Industrial Society.

 II.—The Framework of Economics.
  Production.
  Value.
  Exchange of Commodities.
  International Exchange.
  Consumption.

III.—**The Distribution of Wealth.**
  Sources of Income.
  The Law of Rent.
  The Law of Profits.
  The Law of Interest.
  The Law of Wages.

IV.—**Unsolved Economic Problems.**
  The Unearned Increment.
  The Interest Question.
  International Trade.
  Bimetallism.

V.—**Immediate Industrial Problems.**
  The Labor Question.
  The Eight-Hour Day.
  Monopolies.

VI.—**The Economic Element in Social Questions.**
  The Temperance Agitation.
  The Food Problem.
  Charity Organization.
  The Immigration Question.
  Standing Armies.
  Reciprocity.

Six lectures by Henry W. Rolfe, A.M., on *English Literature of the Nineteenth Century*.

I.—**Charles Lamb.**
  Childhood.
  Youth and Heroism.
  Literary Activity.
  Last years.

II.—**Wordsworth.**
  Introductory.
  Wordsworth's Outward Life.
  Wordsworth's Poetry and its Value.

III.—Scott.
> Ancestry and Childhood.
> Youth and Early Manhood.
> The Poems.
> From Ashestiel to Abbotsford.
> The Novels.
> Adversity and Death.
> Criticism.

IV.—Carlyle.
> Early life.
> The Period of Storm and Stress.
> Entire Devotion to Literature.
> The Closing Years.
> Carlyle's Importance as a Man of Letters.

V.—Thackeray.
> Childhood and Education.
> Seeking a Career.
> Literature as Profession.
> Thackeray's Characteristics as a Writer and as a Man.

VI.—Matthew Arnold.
> His Life.
> His Prose Writings.
> His Poetry.
> Conclusion.

Eight lectures by Professor E. P. Cheyney, of the University of Pennsylvania, on *Modern Industrial History—The Culmination and the Decline of Individualism.*

I.—The Industrial System of the Middle Ages.
> The Manor.
> The Guild :
> > (1) The Guild Merchant.
> > (2) The Craft Guilds.

II.—Breaking up of the Mediæval System.
> The Fall of the Manor System.
> The Fall of the Guild System.
> Industrial Society in the Eighteenth Century.

III.—**The Industrial Revolution of the Eighteenth Century.**
    The New Inventions.
    The New Factories.
    Effect on the Old System.
    Changes in Land-holding.

IV.—**Theoretical Views and the New Industrial Society.**
    Ricardo's Law of Rent.
    Malthus's Law of Population.
    The Wages-Fund Theory.
    The Laissez-faire doctrine.

V.—**Factory Laws.**
    First Factory Act, 1802.
    Second Factory Act, 1819.
    Factory Act of 1833.
    Opposition to these Acts:
      (1) By the Manufacturers.
      (2) By the Political Economists.

VI.—**Trades-Unions.**
    New Position of the Factory Laborer.
    Opposition to Trades-Unions.
    The Growth and Development of Trades-Unions.

VII.—**Co-operation and Profit-Sharing.**
    Tendency of New Industrial Organization to Separate Functions.
    Co-operation.
    Profit-Sharing.

VIII.—**Socialism.**
    Definition of Socialism.
    History of Socialism.

Twelve lectures by Professor C. M. Andrews, of Bryn Mawr College, on *Political History of Europe* (1815 *to the present*).

I.—**From the Fall of Napoleon to the Ushering in of the Era of Reaction.**
    To the Imprisonment at Elba.
    Beginnings of Restoration and the Congress of Vienna.
    The Hundred Days, March 1, 1815, to June 18, 1815.
    The Holy Alliance and the Policy of the Metternich.

II.—France and the Revolution of 1830.
    Restoration and Bourbon Unpopularity.
    Government of Ultras and Priests.
    Revolution of 1830 and an Elective Monarchy.
    Influence of Revolution.

III.—Italy and the Agitation for Unity.
    Italy to 1815.
    From Congress of Vienna to the Rise of Young Italy.
    Work of Mazzini and Young Italy.
    Agitation until 1848–49.

IV.—Germany and a Half-Century of Political Confusion.
    Before the Congress of Vienna.
    Congress of Vienna to Carlsbad Decrees.
    Result of the Carlsbad Decrees.
    Frederick William IV. (1840–61) to Revolution of 1848.

V.—Louis Philippe and the Revolution of 1848.
    The July Monarchy to 1840.
    Ministry of Guizot to Revolution of 1848.
    The Revolution and the Republic.

VI.—Revolution of 1848–49 throughout Europe.
    Wonderful March Days of '48.
    Turning of the Tide.
    Hungary's Death-Struggle.
    General Results.

VII.—The Crimean War and European Political Theories.
    Condition of Europe after 1848–49.
    Progress of the Eternal Eastern Question to 1850.
    Pretexts for War and the Theory of the Balance of Power.
    The War in Crimea and its Results.

VIII.—Cavour and Victor Emmanuel. A United Italy. Growth of Piedmont.
    Austro-Sardinian War.
    An Incomplete Unity.
    The Italian Kingdom.

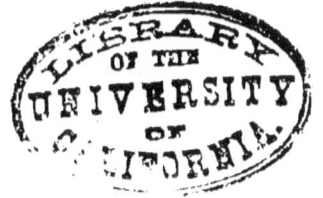

IX.—The Rise and Fall of Imperialism in France.
Louis Napoleon and the Republic. The Coup d'État.
Emperor Napoleon III.
Downfall of Napoleonism.
The Franco-Prussian War.—The Commune and a Republic.

X.—Austria and Prussia—The Struggle for the Hegemony.
Prussia's Last Submission.
A New Regime and a New Attitude.
The Policy of Blood and Iron.
Expulsion of Austria.

XI.—Austria and Prussia—Reconstruction.
Results of the Seven Weeks' War.
The Dual Monarchy.
The German Empire.

XII.—Russia and the Eastern Question.
From the Crimean War to 1875.
Turkish Excesses leading to War of 1877-78.
War of 1877-78 and the Growth of Nationalities.
Recent Difficulties.—The Bulgarian Question.

Questions for weekly exercises from syllabus on *Modern Industrial History. The Culmination and Decline of Individualism*, by Professor E. P. Cheyney.

LECTURE I.
1.—Describe a mediæval manor in England.
2.—Describe a mediæval craft guild in England.
3.—Give the arguments for and against the theory that the villein inhabitants of the manor had formerly been freemen.

LECTURE II.
1.—How did the influence of the Tudor period act in breaking up the earlier industrial organization?
2.—Describe the " domestic" or cottage system of the spinning and weaving industry of England in the nineteenth century.
3.—What was the reason for the great demand for food and manufactured goods in England in the eighteenth century?

LECTURE III.
1.—What is meant by the "industrial revolution" of the eighteenth century?
2.—Name some of the points of difference between the factory system and the industrial organization that preceded it.

LECTURE IV.
1.—What is meant by the Laissez-faire theory of the functions of government, and how is the theory supported?
2.—Compare the good and bad characteristics respectively of the new industrial society.

LECTURE V.
1.—What were the successive steps in English Factory Legislation?
2.—What arguments have been used in favor of, and what opposed to, factory laws?
3.—What do you think is likely to be the future course of factory legislation?

LECTURE VI.
1.—What were the circumstances that led to the formation of Trades-Unions?
2.—Describe the opposition of the English laws to trades-unions and its removal.
3.—What do you think are the good and what are the bad effects flowing from the existence of trades-unions?

LECTURE VII.
1.—Describe and distinguish the three forms of co-operation.
2.—Find and report a full list of one or other of the forms of co-operation in the vicinity of Philadelphia, with the results of each experiment.
3.—What are the probabilities of the future spread of profit-sharing?

LECTURE VIII.
1.—Give a definition of socialism that will not exclude any system claimed to be socialistic, or include any principles not essential.
2.—What is the relation between socialism, communism, and anarchism?
3.—Compare the special ideals of the early part of this century with those most generally prevalent now.

The following papers set for final examinations will assist in showing the grade of the work:

By Professor Paul Shorey, of Bryn Mawr College, upon the course of six lectures entitled *Studies in English Poetry*.

1. Define and illustrate some distinguishing characteristics of Modern English Poetry.
2. State briefly Wordsworth's "Gospel of Nature." Is the doctrine pantheistic? Compare with Shelley. What is the "pathetic fallacy"?
3. In what two ways does Tennyson interpret a Greek myth?
4. Explain the allegory of the Vision of Sin. Is Tennyson a Mystic? In what sense?
5. Comment on the following lines:

> 'O Sylvan Wye! thou wanderer thro' the woods
>   of all the mighty world
> Of Eye and Ear both what they half create
>   and what perceive."

> "Smote the chord of self that trembling passed
>   in music out of sight."

> "Slowly comes a hungry people as a lion
>   creeping nigher
> Glares at one that nods and winks behind
>   a slowly dying fire."

> "Celtic Demos rose a Demon, shrieked and
>   slaked the light with blood."

> "Hesper whom the poet called the bringer—
>   home of all good things—"

> "Have we risen from out the beast? then back
>   into the beast again!"

> "'Passion of the Past' Fancy's Fool.'

> "Tho' some have *gleams*, or so they say,
>   Of more than mortal things."

By Mr. Edward T. Devine upon a course of six lectures on *Political Economy*.

1. What is the most striking difference between primitive and advanced industry?
2. How do you classify the factors of production? What is the special advantage of your classification?
3. What would be the effect on rent of increasing the yield from all poorer lands by the introduction of improved methods of agriculture?
4. Explain what is meant by surplus value.

5. Explain why the cheapening of food, clothing, and other commodities does not always raise the standard of life.
6. What has been the chief gain to the United States of foreign immigration?

By Mr. Henry W. Rolfe upon a course of six lectures on *English Literature of the Nineteenth Century.*

1. Write a careful analysis and criticism of your favorite essay of Lamb.
2. Does Wordsworth's poetry benefit you? If so, how? If not, why?
3. What do you consider the chief value of Scott's poetry?
4. Write a brief but careful criticism of one of Carlyle's books, which you have read.
5. Write an analysis of one of Thackeray's characters.
6. What do you consider the chief excellence and the chief defects of Arnold's poetry?
7. Which one of these writers was the most truly fortunate in his early life, and why?
8. Which one of the six do you most care for?
9. Compare and contrast, briefly, any two of these authors as regards both their life and their work.
10. Which one of them was the most perfect literary artist? Give reasons for your answer.

The following is a list of the centres thus far organized, together with the courses that have been given, and the names of the students passing the examinations:

IN PHILADELPHIA.

ASSOCIATION LOCAL CENTRE.

COURSE I.—Descriptive Astronomy, by Professor Chas. A. Young, of Princeton.

Margaret P. Saunders.

COURSE II.—Shakespeare's Tempest with Companion Studies, by Mr. Richard G. Moulton, of Cambridge University, England.

Clara W. Anable,
Sara C. Dewey,
George Edward Eby,
Ella Faser,
Josephine Hamill,
Mrs. F. H. Taylor.
Augustus J. Loos,
Lucy P. MacIntire,
S. Newlin,
A. H. Saunders,
Margaret P. Saunders,

COURSE III.—Mathematics, with its Applications to Mechanics, by Professor E. S. Crawley, of the University of Pennsylvania.

E. C. Baugher,	Margaret P. Saunders,
S. S. Dewey,	Charles H. Thumbert,
Bessie H. DuBois,	R. H. Trimble,
Mary D. Griffith,	Esther N. Venables.
Jumatsu Matsuo,	E. N. Wigfall,

Helen A. Wilder.

COURSE IV.—Animal Life Considered as a Part of Universal Energy, by Professor Spencer Trotter, of Swarthmore.

Jessie S. Bagg,	Aldrich J. Pennock,
B. P. Flint,	Margaret P. Saunders,

M. D. Woodnutt.

COURSE V.—Milton's Poetic Art, by Mr. Richard G. Moulton, of Cambridge University, England.

Laura J. Ashmore,	Francis W. Kennedy, Jr.,
Sarah C. Dewey,	A. J. Loos,
S. S. Dewey,	Mrs. L. L. Reger,
F. B. Green,	Margaret P. Saunders,

H. M. Smyth.

COURSE VI.—Mathematics, by Professor E. S. Crawley, of the University of Pennsylvania.

H. Gretmar,	William H. Schallioll,
Jumatsu Matsuo,	Charles H. Thumlert,
Robert McLaughlin,	G. P. Tustin,
F. Piers,	E. M. Venables,

Peter Wright.

COURSE VII.—Economics, by Professor F. H. Giddings, of Bryn Mawr.

No examination.

COURSE VIII.—English Literature, by Professor R. E. Thompson, of the University of Pennsylvania.

Lucy C. Conard,	M. M. McCollin,
Lucy P. MacIntire,	E. L. G. Thomas,
F. H. MacIntire,	Mary P. Tunnelle,

K. Fuller Walker.

COURSE IX.—Socialism, by Mr. M. E. Sadler, of Oxford, England.

No examination.

The Report of the American Society.

COURSE X.—The Change in Political Economy, by Mr. M. E. Sadler, of Oxford, England.
No examination.

FRANKFORD CENTRE.

COURSE I.—English Literature, by Professor R. E. Thompson, of the University of Pennsylvania.
E. Augustine Salter.

COURSE II.—American History by Professor F. N. Thorpe, of the University of Pennsylvania.
No examination.

COURSE I.—Political History of Europe, by Professor C. M. Andrews, of Bryn Mawr.

Mary Ekwurzel,	Susanna S. Kite,
Elizabeth Hale,	Mary Rollins Murphy,
Hannah M. Jones,	Benjamin C. Tillinghast,

Eleanor E. Wright.

GERMANTOWN CENTRE.

COURSE I.—Shakespeare's Tempest, with Companion Studies, by Mr. Richard G. Moulton, of Cambridge University, England.

Alice M. Barrett,	Anna Powers,
Adele Marie Beck,	Louisa Randolph,
Jennie T Borton,	Louise Harriett Reger,
Elizabeth W Collins,	Julia Morris Ross,
Margaret Cope,	Laura E. Sampson,
Celia Creeth	Louise Schwartz,
Anna Shinn Doriss,	Annie P. Simmons,
Bessie Ecker Freichler,	Anna W. Smith,
Marion W. Grewcock,	Lydia Starr,
Harriett Harvey	Esther Newlin Stokes,
Fannie C. Hopkins,	Katherine W. Stokes,
Gertrude Houston,	Mary T. Thurler,
Edith F. Kenderdine,	Grace Turner,
Florence P. Middleton,	Isabel S. Vanderslice,
Edith R. Mullen,	Eleanor R. Wagner,
Elizabeth R. Perry,	Sarah Wood Wagner,
Marjorie Plumer,	Annie T. Walker,

Margaret B. Williams.

COURSE II.—Electricity, by Professor Henry Crew, of Haverford College.

Lloyd Balderston, Jr.,   Charles Ingalls Martin,
Louis R. Shellenburger.

244 *The National Conference on University Extension.*

COURSE III.—Modern Industrial History, by Professor E. P. Cheyney, of the University of Pennsylvania.
Lloyd Balderston, Jr., Charles F. Jenkins.
Edward I. H. Howell, G. R. Nichols.

COURSE IV.—Robert Browning, by Mr. Henry S. Pancoast.
Jennie T. Borton, L. L. Reger.

COURSE V.—Socialism, by Mr. Michael E. Sadler, of Oxford, England.
No examination.

NEW CENTURY CLUB GUILD CENTRE.

COURSE I.—English Literature, by Professor R. E. Thompson, of the University of Pennsylvania.
E. G. Banes, Mary J. Thompson,
Adele Sutor, Frances L. Wise,
Florence Yaple.

ROXBOROUGH CENTRE.

COURSE I.—Chemistry, by Professor C. Hanford Henderson, of the Manual Training School
Augustus R. Andrews William B. Hughes,
Tillie J. Barnes Jumatsu Matsuo
Alexander J. Christie, Frank E. Richardson,
Bessie Christie T Elizabeth Slagle,
John Collins Albert Walton,
Alfred Walton.

COURSE II.—Four Studies in Shakespeare, by Mr. R. G. Moulton, of Cambridge University, England.
No examination.

COURSE III.—The People of the United States, by Professor John Bach McMaster, of the University of Pennsylvania.
Results not in.

SOUTH BROAD STREET CENTRE.

COURSE I.—American History, by Professor F. N. Thorpe, of the University of Pennsylvania.
No examination.

SPRING GARDEN CENTRE.

COURSE I.—Stories as a Mode of Thinking, by Mr. R. G. Moulton, of Cambridge University, England.
Miss E. Fraser, Bessie W. McElroy,
Ida C. Levin, Jennie C. McElroy,
L. L. Reger.

The Report of the American Society. 245

COURSE II.—Algebra, by Professor George E. Fisher, of the University of Pennsylvania.

Addison B. Burk,
Addison B. Burk, Jr.,
M. Ethel Burk,
Zeta B. Cundy,
E. J. Donnelly,
Emma A. Holland,
P. J. Lauber,
Jacob Munz,
G. E. Nelson,
J. E. Nethery,
D. O'Brien,
S. J. Owen,
E. Rimmer,
Charles Rowe,
L. K. Siggous,
M. H. Siggous,
Helena A Smith,
Katie Smith,
Horace K. Subers,
Charles H. Thumbert.

COURSE III.—Modern Essayists, by Professor F. E. Schelling, of the University of Pennsylvania.

No examination.

COURSE IV.—Practical Analytical Botany, by Professor J. T. Rothrock, of the University of Pennsylvania.

Harriet W. Adams,
J. S. Bagg,
M. R. Beale,
M. Ethel Burk,
R. A. Child,
D. S. Chrystal,
E. Francis Condit,
Louise Eissler,
Mary Eissler,
Marrianne Ferguson,
Charles F. Guhlmann,
Susan T. Hoopes,
A. E. Hostelly,
Elizabeth James,
Sybil James,
J. A. Jenkins,
Bessie D. Jones,
Julia F. Jones,
Emma L. Karse,
John A. LaFore,
Eliza L. McClure,
James T McClure,
E. McDuffee,
J. B. Murphy,
J. C. H. Newcomer,
Franklin E. Page,
Annie E. Paret,
L. L. Reger,
Maude Remington,
Mary B. Reinhardt,
C. F. Saunders,
M. P. Saunders,
John Smethurst,
Mary E. Smethurst,
S. Smith,
Hannah Streeter,
S. Lillie Twyeross,
William C. Warren,

S. E. Williams.

UNITED CLUB AND INSTITUTE CENTRE.

COURSE I.—American History, by Professor F. N. Thorpe, of the University of Pennsylvania.

No examination.

COURSE II.—American History, by Professor F. N. Thorpe, of the University of Pennsylvania.

No examination.

WAGNER INSTITUTE CENTRE.

COURSE I.—Euripides for English Audiences, by Mr. R. G. Moulton, of Cambridge University, England.

Lida Stokes Adams, Virginia E. Graeff,
C. Belle T. Clay, Helen L. Murphy,
Ella Faser, Susanna M. Price,
Beulah A. Fennimore, Clara G. Rowley,
Mary G. Umsted.

COURSE II.—Four Studies in Shakespeare, by Mr. R. G. Moulton, of Cambridge University, England.

Fanny Binswanger, Helen L. Murphy,
C. Belle T. Clay, Frank H. MacIntire,
Beulah A. Fenimore, Lucy P. MacIntire,
George H. Karder, Clara G. Rowley,
Robert C. Macauley, A. H. Saunders.

COURSE III.—Psychology, by Professor George S. Fullerton, of the University of Pennsylvania.

William H. Arnold, Catherine R. Hansell,
Jessie T. Bagg, Harriet Liebman,
Kate C. Butler, Anna L. Longacre,
Sarah Palmer Byrnes, Mary MacDuffee,
Ella Faser, Paul de Moll,
Anna W. Williams.

COURSE IV.—English Literature, by Professor R. E. Thompson, of the University of Pennsylvania.

Martina de Pierra.

COURSE V.—Poets of America, by Professor Willis Boughton.

Lucy C. Conard, M. V. Haigh,
E. L. G. Thomas.

COURSE VI.—Civil Development of the United States, by Professor F. N. Thorpe, of the University of Pennsylvania.

Lucy C. Conard, Zeta B. Cundy,
E. L. G. Thomas.

Geology and Paleontology, by Professor E. D. Cope, of the University of Pennsylvania.

John G. Johnson, William C. Menough,
E. M. Kenedy, Charles R. Toothaker.

Chemistry, by Professor Henry Leffmann.

No examination.

Zoology, by Professor John A. Ryder, of the University of Pennsylvania.

No examination.

Botany, by Professor J. T. Rothrock, of the University of Pennsylvania.

No examination.

WEST PHILADELPHIA CENTRE.

COURSE I.—American History, by Professor F. N. Thorpe, of the University of Pennsylvania.

No examination.

COURSE II.—Stories as a Mode of Thinking, by Mr. R. G. Moulton, of Cambridge University, England.

Ella C. Alloway, Edith L. Stern,
George E. Eby, Mary C. N. Thomas,
Jennie B. Loos, Mary A. Williamson.

COURSE III.—Psychology, by Professor George S. Fullerton, of the University of Pennsylvania.

Mary A. Albertson, Annie L. English,
Ella C. Alloway, Sue E. Stoever.

COURSE IV.—Change in Political Economy, by Mr. M. E. Sadler, of Oxford, England.

No examination.

COURSE V.—Central Europe in the Nineteenth Century, by Professor E. P. Cheyney, of the University of Pennsylvania.

Results not in.

WISSAHICKON HEIGHTS CENTRE.

COURSE I.—Stories as a Mode of Thinking, by Mr. R. G. Moulton, of Cambridge University, England.

Margaret Cope, Minnie E. Faught,
Jennie T. Borton, Gertrude Houston.

248   *The National Conference on University Extension.*

COURSE II.—Political History of Europe, by Professor C. M. Andrews, of Bryn Mawr.

· Lloyd Balderston, Jr.,   Hannah M. Jones, Susanna S. Kite. ·

COURSE III.—Studies in English Poetry, by Professor Paul Shorey, of Bryn Mawr.

Jennie T. Borton.

COURSE IV.—Chemistry, by Dr. Henry Leffmann.

No examination.

WOMEN'S CHRISTIAN ASSOCIATION CENTRE.

COURSE I.—Botany, by Professor J. T. Rothrock, of the University of Pennsylvania.

David T. Crystal.

COURSE II.—American History and Government, by Professor F. N. Thorpe, of the University of Pennsylvania.

Blanche Baldwin,   Jessie S. Bagg, Antha Knowlton.

COURSE III.—Brook Farm Community, by Mr. Willis Boughton.

Results not in.

OUTSIDE OF PHILADELPHIA.

BRIDGEPORT (CONN.) CENTRE.

COURSE I.—Economics, by Mr. Edward T. Devine, Staff-Lecturer of The American Society.

Results not in.

BRIDGETON (N. J.) CENTRE.

COURSE I.—Economics, by Mr. Edward T. Devine, Staff-Lecturer of The American Society.

Results not in.

BRISTOL (PA.) CENTRE.

COURSE I.—Epochs of American History, by Professor F. N. Thorpe, of the University of Pennsylvania.

Louisa A. Iredell.

COURSE II.—Administration of Government, by Professor F. N. Thorpe, of the University of Pennsylvania.

Results not in.

BRYN MAWR (PA.) CENTRE.

COURSE I.—Typical English Poets, by Mr. Henry S. Pancoast.

No examination.

COURSE II.—Earlier Plays of Shakespeare, by Professor J. O. Murray, of Princeton.

Results not in.

BURLINGTON (N. J.) CENTRE.

COURSE I.—Modern Novelists, by Professor F. E. Schelling, of the University of Pennsylvania.

Margaret M. Gummere,   Margaret Marrs,
Elizabeth D. Howell,   Anna G. Redmond.

COURSE II.—Epochs of the American History, by Professor F. N. Thorpe, of the University of Pennsylvania.

Results not in.

CAMDEN (N. J.) CENTRE.

COURSE I.—Story of Faust by Mr. R. G. Moulton, of Cambridge University England.

Marietta K. Champion,   Henrietta J. Meteer,
George Edward Eby,   Élizabeth C. Reeve,
Anna Farrell,   Esther Schooley,
Norman Grey,   Anna Taylor,
Mary Walsh.

COURSE II.—American History and Government, by Professor F. N. Thorpe, of the University of Pennsylvania.

G. Buckwalter,   Jessie Fulweiler,
Mary A. Burrough,   Loretta Irland,
Lidie Corbon,   Margaret T. Magie,
Anna Farrell,   Emma Thegan,
Clara R. Titus.

COURSE III.—Change in Political Economy, by Mr. M. E. Sadler, of Oxford, England.

No examination.

COURSE IV.—English Literature, by Professor R. E. Thompson, of the University of Pennsylvania.

Results not in.

CARBONDALE (PA.) CENTRE.

COURSE I.—English Poets of the Revolution Age, by Dr. W. Clarke Robinson, Staff-Lecturer of The American Society.

No examination.

CHAMBERSBURG (PA.) CENTRE.

COURSE I.—English Literature of the Nineteenth Century, by Professor Henry W. Rolfe, of the University of Pennsylvania.

Results not in.

CHESTER (PA.) CENTRE.

COURSE I.—American Literature, by Professor A. H. Smyth, of the Central High School.

T. M. Gilbert,	Louise Stern,
S. DuBois Moury,	William H. Stewart,
Charles Palmer,	Aida Pearl Urie,
Walter L. Philips,	Royal W. Urie.

CHESTER SPRINGS (PA.) CENTRE.

COURSE I.—Economics by Mr. E. T. Devine, Staff-Lecturer of The American Society.

No examination.

COATESVILLE (PA.) CENTRE.

COURSE I.—English Literature of the Nineteenth Century, by Mr. H. W. Rolfe of the University of Pennsylvania.

Results not in.

COLUMBIA (PA.) CENTRE.

COURSE I.—English Poets of the Revolution Age, by Dr. W. Clarke Robinson, Staff-Lecturer of The American Society.

Results not in.

CONSHOHOCKEN (PA.) CENTRE.

COURSE I.—American History and Government, by Professor F. N. Thorpe of the University of Pennsylvania.

No examination.

DOYLESTOWN (PA.) CENTRE.

COURSE I.—Representative American Authors, by Mr. J. H. Penniman.

Anna S. Atkinson,
Mary W. Atkinson,
Hannah A. H. Beans,
Elizabeth C. Cox,
Cynthia Doane,
Julia Van Horn,
Miriam Watson,
George Wheeler.

DOWNINGTOWN (PA.) CENTRE.

COURSE I.—American Literature, by Professor A. H. Smyth, of the Central High School.

George Bailey, Jr., Martha G. Thomas,
Isabella F. Worrell.

COURSE II.—English Literature, by Professor A. H. Smyth, of the Central High School.

Mary Ingram, Anna Worrall Kerr,
Martha G. Thomas.

GETTYSBURG (PA.) CENTRE.

COURSE I.—English Poets of the Revolution Age, by Dr. W. Clarke Robinson, Staff-Lecturer of The American Society.

Results not in.

GREEN RIDGE (PA.) CENTRE.

COURSE I.—English Poets of the Revolution Age, by Dr. W. Clarke Robinson, Staff-Lecturer of The American Society.

No examination.

HADDONFIELD (N. J.) CENTRE.

COURSE I.—Central Europe in the Nineteenth Century, by Professor E. P. Cheyney, of the University of Pennsylvania.

Sallie T. Black,
Murray C. Boyer,
Mary A. Crawley,
Minnie A. Moore,
G. Fithian Tatem,
Mary P. Tunnelle,
William Wilcox.

252 *The National Conference on University Extension.*

COURSE II.—Typical English Poets, by Mr. Henry S. Pancoast.

    Mary A. Crawley,   Carrie Stiles,
           Mary P. Tunnelle.

COURSE III.—Civil Development of the United States, by Professor F. N. Thorpe, of the University of Pennsylvania.

    Results not in.

HARRISBURG (PA.) CENTRE.

COURSE I.—English Poets of the Revolution Age, by Dr. W. Clarke Robinson, Staff-Lecturer of The American Society.

    Results not in.

HOLMESBURG (PA.) CENTRE.

COURSE I.—American History, by Professor F. N. Thorpe, of the University of Pennsylvania.

    No examination.

COURSE II.—American Literature, by Professor A. H. Smyth, of the Central High School.

    No examination.

HONESDALE (PA.) CENTRE.

COURSE I.—English Poets of the Revolution Age, by Dr. W. Clarke Robinson, Staff-Lecturer of The American Society.

    No examination.

JENKINTOWN (PA.) CENTRE.

COURSE I.—English Literature, by Professor R. E. Thompson, of the University of Pennsylvania.

    Results not in.

KINGSTON (PA.) CENTRE.

COURSE I.—Political Economy, by Mr. Edward T. Devine, Staff-Lecturer of The American Society.

    Results not in.

The Report of the American Society. 253

LANCASTER (PA.) CENTRE.

COURSE I.—Economics, by Mr. Edward T. Devine, Staff-Lecturer of the American Society.

Emma S. Brimmer,
Mary Byrne,
William S. Gleim,
Elizabeth H. Hager,
Ida R. McMillan,
Emma Powers,
Adaline B. Spindler,
Belle M. Weitzel,
Mary E. Zahn.

COURSE II.—English Poets of the Revolution Age, by Dr. W. Clarke Robinson, Staff-Lecturer of The American Society.

Results not in.

LANGHORNE (PA.) CENTRE.

COURSE I.—Representative American Authors, by Mr. J. H. Penniman.

Results not in.

LANSDOWNE (PA.) CENTRE.

COURSE I.—Electricity, by Professor Henry Crew, of Haverford College.

Morgan Bunting,
Carrie B. Conard,
Thomas P. Conard.
E. W. Davis,

COURSE II.—English Literature, by Professor R. E. Thompson, of the University of Pennsylvania.

No examination.

LEBANON (PA.) CENTRE.

COURSE I.—English Poets of the Revolution Age, by Dr. W. Clarke Robinson, Staff-Lecturer of The American Society.

Results not in.

MEDIA (PA.) CENTRE.

COURSE I.—Modern Essayists, by Professor F. E. Schelling, of the University of Pennsylvania.

No examination.

COURSE II.—Epochs of American History, by Professor F. N. Thorpe, of the University of Pennsylvania.

Results not in.

MOORESTOWN (N. J.) CENTRE.

COURSE I.—Epochs of American History, by Professor F. N. Thorpe, of the University of Pennsylvania.

John C. Beans,
Mary S. Beans,
Irene H. Benyaurd,
Leone E. Benyaurd,
Nathan N. Conrow,
Sarah H. W. Conrow,
Annie Dougherty,
Emily E. Herr,
Frank S. Herr,
Ellwood Hollingshead,
Martha H. Hollingshead,
Elizabeth A. Moore,
Jennie H. Morris,
Lydia H. Morris,
Helen F. Wilson,
Mary R. Wilson.

COURSE II.—Poets of America, by Mr. Willis Boughton.

Results not in.

MOUNT HOLLY (N. J.) CENTRE.

COURSE I.—American History, by Professor F. N. Thorpe, of the University of Pennsylvania.

No examination.

COURSE II.—English Novelists, by Professor F. E. Schelling, of the University of Pennsylvania.

No examination.

COURSE III.—Central Europe in the Nineteenth Century, by Professor E. P. Cheyney, of the University of Pennsylvania.

Ida R. Buzby,   J. Barclay Hilyard,
Charles Evan Merritt.

NEWARK (DEL.) CENTRE.

COURSE I.—Stories as a Mode of Thinking, by Mr. R. G. Moulton, of Cambridge University, England.

Emma V. Blandy,   Margaret W. Blandy,
G. Le Roy Brown.

COURSE II.—English Novelists, by Professor F. E. Schelling, of the University of Pennsylvania.

No examination.

NEWTOWN (PA.) CENTRE.

COURSE I.—Epochs in American History, by Professor F. N. Thorpe, of the University of Pennsylvania.

Fredda H. Bryan,   Hannah E. Holcomb,
Ellie J. Burroughs,   Laura L. Rose,
A. S. Williamson.

The Report of the American Society. 255

NORRISTOWN (PA.) CENTRE.

COURSE I.—English Literature, by Professor R. E. Thompson, of the University of Pennsylvania.

No examination.

COURSE II.—Stories as a Mode of Thinking, by Mr. R. G. Moulton, of Cambridge University, England.

Jacob Lynchenheim,   Frederick I. Naile.

COURSE III.—Political Economy, by Professor R. E. Thompson, of the University of Pennsylvania.

A. D. Eisenhower,   Lidie R. Jones,
Esther B. Eisenhower,   Emma J. Kuder,
Clandia B. Gurie,   Frederick I. Naile,
Mattie J. Zimmerman.

COURSE IV.—Civil Development of the United States, by Professor F. N. Thorpe, of the University of Pennsylvania.

Harriet E. Hallman.

NORTH WALES (PA.) CENTRE.

COURSE I.—Europe finds America, by Professor F. N. Thorpe, of the University of Pennsylvania.

Lizzie A. Brooke,   Carrie A. Lukens,
Mary Davlin,   Esther Newlin.

PHŒNIXVILLE (PA.) CENTRE

COURSE I.—English Literature of the Nineteenth Century, by Mr. H. W. Rolfe, of the University of Pennsylvania.

Results not in.

PLYMOUTH (PA.) CENTRE.

COURSE I.—Political Economy, by Mr. Edward T. Devine, Staff-Lecturer of The American Society.

Results not in.

READING (PA.) CENTRE.

COURSE I.—Political Economy, by Mr. Edward T. Devine, Staff-Lecturer of The American Society.

William T. Arnold,   May Miller,
George Auchy,   Bessie H. McLenegan,
Henry T. Conard,   William H. Price,
Minta Fulton,   Charles S. Prizer,
Mary S. Thomas.

COURSE II.—English Literature of the Nineteenth Century, by Mr. H. W. Rolfe, of the University of Pennsylvania.

Results not in.

SCRANTON (PA.) CENTRE.

COURSE I.—English Poets of the Revolution Age, by Dr. W. Clarke Robinson, Staff-Lecturer of The American Society.

No examination.

TRENTON (N. J.) CENTRE.

COURSE I.—English Literature, by Professor R. E. Thompson, of the University of Pennsylvania.

Ella D. Hankinson,   Annie L. Hughes,
Elizabeth Hughes.

COURSE II.—The Earlier Plays of Shakespeare, by Professor J. O. Murray, of Princeton.

No examination.

COURSE III.—Geology, by Professor W. B. Scott, of Princeton.

William R. Wright.

COURSE IV.—Political Economy, by Professor R. E. Thompson, of the University of Pennsylvania.

Results not in.

VINELAND (N. J.) CENTRE.

COURSE I.—Electricity, by Professor A. W. Goodspeed, of the University of Pennsylvania.

No examination.

WAYNE (PA.) CENTRE.

COURSE I.—English Literature in the Nineteenth Century, by Professor H. W. Rolfe, of the University of Pennsylvania.

J. Charles Aiken,   Caroline T. Martin,
Elizabeth C. Crumley,   Mary L. Roberts,
Mary T. Dunn,   Etta M. Stauffer,
Leila Wetherill.

COURSE II.—A Bird's-Eye View of European History, by Ida M. Gardner.

Results not in.

The Report of the American Society. 257

WEST CHESTER (PA.) CENTRE.

COURSE I.—History of Europe, 1815-49, by Professor Charles M. Andrews, of Bryn Mawr.

Sue Henderson, William T. Sharpless,
Catherine S. Monaghan, Mary Butler Windle.

COURSE II.—American Literature, by Professor A. H. Smyth, of the Central High School of Philadelphia.
No examination.

COURSE III.—The People of the United States, by Professor John Bach McMaster, of the University of Pennsylvania.
No examination.

WILKES-BARRE (PA.) CENTRE.

COURSE I.—Political Economy, by Mr. Edward T. Devine, Staff-Lecturer of The American Society.
Results not in.

WILMINGTON (DEL.) CENTRE.

COURSE I.—English Literature, by Mr. R. G. Moulton, of Cambridge University, England.
No examination.

COURSE II.—Electricity, by Professor A. W. Goodspeed, of the University of Pennsylvania.
No examination.

COURSE III.—France During the Struggle for Freedom of Conscience, by Rev. William H. Johnson.

Gertrude C. Pyle, Isabel B. Wales,
Mary R. D. Withers.

WINCHESTER (VA.) CENTRE.

COURSE I.—English Literature in the Nineteenth Century, by Mr. H. W. Rolfe, of the University of Pennsylvania.
Results not in

YORK (PA.) CENTRE.

COURSE I.—English Poets of the Revolution Age, by Dr. W. Clarke Robinson.
Results not in.

17

TABLE OF RESULTS, NOVEMBER, 1890, TO JUNE, 1891.

CENTRE.	PLACE.	HOUR.	LECTURER.	SUBJECT.	Number of Course at the Given Centre.	Number of Lectures in the Course.	Fee.	Average Number at Lecture.	Average Number at Class.	Average Number of Weekly Papers.	Passed Examination.	Rejected.
Association Local (Philadelphia).†	Y. M. C. A. Building.	8.00	C. A. Young, Ph.D. (Princeton).	Descriptive Astronomy.	1	6	$1.00	135	130	1	1	0
Association Local (Philadelphia).†	Y. M. C. A. Building.	8.00	R. G. Moulton, A.M. (Cambridge, Eng.).	Shakespeare's Tempest, with Companion Studies.	2	6	1.00	959	700	42	9	3
					3	12	3.00	70	45	23	11	1
Association Local (Philadelphia).†	Y. M. C. A. Building.	8.00	Edwin S. Crawley, B.S. (Univ. of Penna.).	Mathematics.	4	6	1.00	165	45	6	5	0
Association Local (Philadelphia).†	Y. M. C. A. Building.	8.00	Spencer Trotter, M.D. (Swarthmore).	Animal Life Considered as a Part of Universal Energy.	5	6	1.00	1000	750	51	9	0
Association Local (Philadelphia).†	Y. M. C. A. Building.	4.30	R. G. Moulton, A.M. (Cambridge, Eng.).	Milton's Poetic Art.		6	1.00	200	200			
Frankford (Philadelphia).†	Wright's Institute.	8.00	R. E. Thompson, D.D. (Univ. of Penna.).	English Literature.	1	7	1.00	200	150			
Frankford (Philadelphia).†	Wright's Institute.	8.00	F. N. Thorpe, Ph.D. (Univ. of Penna.).	American History.	2	6	1.00	192	150			
Germantown (Philadelphia).†	Workingmen's Club.	4.00	R. G. Moulton, A.M. (Cambridge, Eng.).	Shakespeare's Tempest, with Companion Studies.	1	6	1.00	600	350	46	35	1
					2	8	1.00	150	75	6	3	2
Germantown (Philadelphia).†	Workingmen's Club.	8.00	Henry Crew, Ph.D. (Haverford College.)	Electricity.	1	6	1.50	150	30	1		
Holmesburg (Philadelphia).†	Holme Library.	8.00	F. N. Thorpe, Ph.D. (Univ. of Penna.).	American History.	1	6	1.50	150	30			
Holmesburg (Philadelphia).†	Holme Library.	8.00	A. H. Smyth, A.M. (Central High School).	American Literature.	2	6	1.50	40	20	5	11	0
Roxborough (Philadelphia).†	St. Timothy's Hall.	8.00	C. Hanford Henderson, A.M. (Manual Training School).	Chemistry.	1	6	.50	83	60			
Roxborough (Philadelphia).†	St. Timothy's Hall.	8.00	R. G. Moulton, A.M. (Cambridge, Eng.).	Four Studies in Shakespeare.	2	4	1.00	250	150	13	5	0
Spring Garden (Philadelphia).†	Spring Garden Institute.	8.00	R. G. Moulton, A.M. (Cambridge, Eng.).	Stories as a Mode of Thinking.	1	6	1.00	150	125	20	20	3
Spring Garden (Philadelphia).†	Spring Garden Institute.	8.00	Geo. H. Fisher, A.B. (Univ. of Penna.).	Algebra.	2	12	1.00	40	20	1		
Spring Garden (Philadelphia).†	Spring Garden Institute.	8.00	F. E. Schelling, A.M. (Univ. of Penna.).	Modern Essayists.	3	6	1.00	20	20			
Spring Garden (Philadelphia).†	Spring Garden Institute.	8.00	J. T. Rothrock, M.D. (Univ. of Penna.).	Practical Analytical Botany.		6	1.00	130	130	1	5	0
South Broad Street (Philadelphia).†	Southern Branch, Y. M. C. A.	8.00	F. N. Thorpe, Ph.D. (Univ. of Penna.).	American History.	4	6	1.50	100	100	2	20	3
					1	6					39	0

The Report of the American Society.

Location	Place	Time	Instructor	Subject							
United Club and Institute (Philadelphia).†	United Club and Institute Hall.	8.00	F. N. Thorpe, Ph.D. (Univ. of Penna.).	American History.	1						1
Wagner Institute (Philadelphia).†	Seventeenth and Montgomery Avenue.	8.00	R. G. Moulton, A.M. (Cambridge, Eng.).	Euripides for English Audiences.	1	6	1.00	775	125	2	9	1
Wagner Institute (Philadelphia).†	Seventeenth and Montgomery Avenue.	8.00	R. G. Moulton, A.M. (Cambridge, Eng.).	Four Studies in Shakespeare.	2	6	.75	300	200	11	10	0
Wagner Institute (Philadelphia).†	Seventeenth and Montgomery Avenue.	8.00	G. S. Fullerton, A.M. (Univ. of Penna.).	Psychology.	3	6	1.00	205	200	17	11	0
Wagner Institute (Philadelphia).†	Seventeenth and Montgomery Avenue.	8.00	E. D. Cope, Ph.D. (Univ. of Penna.).	Geology and Paleontology.	*	20	*	76	103	*		
Wagner Institute (Philadelphia).†	Seventeenth and Montgomery Avenue.	8.00	Henry Leffmann, M.D.	Chemistry.	*	20	*	154	40	*	5	0
Wagner Institute (Philadelphia).†	Seventeenth and Montgomery Avenue.	8.00	Jno. A. Ryder, Ph.D. (Univ. of Penna.).	Zoology.	*	10	*	65		*	4	0
Wagner Institute (Philadelphia).†	Seventeenth and Montgomery Avenue.	8.00	J. T. Rothrock, M.D. (Univ. of Penna.).	Botany.	*	10	*	105		*		
West Philadelphia (Philadelphia).	College Hall, University of Pennsylvania.	8.00	F. N. Thorpe, Ph.D. (Univ. of Penna.).	American History.	1	6	1.00	225	225	3	6	0
West Philadelphia (Philadelphia).†	College Hall, University of Pennsylvania.	4.30	R. G. Moulton, A.M. (Cambridge, Eng.).	Stories as a Mode of Thinking.	2	6	1.00	550	125	14	6	2
Wissahickon Heights (Philadelphia).†	St. Martin's in the Fields.	3.15	R. G. Moulton, A.M. (Cambridge, Eng.).	Stories as a Mode of Thinking.	1	6	.75	150	100	7	4	0
Wissahickon Heights (Philadelphia).†	St. Martin's in the Fields.	8.05	C. M. Andrews, Ph.D. (Bryn Mawr).	Political History of Europe.	2	6	.75	50	30	4	3	0
Women's Christian Association (Philadelphia).†	Women's Christian Association Hall.	8.00	J. T. Rothrock, M.D. (Univ. of Penna.).	Botany.	1	6	1.00	100	100	3	1	1
Camden (New Jersey).†	St. Paul's Church.	8.00	R. G. Moulton, A.M. (Cambridge, Eng.).	Story of Faust.	1	6	1.00	250	225	16	9	2
Downingtown (Pennsylvania).	Central Hall.	8.00	A. H. Smyth, A.M. (Central High School).	American Literature.	1	6	1.00	200	75	8	3	0
Haddonfield (New Jersey).†	Athenaeum Hall.	8.00	E. P. Cheyney, A.M. (Univ. of Penna.).	Central Europe in the Nineteenth Century.	1	6	1.00	225	200	10	7	0
Lansdowne (Pennsylvania).†	Public Hall.	8.00	Henry Chew, Ph.D. (Haverford).	Electricity.	1	8	.75	100	75	4	4	1
Media (Pennsylvania).	Delaware County Institute of Science.	8.00	F. E. Schelling, A.M. (Univ. of Penna.).	Modern Essayists.	1	6	1.25	140	140	3	3	
Mt. Holly (New Jersey).	Court-House.	8.00	F. N. Thorpe, Ph.D. (Univ. of Penna.).	American History.	1	6	1.00	175	50			
Newark (Delaware).†	Delaware State College.	4.00	R. G. Moulton, A.M. (Cambridge, Eng.).	Stories as a Mode of Thinking.	1	6	1.00	250	150	3	3	0
Norristown (Pennsylvania).	Public High School.	3.15	R. E. Thompson, D.D. (Univ. of Penna.).	English Literature.	1	7	1.50	159	140			
Norristown (Pennsylvania).†	Public High School.	8.00	R. G. Moulton, A.M. (Cambridge, Eng.).	Stories as a Mode of Thinking.	2	6	1.00	225	120	3	2	0
Trenton (New Jersey).	Women's Christian Temperance Union Hall.	8.00	R. E. Thompson, D.D. (Univ. of Penna.).	English Literature.	1	7	1.00	350	125	5	5	1
West Chester (Pennsylvania).†	Public Library.	8.00	Chas. M. Andrews, Ph.D. (Bryn Mawr).	History of Europe, 1815–1849.	1	6	1.00	166	115	3	3	1
Wilmington (Delaware).	High School Building.	4.30	R. G. Moulton, A.M. (Cambridge, Eng.).	English Literature.	1	4	.75	286	230	5	5	1

* These were given by The Wagner Free Institute of Science.   † Examination held.   ‡ Practical exercises instead of weekly papers.

NAMES AND ADDRESSES OF LOCAL SECRETARIES.

Association Local.—MR. HORACE G. THOMAS, Fifteenth and Chestnut Streets.
Bridgeport, Conn.—MISS M. F. SOMERSET, 206 Lafayette Street, Bridgeport.
Bridgeton, N. J.—MR. PHŒBUS W. LYON, Bridgeton.
Bristol, Pa.—MR. WILLIAM V. LEECH, Bristol.
Bryn Mawr.—MRS. EDNA WITHERSPOON, Haverford College, Pa.
Burlington, N. J.—MRS. J. B. HOWELL, Burlington.
Camden, N. J.—MISS ELIZABETH C. REEVE, 301 State Street, Camden.
Carbondale, Pa.—MR. H. F. SWARTZ, Carbondale.
Chambersburg, Pa.—REV. HERBERT ALLEMAN, Chambersburg.
Chester, Pa.—PROF. THOMAS S. COLE, Chester.
Chester Springs, Pa.—MISS ANNIE J. DAVIS, Chester Springs.
Coatesville, Pa.—MR. LEWIS B. HENSON, Coatesville.
Columbia, Pa.—MISS MARY WELSH, 532 Chestnut Street, Columbia.
Conshohocken, Pa.—WM. A. COOPER, Conshohocken.
Doylestown, Pa.—MR. HUGH B. EASTBURN, Doylestown.
Downingtown, Pa.—DR. EDWARD KERR, East Lancaster Avenue, Downingtown.
Frankford, Pa.—MR. GEORGE W. WRIGHT, 237 South Fourth Street, Philadelphia.
Germantown, Pa.—MRS. LOUISA RANDOLPH, 132 Price Street, Germantown.
Gettysburg, Pa.—MR. C. F. SANDERS, Gettysburg.
Green Ridge, Pa.—MR. H. B. REYNOLDS, Green Ridge.
Haddonfield, N. J.—MISS MARY TUNNELLE, Haddonfield.
Harrisburg, Pa.—MISS VIRGINIA HOAGLAND, Harrisburg.
Holmesburg, Pa.—MR. W. W. BROWN, Holmesburg.
Honesdale, Pa.—HON. R. BRUCE WILSON, Honesdale.
Jenkintown, Pa.—MISS BELLE VANSANT, Jenkintown.
Kingston, Pa.—MR. S. R. SMITH, Kingston.

Lancaster, Pa.—REV. CHAS. S. FRY, Lancaster.
Langhorne, Pa.—MISS LILLIE ALLEN, Langhorne.
Lansdowne, Pa.—MR. EDWARD V. KANE, Lansdowne.
Lebanon, Pa.—REV. THEODORE E. SCHMAUK, Lebanon.
Media, Pa.—MR. J. T. REYNOLDS, Media.
Moorestown, N. J.—DR. JOSEPH STOKES, Moorestown.
Mount Holly, N. J.—MR. B. F. HEYWOOD SHREVE, Mount Holly.
New Century Club Guild, Philadelphia.—MRS. E. S. TURNER, 2102 Mt. Vernon Street.
Newark, Del.—MR. HARLOW H. CURTIS, Newark.
Newtown, Pa.—MISS LAURA W. WHITE, Newtown.
Norristown, Pa.—MR. WALTER M. SHAW, Penn and Swede Streets, Norristown.
North Wales, Pa.—MRS. W. R. CHILDS, North Wales.
Phœnixville, Pa.—MR. D. F. MOORE, Phœnixville.
Plymouth, Pa.—MR. J. I. CREVELING, Plymouth.
Reading, Pa.—MR. CHARLES S. PRIZER, Reading.
Roxborough, Pa.—MR. A. C. GOELL, Ridge Avenue and Vassar Streets, Philadelphia.
Scranton, Pa.—MR. H. B. COX, Scranton.
South Broad Street, Philadelphia.—MR. S. K. CAMPBELL, 1156 South Broad Street, Philadelphia.
Spring Garden Institute, Philadelphia.—MR. JAMES HAWORTH, 641 Arch Street, Philadelphia.
Trenton, N. J.—MR. J. H. WOOD, 223 N. Warren Street, Trenton.
United Club and Institute, Philadelphia.—MR. J. L. STEWART, 1726 South Fifteenth Street, Philadelphia.
Vineland, N. J.—MR. C. K. LANDIS, Vineland.
Wagner Institute, Philadelphia.—MR. THOMAS L. MONTGOMERY, Seventeenth and Montgomery Avenue.
Wayne, Pa.—MRS. R. ESTRADA, Wayne.
West Chester, Pa.—MR. JAMES MONAGHAN, West Chester.
West Philadelphia.—MISS HENRIETTA LEONARD, 4300 Walnut Street, Philadelphia.
Wilkes-Barre, Pa.—MR. SYDNEY R. MINER, Wilkes-Barre.

Wilmington, Del.—Mr. Enos L. Doan, 511 Washington Street, Wilmington.
Winchester, Va.—Mr. W. Roy Stephenson, Winchester.
Wissahickon Heights, Pa.—Dr. L. Ashley Faught, 1331 Arch Street, Philadelphia.
Women's Christian Association, Philadelphia.—Mrs. William S. Stewart, 1801 Arch Street.
Wyoming, Pa.—Dr. Charles P. Knapp.
York, Pa.—Mr. A. Wanner, York.

COMPARATIVE STATISTICS.

TOTAL NUMBER OF COURSES.			Total Number of Lectures Given.	Average Number of Lectures in Each Course.	Average Attendance at the Lectures.	Average Attendance at each Course.	Total Attendance at the Lectures.	Number of Certificates Awarded.
Cambridge	Of 6 Lectures,	4						
	Of 7 or 8 "	0						
1889–90.	Of 11 or 12 "	115						
		— 119	1404	11.7	11,301	95	132,221	1585
London	Of 6 Lectures,	3						
	Of 7 or 8 "	0						
1889–90.	Of 10 or 12 "	99						
		— 102	1028	10	12,067	118	120,670	1384
Oxford	Of 6 Lectures,	113						
	Of 7 or 8 "	24						
1889–90.	Of 10 or 12 "	11						
		— 148	979	6.6	17,904	121	118,166	927
Victoria	Of 8 Lectures,	8						
1889–90.		— 8	64	8	1,040	130	8,320	31
American Society .	Of 3 Lectures,	6						
	Of 4 "	4						
	Of 6 "	67						
	Of 7 "	3						
	Of 8 "	4						
	Of 10 "	2						
	Of 12 "	4						
1891. Jan. 1–Dec. 31.	Of 20 "	2						
		— 92	597	6.5	15,795	172	134,257	366

SUBSCRIBERS TO THE GUARANTEE FUND OF THE AMERICAN SOCIETY.

BAER, MR. GEORGE F.,
BAIRD, MR. JOHN,
BAIRD, MRS. MATTHEW,
BARRETT, MISS G. A.,
BELL & SONS, SAMUEL,
BLAIR, MRS. ANDREW A.,
BLANCHARD, MISS MARIA,
BODINE, MR. SAMUEL,
BOHLEN, MRS. JOHN,
BORIE, MR. BEAUVEAU,
BROWN, MR. ALEXANDER,
BRUSH, MRS. C. H.,
BRYAN, MISS MARY T.,
BURNHAM, MR. GEORGE, SR.,
BURNHAM, MR. WILLIAM,
BUSHNELL, MR. CHARLES E.,
CLOTHIER, MR. ISAAC H.,
CONVERSE, MR. JOHN H.,
COPE, MRS. ALEXIS G.,
COPE, MRS. FRANCES R.,
COWIE, MISS ISABEL,
DELANO, MR. EUGENE,
DOUGHERTY, MRS. T. H.,
EDELHEIM, MR. CARL,
EVANS, MISS H. B.,
EVANS, MRS. J. W.,
FOULKE, MRS. W. G.,
GARRETT, MISS E. N.,
HACKER, MISS ELIZABETH M.,
HALL, MR. AUGUSTUS R.,
HARRIS, MR. W. T.,
HARRISON, MR. ALFRED C.,
HARRISON, MR. CHARLES C.,
HEAD, MRS. E. L.,
HENSZEY, MR. WILLIAM P.,
HOUSTON, MR. H. H.,
HUTTON, MR. ADDISON,
JOHNSON, MRS. JOSEPH
JOHNSON, MISS,
JENKS, MRS. W. F.,
KOHN, ADLER & CO., MESSRS.
LEVY, MRS. MAX,
LIPPINCOTT, MRS. J. B.,
LIPPINCOTT, MR. J. DUNDAS,
MASON, MR. A. HEYWOOD,
MILES, MR. FREDERICK B.,
MILNE, MR. F. F.,
PARDEE, MR. & MRS. CALVIN,
PARDEE, MISS,
PEABODY, MR. CHARLES,
PEPPER, DR. WILLIAM,
PFAELZER, MR. MAURICE,
RANDOLPH, MRS. LOUISA,
RITCHIE, MR. CRAIG D.,
ROSENGARTEN, MR. JOSEPH G.,
SAMPSON, MISS EDITH F.,
SCHMIDT, MR. HENRY,
SELLERS, MR. WILLIAM,
SHOEMAKER, MRS. BENJAMIN,
SILL, MRS. H. M.,
SMITH, MISS ANNA W.,
SMITH, MR. BENJAMIN R.,
SMITH, MISS E. N.,
SMYTH, MR. LINDLEY,
STOTESBURY, MR. E. T.,
THOMAS, MR. GEORGE C.,
THOMPSON, MRS. J. E.,
TOWNE, MRS. J. H.,
TOWER, MR. C., JR.
VAIL, MISS,
VON UTASSEY, MR. A. W.,
WARNER, MR. REDWOOD F.
WEIDENER, MR. A. J.,
WHARTON, MRS. CHARLES W.,
WHARTON, MRS. JOSEPH,
WHARTON, MR. JOSEPH,
WHARTON, MRS. J. LOVERING,
WHELEN, MR. EDWARD S.,

WHITALL, MRS. J. M.,
WHITNEY, MRS. W. B.,
WILLIAMS, DR. EDWARD H.,
WOOD, REV. DR. CHARLES,
WRIGHT, MISS BESSIE.

COUNCILLORS FOR PHILADELPHIA.

ALBERTSON, MR. HENRY,
BAIRD, MRS. MATTHEW,
BAIRD, MR. JOHN,
BARTLETT, REV. EDWARD T.,
BLAIR, MRS. ANDREW A.,
BURK, MR. ADDISON B.,
BURNHAM, MR. GEORGE, JR.,
BUSHNELL, MR. CHARLES E.,
DOUGLAS, MR. WALTER C.,
GUMMERE, PROFESSOR FRANK B.,
HARRISON, MR. CHARLES C.,
HEAD, MRS. E. L.,
HOFFMAN, MRS. EDWARD F.,
HOUSTON, MISS GERTRUDE,
JAYNE, DR. HORACE,
JENKS, MRS. WILLIAM F.,
KEEN, DR. W. W.,
LAMBDIN, DR. ALFRED C.
LEONARD, MR. JAMES B.,
MACINTOSH, REV. DR. JOHN S.,
MACALISTER, DR. JAMES,
MACVEAGH, MRS. WAYN
MAGILL, DR. EDWARD A.
MARSHALL, DR. CLARA,
MCMURTRIE, MISS MARY D.,
MILES, MR. FREDERICK B.,
MORLEY, PROFESSOR FRANK,
MUMFORD, MRS. MARY E.,
PATTEN, PROFESSOR SIMON N.,
PEPPER, MRS. GEORGE W.,
PEPPER, DR. WILLIAM,
RHOADES, DR. JAMES E.,
ROSENGARTEN, MR. JOSEPH G.,
SAMPSON, MISS EDITH F.,
SAYRE, MR. W. L.,
SELLERS, MR. WILLIAM,
SHARPLESS, DR. ISAAC,
SKIDMORE, MR. SYDNEY T.,
STETSON, MR. JOHN B.,
STEWART, MISS SARAH A.,
STITT, MRS. SETH B.,
STRAWBRIDGE, MR. JUSTUS C.,
STUART, MR. EDWIN S.,
SULZBERGER, MR. MAYER,
THOMAS, DR. CHARLES H.,
THOMAS, MISS M. CAREY,
THOMSON, DR. WILLIAM,
WAGNER, MR. SAMUEL,
WHARTON, MR. JOSEPH,
WHITE, DR. FRANCIS E.,
WILLIAMS, MR. TALCOTT,
WILSON, MR. JOSEPH M.,
WOOD, MISS IDA,
WOOD, REV. DR. CHARLES,

DELEGATES.

BEARDSLEY, PROFESSOR ARTHUR, Swarthmore College, Swarthmore, Pa.
BIGELOW, MR. R. B., Johns Hopkins University, Baltimore, Md.
BIRNES, PROFESSOR WILLIAM P., Franklin and Marshall College, Lancaster, Pa.
BLACK, PRESIDENT WILLIAM H., Missouri Valley College, Marshall, Mo.
BOURNE, PROFESSOR HENRY E., Norwich Free Academy, Hartford, Conn.
BUCKHAM, PRESIDENT M. H., University of Vermont, Burlington, Vt.
BUDD, MR. H. I., Mount Holly Centre, Mount Holly, N. J.
BUEHRLE, SUPERINTENDENT B. K., Lancaster, Pa.
BUTTZ, PRESIDENT H. A., Drew Theological Seminary, Madison, N. Y.
COLEMAN, RT. REV. LEIGHTON, Bishop of Delaware, Wilmington, Del.
CORSE, MR. F. M., University of Vermont, Burlington, Vt.
DAVENPORT, MR. CHARLES B., Harvard University, Cambridge, Mass.
DAY, MR. B. C., Columbia College, New York City, N. Y.
DEGARMO, PRESIDENT CHARLES, Swarthmore College, Swarthmore, Pa.
DEWEY, MR. MELVIL, Secretary of University of the State of New York, Albany, N. Y.
DIMM, PRINCIPAL J. R., Missionary Institute, Selin's Grove, Pa.
DOWLING, PROFESSOR F. N., Bethany College, Bethany, West Va.
DUBBS, PROFESSOR JOSEPH H., Franklin and Marshall College, Lancaster, Pa.
DUNCAN, MR. GEORGE S., Harrisburg Centre, Harrisburg, Pa.
EDGAR, PRESIDENT J., Wilson College, Chambersburg, Pa.
ETTINGER, PROFESSOR GEORGE T., Muhlenberg College, Allentown, Pa.
FELL, PRESIDENT THOMAS, St. John's College, Annapolis, Md.

FERGUSON, PROFESSOR HENRY, Trinity College, Hartford, Conn.
FISHER, PROFESSOR GEORGE P., Yale University, New Haven, Conn.
FOSTER, SUPERINTENDENT CHARLES F., Chester, Pa.
FRY, REV. CHARLES L., President Extension Society, Lancaster, PA.
GILBERT, PROFESSOR GEORGE, President Chester Centre, Chester, Pa.
GREEN, MR. D. I., Johns Hopkins University, Baltimore, Md.
GRINE, MR. R. W., Johns Hopkins University, Baltimore, Md.
HAGER, MISS, Lancaster Centre, Lancaster, Pa.
HALL, PRESIDENT G. STANLEY, Clark University, Worcester, Mass.
HARE, REV. J. M., Phœnixville Centre, Phœnixville, Pa.
HARK, REV. J. MAX, Lancaster Centre, Lancaster, Pa.
HARRIS, HON. WILLIAM T., U. S. Commissioner of Education, Washington, D. C.
HARTER, PROFESSOR GEORGE A., Delaware College, Newark, Del.
HARTRANFT, REV. F. B., Hartford Theological Seminary, Hartford, Conn.
HATCH, SUPERINTENDENT WILLIAM E., New Bedford, Mass.
HINES, PROFESSOR CHARLES F., Dickinson College, Carlisle, Pa.
HOLLANDER, MR. J. H., Johns Hopkins University, Baltimore, Md.
HOOPER, PROFESSOR FRANKLIN W., Brooklyn Institute, Brooklyn, N. Y.
HOOVER, SECRETARY S. R., Lebanon Centre, Lebanon, Pa.
HOVEY, PRINCIPAL E. O., Newark Centre, Newark, N. J.
HOWELL, MR. J. R., Mount Holly Centre, Mount Holly, N. J.
HYATT, COL. CHARLES E., President Penna. Military Academy, Chester, Pa.
JOHANN, PRESIDENT CARL, Eureka College, Eureka, Ill.
JONES, MR. ADDISON, Chairman of West Chester Centre, West Chester, Pa.

KAIGHN, MR. E. P., Secretary Y. M. C. A., Springfield, Mass.
KERR, PRESIDENT D. R., Omaha College, Omaha, Neb.
KERSHNER, PROFESSOR J. E., Franklin and Marshall College, Lancaster, Pa.
KIEFFER, PROFESSOR JOHN B., Franklin and Marshall College, Lancaster, Pa.
KINLEY, MR. DAVID, Johns Hopkins University, Baltimore, Md.
LEASE, MR. E. B., Baltimore, Md.
LIBBEY, JR., PROFESSOR WILLIAM, College of New Jersey, Princeton, N. J.
MARTIN, PROFESSOR S. A., Lincoln University, Lincoln University P. O., Pa.
MCDIARMID, PRESIDENT H., Bethany College, Bethany, West Va.
MCKNIGHT, PRESIDENT H. W., Pennsylvania College, Gettysburg, Pa.
MELOY, PROFESSOR ANDREW E., State Normal, Lock Haven, Pa.
MERRILL, PROFESSOR W. A., Miami University, Oxford, Ohio.
MILLER, MR. EDGAR G., Baltimore, Md.
MILLIGAN, SUPERINTENDENT WILLIAM, Woodbury, N. J.
MITCHELL, PRESIDENT EDWARD C., Leland University, New Orleans, La.
MOORE, REV. W. W., Rector of Franklin and Marshall College, Lancaster, Pa.
MORSE, MR. F. L., Hanover, Ind.
MOTTER, DR. MURRAY GALT, Lancaster Centre, Lancaster, Pa.
MULL, MR. GEORGE F., Lancaster Centre, Lancaster, Pa.
MUNRO, PROFESSOR WILFRED H., Brown University, Providence, R. I.
OGDEN, PROFESSOR HOWARD N., University of West Virginia, Morgantown, West Va.
PAHLMANN, PROFESSOR AUGUST, Lutheran Theological Seminary, Gettysburg, Pa.
PHILPUTT, REV. A. B., New York City, N. Y.
PRATT, PRINCIPAL F. B., Pratt Institute, Brooklyn, N. Y.
PRIZER, MR. CHARLES S., Reading Centre, Reading, Pa.
PURINTON, PRESIDENT D. B., Denison University, Granville, Ohio.

RAINE, SUPERINTENDENT CHARLES D., Mount Holly, N. J.
RAUB, PRESIDENT ALBERT N., Delaware College, Newark, Del.
RAYMOND, PRESIDENT S. P., Wesleyan University, Middletown, Conn.
RICE, PROFESSOR WILLIAM NORTH, Wesleyan University, Middletown, Conn.
RICHARDS, PROFESSOR M. H., Muhlenberg College, Allentown, Pa.
ROGERS, PROFESSOR ROBERT W., Dickinson College, Carlisle, Pa.
SANFORD, PROFESSOR M. L., University of Minnesota, Minneapolis, Minn.
SCHMAUK, REV. T. E., President Extension Society, Lebanon, Pa.
SHERLEY, MR. FRED., University of the State of New York, Albany, N. Y.
SMITH, PRESIDENT W. W., Randolph-Macon College, Ashland, Va.
SPROULL, PROFESSOR W. O., University of Cincinnati, Cincinnati, Ohio.
STAHR, PRESIDENT JOHN S., Franklin and Marshall College, Lancaster, Pa.
STILES, DR. CHARLES W., Washington, D. C.
SUPER, PRESIDENT CHARLES W., Ohio University, Athens, Ohio.
THOMAS, MR. RALPH W., University of the State of New York, Albany, N. Y.
VANMETER, DEAN JOHN B., Women's College, Baltimore, Md.
VENTER, MR. W. A., Secretary Y. M. C. A., Trenton, N. J.
VINCENT, BISHOP JOHN H., Chancellor of the Chautauqua System, Buffalo, N. Y.
WARD, PROFESSOR HENRY BALDWIN, Harvard University, Cambridge, Mass.
WHITCOMB, DR. HENRY B., Norristown Centre, Norristown, Pa.
WOODBURN, PROFESSOR JAMES A., University of Indiana, Bloomington, Ind.
WOOLEY, PROFESSOR L. C., Bethany College, Bethany, West Va.
ZULLIG, PROFESSOR ARNOLD, High School, Watertown, Mass.

APPENDIX A.

UNIVERSITY EXTENSION IN NEW YORK.

BY MELVIL DEWEY,

Secretary of the University of the State of New York.

BEFORE submitting the University Extension plans of the University of the State of New York, I must make sure that you do not misunderstand what that University is. It is not a teaching body, and has neither professors, class-rooms, nor students in the ordinary sense. May 1 is celebrated in New York as University Day because on that day, in 1784, as a result of the labors of a committee, of which Alexander Hamilton was the most prominent member, this unique University had its birth. The idea of federal government, of which Hamilton's mind was full, is deeply stamped on our University. It is really a federation of all incorporated academies, colleges, universities, professional and technical schools, and other institutions of higher education in New York State, though each has its independent trustees and government, just as the forty-four States of the Union are all sovereign and independent, and yet together make up this nation. As the United States government has no territory except the little District of Columbia, so the University of the State of New York has only the forty or fifty rooms occupied by its departments and offices at the State Capitol. The University, however, is governed by its regents, the federated institutions having only an advisory voice in its administration. Many of its functions are those of a State department of higher education, distinct from the department of public instruction in charge of common schools. It began with only a single institution, Columbia College.

The great common-school system of New York is an outgrowth of the University, which urged on the government the need of establishing elementary schools at the cost and under the supervision of the State. The germs of the greatest possibilities were in Hamilton's original idea, but for three-quarters of a century they lay largely dormant. During the civil war two important steps were taken. In 1863 began the series of University Convocations, annual gatherings, in the second week of July, of the representatives of the colleges and academies of the State, which have grown more and more important, till recent sessions have been pronounced by the most competent judges the best of American educational meetings. Two years later, in 1865, began the system of State examinations, which from the smallest beginnings has steadily grown till it now uses half a million question papers annually for examinations conducted simultaneously in three hundred and fifty different centres in the State. At first only the common-school studies,—arithmetic, geography, grammar, reading, writing, and spelling were tested, in order to show what pupils had completed elementary work and could properly be classed as academic students, and therefore as properly belonging to the University. In 1878, twenty academic studies were added, and this number was increased in 1879 to thirty-five, in 1881 to thirty-six, in 1883 to thirty-nine, in 1885 to forty-one, in 1889 to forty-two, in 1890 to fifty-eight. With the present year the University is giving examinations also in law, medicine, literary science, and announces the early opening of examinations in all ordinary college and university subjects.

In 1889 there was a general reorganization of the University, and the forty-four laws which had grown up during the one hundred and five years of its existence were all replaced by a single law greatly enlarging its scope and powers. Our great State library of one hundred and sixty thousand volumes, beside one hundred thousand duplicates, and our great State museum, with the work of the various State scientific officers, paleontologist, geologist, botanist, entomologist, zoologist, etc., are now integral departments of the University. Universities, colleges, academies, libraries and museums, and other institutions of

Appendix A. 271

higher education, are chartered by the University, instead of by the legislature as in all other States, and questions of change in name, or alteration, suspension, or revocation of charters of such institutions come to the regents instead of to the legislature or courts. The functions of the University are therefore manifold, and will be recognized as combining those of various well-known English institutions,—the State Library and the State Museum correspond to the British Museum and the natural history departments at South Kensington; the Examinations department has the functions of London University, the local examinations of Oxford and Cambridge, and of the Science and Art department; while the executive work corresponds to much of that of the general education department. A law of last year authorized a fifth department, so that the departments of the University are now Executive, Examinations, University Extension, State Library, and State Museum. To those interested we are always glad to send without charge publications explaining the peculiar New York system. This brief mention will show its remarkable adaptation for undertaking the work of University Extension.

Extension work can have no permanent success unless it utilizes fully the facilities of existing institutions and is conducted in close relations with them. On the other hand, if each college or university undertook to maintain an administrative department for University Extension purposes, the cost would be prohibitive. Only those who have studied the elaborate machinery necessary to secure the best results can understand how much time and expense are involved in a central organization for such work. With us, the University itself, being a central office in the interest of all the separate institutions, becomes the ideal administrative Extension centre.

Now, a word of warning: University Extension is a great permanent force in education which has come to stay, but it is clearly destined to go through a period of misapprehension and to suffer, probably, more from its friends than from its enemies, till Extension workers and the public shall both come to a clear understanding of what the work is and how it can best be done.

Just at present it is the fashion, and is spreading through the country like the craze of twenty years ago for velocipedes, and later for roller-skates, when even little villages built rinks for the new amusement. Unhappily, all sorts of things, more or less resembling University Extension, are being called by its name. There is a large class of people who seize on any taking phrase or name and try to ride upon it into popular favor. A man with a course of lectures that he could get no opportunity to deliver, brushes off the dust and writes " University Extension" at the head, and immediately it is in demand. They are the old lectures without the alteration of a word. It is simple abuse of the new name, and an effort to ride into popular favor at the very front of the movement. This is the cow-catcher danger.

Then there is the kindling-wood danger. In lighting a hard-coal fire there is a great blaze and roar, and not a little heat as the shavings and kindlings blaze fiercely up. We are now in just this period of University Extension, and it is altogether probable that after a little the blaze and roar and heat will die down, and the casual observer will say, " That is ended," and turn to the next new fad; but as with the fire, if we handle it properly it will mean only that the coal is just kindling. After a little will come the strong heat, and we shall be in an era of real University Extension.

I met a man last week a little ailing. To my query he answered, "I have the grippe," and then added, "I have had exactly the same difficulty for the last forty years, but this year it is the grippe." Just in this random, popular way everything good, bad, and indifferent, connected in any way with reading, studying, lecturing, examinations, etc., is called University Extension.

We must face facts, and shall accomplish more in the end by not attempting too much at the beginning. I am constrained to enter my personal protest when over-zealous friends of the new movement propose to create new and unnecessary institutions, and to ignore the fact that the work can be done better and cheaper by using existing plants. I object to the proposed use of the name "college" in connection with institutions that are desirable in many localities. The word college has in the

American mind a distinct meaning, and will only be belittled by applying it loosely to other things, however good. Call it an institute, seminary, anything you please, except to take the word college or university, which conveys to the ordinary mind a sense of protracted study in residence.

Finally, I wish to lay the greatest possible emphasis on a fact that many seem to forget. The public library is the real cornerstone of University Extension. The mission of the University Extension lecturer is less to instruct than to inspire. He should lead both auditors and students to feel an interest in the subject that will force them to read during the week from the books and articles he has recommended, and to come to the class the next week full of the fruits of this reading. An institution to which the name library will usually be given, may well be built in the form of a Greek cross, of which the four arms shall be used, one for a reference library and reading-room, another for the circulating library, the third for a museum of science, and the fourth for a museum of history and art, while in the second story will be rooms of different sizes for University Extension classes. The library is the real people's university of this age, but it can never do its highest work unless the public can have the inspiration of personal contact with teachers who will guide, and interest, and help them to get most good from the books. What we need is a well-selected library in every town, with rooms for Extension classes, to which there shall come frequently from the universities Extension teachers freighted with inspiration. These libraries in such vital connection with the universities will be like hydrants connected with a great reservoir on the hill-tops. How vastly better in a city is a series of such hydrants, with power enough to throw a stream to the roof of the tallest house, than it would be to have an old-fashioned hand fire-engine standing before every door, with a score of men to work the brakes. Our University Extension centres are educational hydrants connected with the high reservoirs, the universities.

As to the definite plan of work which we have laid out for the State University Extension department, I must remind you that we mean to go slowly, to build carefully, feeling that we are erecting a permanent structure that must have broad and strong foundations. You can build a temporary tabernacle for a camp-meeting in a week or two; but when you build a pile of granite like your great city hall, which centuries hence will be looked on with admiration, you do not hesitate to give years to its construction. Our department includes not only University Extension proper, but all other educational work not covered by our schools, academies, colleges, libraries, and museums. The following statements from our first circular will make clear our plans:

PLAN OF WORK.

Publications, to be had free from the University Extension department, give a brief history of the movement, and detail the methods found most successful in its workings. The present circular aims to outline briefly the work of the new department, for which the last legislature appropriated ten thousand dollars. The State fiscal year begins October 1, but in establishing a new department it was deemed more important to utilize fully the experience of those who had been conducting similar work during the past twenty years than to start at the earliest possible day. As the secretary returned late in October from a second study of the methods and workings of the Extension system in the English universities, the department was not formally organized till November, 1891.

Use of State Appropriation.—There has been serious misapprehension in many quarters as to the method of spending the new appropriation, some supposing that on application the regents would send about the State, without charge, university professors to deliver free courses of lectures. The law distinctly provides that no part of the money shall be so spent, it being the intent of the act that such expenses shall be borne by the localities benefited. The appropriation is for expenses of such administrative and other work as can be done better and cheaper in the central office at the capitol for the whole State than by individual centres. Besides doing such administrative work for its colleges and academies, the State annually distributes one hundred and six thousand dollars to its academies to buy books and apparatus, and to pay teachers' wages. For University Extension, however, it makes no such provision, but only lends necessary books and apparatus to communities needing such assistance in increasing educational facilities. The Extension department has already received some aid from private sources, and invites gifts either for immediate use or for permanent endowments, which will enable it to contribute toward the salaries of competent Extension teachers, for which State money cannot be used.

Rigid economy in the use of this money is necessary, because:

(*a*) The appropriation is so small in comparison with the extent of the work to be undertaken, averaging less than one dollar to each school district in the State.

(*b*) Permanent success of the movement requires that conservative and doubtful legislators shall see that every dollar is needed and has been expended wisely and economically.

Subjects Properly Covered by Extension Courses.—The word "university" misleads many into thinking only of ordinary college studies. The law intentionally omits the limiting words, and says only "opportunities and facilities for education for the people at large, adults as well as youth." It includes, therefore, any subject which can be included under the broadest conception of education, whether it is taught usually in academy, college, university, professional or technical school, or even if it is taught in no other institution.

Location of Office.—The office of the Extension department is in the southwest corner of the fourth floor of the capitol, between the upper rooms of the State library and the examinations department, with both of which its work will be very intimately connected.

The notes below show what the work of the department is, and how much the State furnishes free to localities willing to pay the teacher's fees and expenses.

1. *Information Bureau.*—This answers, either personally or by correspondence, questions of all kinds pertaining to any phase of Extension work, including not only University Extension in its more limited sense, but also courses of reading, home study,

examinations and credentials, self-culture, and all reputable movements at home and abroad for providing larger facilities for higher education outside the schools.

An important part of the work at present is in putting those needing such aids into communication with the best of the many agencies which have sprung up in recent years for helping those who wish to help themselves, notably the great Chautauqua system of guided reading. Instead of duplicating existing facilities, the department prefers to have every institution do all it can do well, and therefore gladly refers inquirers to the place where they can find the needed help already provided.

2. *Extension Library.*—This includes not only books, pamphlets, and serials pertaining to the various phases of Extension work, but also syllabuses, circulars, programmes, blanks, and forms illustrative of methods, and everything else obtainable in print which the most thorough student of the movement would find of interest. This Extension library is to be made as complete as possible, including all languages, and will be an important attraction to those engaged in Extension work to attend the annual Extension conferences at the time of University Convocation. To increase its convenience, it is minutely classified by subjects, so that any student of Extension methods, experiments, and experience can see what the rest of the world has done and is doing on any of the hundreds of phases of the movement. All syllabuses, both American and foreign, are also brought together and minutely classified by subjects treated.

The complete file of publications can always be found in the building for reference; but as most of the Extension library is duplicated, the second copies will be available for lending to Extension workers throughout the State who are unable to come to Albany to consult them. This library is for the promoters and managers of the movement. For students, provision is made in travelling libraries and in loans of books on the special subject under consideration at any given time.

3. *Publications.*—As the Extension movement is comparatively so new, one of the greatest needs is full information in print for the increasing number desirous of knowing its

history, methods, advantages, and limitations. Besides explanatory and descriptive circulars and other documents which are sent post-free to all applicants, there are kept constantly on hand the best periodicals, pamphlets, and books from the whole field of extension literature, to be lent to interested applicants free, or sold at wholesale cost. Books lent are unmarked, so that the reader has the option of returning them post-paid, or of retaining them and sending the wholesale price. Each book lent has next the front cover a slip lightly pasted at one end, reading, "This book is charged at Albany to a responsible borrower. It must be returned post-paid within two weeks, or this slip, the number on which identifies the charge, may be torn out and returned with............cents to pay its wholesale cost. The charge will then be cancelled and the book recorded as paid for." Borrowers not known to the office as responsible deposit the value of books taken, which is refunded on their return.

The cost of securing needed publications is thus greatly reduced, and the department can promptly furnish the best publications on every phase of the subject in a single package, when otherwise those interested might be compelled to write to a dozen different sources, and, as some of the matter must be imported, to wait several weeks for its arrival, besides suffering the annoyance of custom-house routine. The small price affixed to certain publications guards against the waste inevitable if they are given free to all applicants, and also guards against the criticism that State money is used to print or buy books to be given away. Local committees and others desiring to distribute documents in aid of Extension work will be supplied at mere cost of paper and press-work, *i.e.*, one cent for each sixteen pages like this circular.

A list of the best publications is supplied free, and notes under each title indicate its character, so that inquirers may select what they need and order it by simply giving the number prefixed in the check list.

4. *Organizing*.—To any locality wishing to establish Extension courses, the department undertakes to give expert assistance in selecting subjects, teachers, and dates, arranging terms, and per-

fecting any needed organization for doing the work in the way experience has shown to be best. This may be done by correspondence, though it can usually be better done if the organizer visits the centre in person, so that he can study local conditions, become acquainted with those in the community interested in such work, and personally assist in the preliminary organization. The organizers are provided with all needed blanks and forms for this work. The department hopes to be able to send to any place in the State a suitable person to give a public address to stimulate general interest, or meet a smaller number chosen as a local committee, or render any assistance in the power of a competent specialist. No charge is made for such service, beyond actual travelling expenses. In case of the illness of a lecturer during the course, the department will try to provide the most satisfactory substitute available.

Expenses for which provision must be made by the centre are the teacher's fee, travelling expenses, and local expenses, such as hall, heat, light, and advertising. The department will supply any of these lecturers with thousand-mile tickets, as any parts of tickets left over can be used in other places, and the centre be charged only for the amount used in its service. The fee for the course should be provided for in advance, and, if intrusted to the department, one-half should be sent before the course begins and the remainder before the sixth lecture. College professors, as a rule, prefer to have terms arranged and to receive their compensation from the Extension department, rather than conduct negotiations and collect fees in person. As the supply of competent teachers is far less than the demand, it is folly to waste any of their time and strength on business details. That there may be no misunderstanding, blank forms filled with an explicit statement of exact terms in writing are supplied both to teachers and local secretaries. Obviously it will be pleasanter and better for all parties to have financial arrangements made through the department. All this work is done by the office without charge or commission, and it will often be able so to arrange courses in circuits or on succeeding nights as to reduce materially the travelling expenses or time taken, and therefore the amount of fees to be paid. (See also "Expenses," in *How to begin University Extension.*)

5. *Supervising.*—As in organizing, the department will on request endeavor to send an expert to inspect the workings of centres and give such practical suggestions as may enable them to accomplish better work with the time and money at their disposal. It constantly happens, specially in the early years, that centres accomplish only half the work possible, or sometimes are wholly abandoned, when one thoroughly familiar with Extension methods could readily have pointed out mistakes and introduced new elements which would have insured high success.

Though Extension teaching is a new and peculiar form of education, its methods have already been worked out with great care. Centres, however, are springing up in many places with very imperfect notions of what these methods are, and as a result are giving courses of lectures with more or less work resembling University Extension proper, but by no means entitled to the name. Perhaps no work of the department will be more important for the first years than this advisory supervision for enabling local centres to utilize fully the experiments and experiences of the remarkable work carried on for the past twenty years by the English universities.

6. *Supplies.*—Specially ruled and printed books and forms for recording attendance at lectures, classes, and clubs, for marks of papers and examinations, and other needed records, are furnished free. The department furnishes syllabuses for less than centres can print them, as it divides their cost among the various centres using the same syllabus. For protection of the syllabuses, it further provides, if requested, manilla pockets containing also note-books of uniform size, costing at wholesale only five dollars per hundred, so that centres can furnish a manilla pocket, holding ticket, syllabus, and note-book, to each person buying a ticket. For centres preferring, the syllabus will be printed with blank pages for notes, but the separate note-book, uniform in size, is preferable, and, if supplied with the ticket, many more students will take notes and profit more from the course.

Tickets for the course can be had at twenty-five cents per hundred, and blanks (described in circular 11, page 5) for securing members and students, at ten cents per hundred.

Every centre is of course free to get its supplies where it chooses. The department aims simply to save time and money by getting at wholesale supplies needed by many centres, and distributing them without profit among centres asking such service.

7. *Extension Teachers.*—Two lists are kept of all available lecturers, and class or correspondence teachers, with notes of education, academic degrees, experience in teaching, subjects, length of each course, months and days when service is available, price, and any other items that would help in making a selection. One of these lists is arranged alphabetically, the other is classified by subjects. These lists of teachers may be consulted by all interested.

Later there will doubtless be a distinct University Extension faculty, representing the most successful teachers available for the work. This, however, cannot take permanent form until after a year or two's experience, for some of the most eminent university professors may be less successful in this new and peculiar form of teaching, while experience has proved that some of the very best work will be done by young men whose reputation is not yet made.

While the best work is always done by lecturers who also conduct classes and correct weekly papers, there may be some desirable teachers who will give only inspirational lectures, leaving pupils to get their instruction chiefly from the books recommended; others may be more successful in class-work than in lecturing, while still others may accomplish most by correspondence, giving needed guidance to their pupils by mail. The most desirable and efficient teachers, of course, combine all these methods.

The State pays no part of the teacher's fees or travelling expenses; but it furnishes teachers in regents' centres with needed blanks, circulars for distribution, etc., and lends books, apparatus, or illustrative material if needed. While the unusual number of competent professors and specialists in our own State, and economy in time and travelling expenses to be gained by using teachers as near home as possible, will insure that the great majority of teachers will be New Yorkers, the department makes no limitation, but aims to recommend to each community the best teacher available for its purpose, regardless of his residence. Near the borders of another State it will often be wiser to combine with towns over the line, and perhaps to use their teachers.

8. *Examinations.*—Examinations are one of the most essential features of the plan, because of their great influence in holding Extension students up to continuous and systematic work, and of their necessity as a test in determining the quality of teaching and the success of the study done.

A successful Extension teacher must be able to do two things: to hold the interest of his audience; to give them such instruction that at the end of the course they will have a fund of valuable knowledge on the subject. Interest is readily tested by attendance, for people come regularly only when the teacher interests them. The second and more important part, the knowledge gained, is tested by means of examinations conducted quite independently of the teacher.

When a course is completed, the University will give an examination prepared by skilful and experienced examiners, and covering only the ground specified in the syllabus, so that nothing shall be asked which should not readily be answered by any person who has attended the lectures and done the class and paper work satisfactorily. Extension students thus have a test which experience has proved much more valuable than it would be if the teacher who had given the instruction also gave the examination. The department prepares and prints the papers, sends an examiner who conducts the test by the most approved methods, revises and grades all the answers, and awards to those who attain the prescribed standards suitable credentials under the seal of the University. Any local or other prizes offered for excellence in the course will also be awarded. The favorite form of prize has been a collection of books on the subject of the course up to the amount of the prize. Each of these books has inside its cover an official book-plate showing that it was awarded by the University to the most successful student in a specified course and centre. Many are stimulated to do the class and paper work and take the examination by the possible honor of winning one of these prizes, and some one in almost every centre can be found to give enough to buy one, two, or three prizes, for the wholesale cost of suitable books is small. The result of the examinations becomes a part of the permanent State records in the capitol, and the names of those who receive credentials are printed in the next report of the regents to the legislature. Those who pass with honors have the fact recorded on their credentials. Usually students' weekly papers are marked on a scale of 10, the ten papers of the course thus aggregating a possible 100. The examination at the end is marked on a scale of 100, and combined with the results of the paper-work in determining a student's proficiency. This has been found a fairer test than to depend wholly on the results of a single examination.

The Extension teacher will give permits to enter this examination only to such students as have satisfactorily done the paper-work of the course. Others will be admitted only after written application at least ten days before the examination, showing to the satisfaction of the chief examiner that they have pursued such studies as would entitle them to the official test provided by the State. The whole plan has been worked out with exceeding care, and is pronounced by experts to be the fairest and most completely-organized system of examinations now in operation. A forty-page hand-book, fully explaining the system as used in the three hundred and fifty-five academies of the State, can be had free on application. The same general methods are used in the law, medical, library, and other examinations conducted by the University. So that this academic hand-book will make clear the general features of University Extension examinations and the rules and directions for credentials. Special circulars will give subjects and other details peculiar to Extension work.

Every precaution is taken to avoid the serious faults of most extensive and fully-organized systems. Room is left for the individuality of the teacher, and if in any subject reasonable cause can be shown for using a different form of treatment, an examination will be given on a syllabus drawn up in accordance with the teacher's plan, provided that it shall represent an equal quantity and quality of work, and so shall not lower the standard.

9. *Loans.*—As noted in 2 and 3, books are lent from the Extension library as from other departments of the State library. By a much larger system the necessary books, apparatus, lantern-slides, or other illustrative material needed for the best educational work, but beyond the resources of the centre to buy for itself, are lent from the State Extension department for use during the course. The centre must be responsible for any injury beyond reasonable wear and must pay transportation. Beyond this there is no charge. Obviously some books and apparatus required for a course in one town may be used a hundred times before they are worn out, thus involving only one per cent. of the expense required, if each of the hundred localities were compelled to buy its own. In some cases these loans will include several copies of the same book, so that instructors can put into the hands of pupils not having their own copies the books most important for them to read. Even where there is an excellent local library, it cannot, of course, furnish as many copies as are needed by the class. The loan system of the Extension department is designed to meet this need in the most economical way.

Books which many or all of the class need to have at hand during the entire course can be provided by a loan system in the centre itself. The managers can buy any needed books at the lowest wholesale price, and should supply students without profit, as some who would not buy a book at three dollars will buy it if it can be had for two dollars, and owning the work itself will greatly increase the value of the course and the chances of permanent interest. To any student unable to buy, a book should be lent for the entire course at perhaps one-fifth of its cost, thus enabling practically every student to have always at hand one or two of the most necessary books. At the close of the course the managers can send these books to the department for exchange and probably get nearly all they have cost, when the money paid for their use is deducted. Students not known to the local secretary would of course deposit the value of the book, four-fifths of which would be refunded on return of the book in good condition, reasonable wear excepted.

10. *Travelling Libraries.*—For centres distant from a public library, and needing such assistance, it is arranged to send small carefully-selected libraries to be kept according to circumstances, from a month to a year, so that those for whose benefit they are sent shall have ample opportunity for their satisfactory use. Some responsible real-estate owner must guarantee to make good any loss or injury beyond reasonable wear, and to return the library when called for, freight prepaid. Also, some competent person must agree in writing to act as librarian, to observe strictly the rules sent with the library, and to keep on the blanks provided the record of its use.

The books will be sent in suitable cases with complete catalogues and directions, and as fast as practicable the department will add such aids and guides to the most profitable reading as it is possible to put in print. The selection of the books themselves will represent the judgment of experts, and will be revised as experience shows how to improve at any point. The co-operation of all interested is invited, and suggestions as to these travelling libraries will be specially welcomed.

11. *Circuit Books and Apparatus for Use during the Course.*—Centres wishing more books and apparatus than can be furnished by the department in the form of travelling libraries or loans may greatly reduce the cost of this extra material by co-operation with other centres requiring the same at a different time. For books or apparatus likely to be required by at least five centres the department will arrange a circuit on the same plan found so valuable in reducing the cost of lectures. Each of five centres requiring the material will be charged one-fifth its wholesale cost, and each will be entitled to its use during one full course. The department assumes the responsibility and makes all the arrangements, so that the centre has simply to pay its fifth of the cost, and return the material to Albany or ship it to the next

centre, as directed at the close of the course. Should any books be injured beyond reasonable wear, the centre must pay for damage, and if any are unreturned must pay the other four-fifths of their value, thus enabling the department to replace them. Very often students who borrow a book at the beginning of the course will prefer at its close to pay the remaining four-fifths of its wholesale cost and retain it permanently. We wish to avoid even apparent rivalry with local booksellers, whose business ought to be stimulated as a result of Extension courses, but we find it necessary for the success of the movement to undertake this co-operative system of supply, which booksellers would find quite impracticable.

12. *Exchanges.*—Through the agency of the department, books, apparatus, or other material which any centre may have bought for one course and no longer needs, will, if practicable, be exchanged with some other centre for an equivalent in what it requires for the next year's work. The value of what is received and sent will be determined by an appraiser having no personal interest in the matter, and there will be no charge for the work. The centre, of course, pays for packing and transportation both ways.

13. *Regents' Centres.*—The facilities provided by the department are available to all localities or associations in the State which conform to the necessary rules, keep the records of the centre, and make an annual report to the regents in the form prescribed. As the department is doing the work of the State, it has no rivalry or competition with any other organization. Its officers are glad to find any person or association doing creditable work in the interest of higher education, and to give any assistance in their power. Obviously, however, the examinations, loans, travelling libraries, facilities for exchange, and the right to use the name of the department in connection with the centre should be given only where there is an organized local centre meeting at least the regents' minimum requirements. A register has been opened for such centres as shall maintain a course of not less than ten weeks during the academic year under direction of an accredited teacher, giving each week not only instruction,

but also satisfactory class and paper work. Experience has proved that as a rule localities which think that they are unable to maintain a systematic course of study, and that they must begin with a few popular lectures without attempting class or paper work, if required to do so, usually find it possible to establish a regular Extension course. While the weekly meetings are the rule, bi-weekly meetings for twenty weeks, or semi-weekly meetings for five weeks, will be accepted as the equivalent.

Regular regents' centres are recorded and numbered in order of establishment. A letter following the number indicates extent of work undertaken. Centres maintaining only one course are marked " E ;" two courses, " D ;" three or four courses, " C ;" five to nine courses " B ;" and the largest and most active centres which maintain ten or more courses annually are marked " A." Every centre which on inspection is found to maintain at least the minimum standard required will receive a certificate that it is officially registered as " Regents' Centre, No. —." This entitles it to use that name, or, if preferred, the fuller form, " University of the State of New York, University Extension Department, Centre No. —." The public will recognize that any centre using this official name is maintaining a standard of teaching and work which has been formally approved by the Extension Department of the University of the State.

All are urged to try, if possible, to reach at least the minimum standard required for a regents' centre, and it is highly desirable that every centre maintaining instruction worthy of registration should secure it. The department, however, interprets its duties broadly, and will gladly be of any practicable service to organized effort outside the regents' centres, assisting so far as in its power all efforts toward creditable work in extending educational opportunities more widely to the people.

14. *Registry.*—Beside regular centres, the department will register each club, society, or other organization engaged in any phase of Extension work in its broadest sense. This will include lecture courses which lack the necessary elements for registry as University Extension courses, but which the department wishes to know about and to encourage. It is hoped that year by year

these smaller organized movements can be fostered and made larger and stronger, till they can meet the requirements of regular regents' centres.

The department asks every literary, scientific, historical, art, or other club, society, or association engaged in work allied to University Extension, to send for the department files any programmes, circulars, or other publications illustrating its work, and to report its address, number of members, annual fees, number of meetings held yearly, average attendance, subjects of study and method pursued,—*e.g.*, addresses, papers, readings, discussions with leaders, conversation, class instruction, etc.

A similar record of lecture courses maintained in the State is kept, and we ask a report of the number of lectures, each speaker's name and subject, price of tickets, and average attendance.

Blanks for these reports will be sent free to any secretary or officer whose address is received.

For definite suggestions about details, see Circular 11, "*How to begin University Extension*," to be had free on application to University Extension Department, Regents' office, Albany, N. Y.

For explanations of what University Extension really is, see the circular on the "*Seven Elements of University Extension proper*," viz., lecture, syllabus, class, paper work, guided reading, students' clubs, and examinations.

APPENDIX B.

GENERAL ANNOUNCEMENT OF THE AMERICAN SOCIETY FOR THE EXTENSION OF UNIVERSITY TEACHING.

THE American Society for the Extension of University Teaching was founded in response to a deeply-felt want for a National Association which might assist in promoting the work of University Extension. The friends of popular education feel that the time has come for a better utilization of the facilities for instruction found in our existing educational institutions.

Experience has shown that this object is accomplished with great measure of success by the movement popularly known as University Extension. The results of this system in several countries, notably in England and the United States, have attracted much attention and its merits are now widely known.

To do this work efficiently will require large funds. The only sources of income at present are the fees of members ($5 annual fee, $50 life-membership fee) and the voluntary contributions of friends of the movement. You are cordially invited to become a member of the Society, and to present its claims to your friends and acquaintances who are, or should be, interested in the work. A national movement like this can succeed only when the people on the one hand and the colleges on the other take hold of it in earnest.

The membership fee and all other contributions may be sent by postal order, or draft on Philadelphia, or by draft on New York, payable to the order of Frederick B. Miles, Treasurer of the American Society for the Extension of University Teaching, Fifteenth and Chestnut Streets, Philadelphia.

The American Society is doing a two fold work. It is, in the first place, collecting information as to the progress of the movement in all countries, and through its monthly journal making it accessible to those interested in this system of instruction. In the second place, it is carrying on an extensive experiment in University Extension instruction. This work is a persistent effort to solve the difficult problems involved in the training of lecturers, the conduct and sequence of courses, and the financial support of centres. In this way the work of the Society becomes a series of illustrative experiments in adapting University Extension teaching to American conditions. It is plain that if the Society can successfully solve these difficult problems it will render a great service to American education, making the introduction of the work throughout the country a matter of comparative ease. Every one interested in the ultimate success of this great movement for popular education should, therefore, to the extent of his ability, contribute to the support of the American Society.

THE UNIVERSITY EXTENSION SEMINARY FOR THE STUDY OF AMERICAN EDUCATIONAL PROBLEMS AND FOR THE TRAINING OF UNIVERSITY EXTENSION LECTURERS.

IT is plain to those who have given serious attention to the subject that the movement for popular education known as University Extension has in it the possibility of valuable and permanent improvement of our educational system. It is also equally plain that to make the work as efficient as it may be, there should be a strong nucleus of persons engaged in the task of organization and instruction who have peculiar gifts or taste for this sort of labor, and who have received special training for it before they enter it. Their services are necessary to co-operate with and supplement the efforts of the University professor and instructor.

Many prominent educators have expressed the fear that it will not be possible to find men and women of suitable education and training to undertake this special work, and, indeed, have rightly insisted that there is at present no opportunity for those who would be inclined to enter the field to secure a suitable training for it.

It is believed, however, by the friends of the movement that there are many young men and women now studying in our colleges who are especially suited to this work, and who would prefer it to any other if they were sure they could thereby make a modest living, and if they knew how properly to prepare themselves. There are doubtless many professors and instructors in our colleges and universities, many teachers in our normal schools and high schools, and many college men and women in other careers, who would be admirably adapted to succeed in this field if they had the necessary technical preparation. It is furthermore clear, that the work of University Extension offers a new road to permanent college positions besides the ordinary one now travelled, of starting in as instructor, for the knowledge of University Extension work on the part of candidates for college positions will constitute a valuable recommendation to boards of trustees.

Acting on this belief, the American Society for the Extension of University Teaching has decided to establish a University Extension Seminary for the training of University Extension lecturers and organizers.

It will be under the direction of Professor Edmund J. James, President of the Society, assisted by leading university men of this country and Europe.

The term will open October 1, 1892, and last until June 1, 1893. The price for tuition will be fifty dollars per year. A certain number of free scholarships will be awarded to suitable candidates.

Members of the Seminary can pursue advanced studies for the degrees of A.M. and Ph.D. in the institutions near enough to Philadelphia to enable them to attend the work of the Seminary.*

---

* Arrangements have been made with the University of Pennsylvania by which members of the Seminary can enter that institution and carry on such studies for the higher degrees as they may be fitted for. It will thus be possible for the graduate student to enter on his course for the A.M. or Ph.D.

Each member of the Seminary will be expected to prepare and deliver a course of Extension lectures on a subject to be selected by himself, with the advice and consent of the Director of the Seminary.

It will be possible in many cases to secure an opportunity to deliver these lectures at different places and obtain a remuneration for them. In the case of mature and properly qualified members it will doubtless be possible to earn enough money in this way to defray a considerable portion, if not all, of the year's residence. No guarantee of such remuneration is, however, given, and no one is advised to enter the Seminary with this expectation. The members of the Seminary will be expected to aid in the work of the Society when possible, and every facility will be offered them to make themselves thoroughly acquainted with the theory and practice of University Extension work.

A certificate will be given at the end of the year to properly qualified members who have complied faithfully with the rules and regulations of the Seminary.

It is the opinion of the Society that no one can do the best work in the University Extension field who is not thoroughly interested in the problems of education,—more especially of American education. The University Extension lecturer and organizer should be thoroughly acquainted with the whole educational system of the country, since only in this way can he co-ordinate his work with that of the other educational agencies in the field. With this fact in view, the work of the Seminary, aside from the technical subjects relating to University Extension, will be devoted to a thorough examination and discussion of modern educational problems.

The University Extension Seminary will thus offer, for the first

---

immediately, or continue it if he has already begun it. A deduction in tuition of fifty dollars will also be made to members of the Seminary.

Women are admitted to the Graduate Department of the University of Pennsylvania on the same terms as men.

For further information, address Dr. Horace Jayne, Dean of the Faculty of Philosophy, University of Pennsylvania, Philadelphia.

It is hoped that similar arrangements can be made with other institutions.

time in the history of American education, an opportunity to the teacher, or the college student looking forward to teaching, whether in public or private school, whether in college or primary grade, to prepare himself thoroughly for the work of educational leadership in the various departments of our national life. The man or woman who desires not merely to be a good teacher, but also a real leader in educational thought and action, will find here an opportunity to put himself in touch with the latest and best thought on educational topics, and take away with him not merely increased knowledge, but a deeper insight and wider outlook than ever before.

Among the men who will take part in the work of instruction may be mentioned: Hon. W. T. Harris, United States Commissioner of Education; Dr. James MacAlister, President of the Drexel Institute; Dr. Charles DeGarmo, President of Swarthmore College; Dr. Isaac Sharpless, President of Haverford College; Professor Simon N. Patten, of the University of Pennsylvania; and Rev. Hudson Shaw, of Oxford University, England.

The following courses have already been arranged for, and others will be announced later:

1. Educational Administration.—*Professor Edmund J. J es, Ph.D.*
2. Educational Ideals.—*Professor Simon N. Patten, Ph.D.*
3. Science of Instruction.—*President Charles DeGarmo, Ph.D., of Swarthmore College.*
4. English Educational Institutions and their Lessons for us.—*President Isaac Sharpless, Ph.D., of Haverford College.*
5. The Place and Function of the Normal School in American Education.—*Principal George M. Philips, Ph.D., State Normal School, West Chester, Pa.*

For further information as to the Seminary, address

UNIVERSITY EXTENSION SEMINARY,
Fifteenth and Chestnut Streets,
Philadelphia.

Honorary President, William Pepper, M.D., LL.D.
President,   Treasurer,   Gen'l Secretary,
Edmund J. James.   Frederick B. Miles.   George Henderson.

THE AMERICAN SOCIETY.

THE American Society for the Extension of University Teaching was founded in response to a deeply-felt want for a National Association which might assist in promoting the work of University Extension. The friends of popular education feel that the time has come for a better utilization of the facilities for instruction which are to be found in our existing educational institutions.

Experience has shown that this object is accomplished with great measure of success by the movement popularly known as University Extension. The results of this system in several countries—notably in England and the United States—have attracted much attention, and its merits are now widely known.

The American Society has a twofold work. It is, in the first place, collecting information as to the progress of the movement in all countries, and making it accessible through its monthly journal to all interested in this system of instruction. In the second place, it is carrying on in not less than six States, nearest its General Offices, an object lesson in Extension teaching for the benefit of the whole country. Slowly and carefully it is testing the various elements of the system and adapting them to American conditions, and at the same time solving one after another the difficult problems of the work in the training of lecturers, the sequence of courses, and the financial support of centres.

To do this work efficiently will require large funds. The only sources of income at present are the fees of members ($5.00 annual fee, $50.00 life-membership fee) and the voluntary contributions of friends of the movement. You are cordially invited to become a member of the Society, and to present its claims to your friends and acquaintances who are, or should be, interested in the work. A national movement like this can only succeed when the people take hold of it in earnest, on the one hand, and the colleges on the other.

The membership fee and all other contributions may be sent by postal order or draft on Philadelphia, or by draft on New York, payable to the order of Frederick B. Miles, Treasurer of the American Society for the Extension of University Teaching, Fifteenth and Chestnut Streets, Philadelphia.

UNIVERSITY EXTENSION.

A Monthly Journal, giving full information as to the methods and results of Extension teaching in all countries, with special reference to the development of the movement in the United States.

Yearly Subscription, $1.50.   Single Numbers, 15 Cents.

Vol. I.—July, 1891, to July, 1892—will be issued in full black cloth binding at ONE DOLLAR. READY JUNE FIFTEENTH.

Address   UNIVERSITY EXTENSION,
15th and Chestnut Sts., Philadelphia.

☞ Send for list of publications of The American Society.

UNIVERSITY EXTENSION.

CONTENTS:

JULY, 1891.
- THE AMERICAN SOCIETY.
- THE FUNDAMENTAL DISTINCTIONS BETWEEN ELEMENTARY AND HIGHER INSTRUCTION.
- THE ENDOWMENT OF UNIVERSITY EXTENSION.
- THE HISTORY OF A BRANCH SOCIETY.
- THE FORMATION OF A LOCAL CENTRE.
- NOTES.
- CURRENT LITERATURE.

AUGUST, 1891.
- THE PROSPECTS OF UNIVERSITY EXTENSION IN ENGLAND.
- AMERICAN WOMEN AND UNIVERSITY EXTENSION.
- EXTENSION TEACHING AT BROWN UNIVERSITY.
- WHAT IS UNIVERSITY EXTENSION?
- WHY TEACHERS SHOULD BE INTERESTED IN UNIVERSITY EXTENSION.
- NOTES.
- THOUGHTS ON UNIVERSITY EXTENSION.

SEPTEMBER, 1891.
- UNIVERSITY EXTENSION IN THE SOUTH.
- THE UNIVERSITY AND UNIVERSITY EXTENSION.
- UNIT COURSE.
- OXFORD ANNUAL REPORT.
- NOTES.

OCTOBER, 1891.
- THE OXFORD SUMMER MEETING OF 1891.
- SUMMER SCHOOLS IN BOTANY.
- STUDENTS' ASSOCIATIONS IN GREAT BRITAIN.
- NOTES.

NOVEMBER, 1891.
- THE EDUCATIONAL VALUE OF EUROPEAN HISTORY.
- RECENT DEVELOPMENTS IN ENGLAND.
- THE LOWELL INSTITUTE IN BOSTON.
- INTRODUCTION TO UNIVERSITY EXTENSION STUDY OF POLITICAL ECONOMY.
- SOME TYPICAL COURSES.
- NOTES.

DECEMBER, 1891.
- THE NATIONAL CONFERENCE.
- THE SHAM AND THE REAL IN UNIVERSITY EXTENSION.
- INTRODUCTION TO THE UNIVERSITY EXTENSION STUDY OF POLITICAL ECONOMY.
- THE ENGLISH MINERS AND UNIVERSITY EXTENSION.
- UNIVERSITY EXTENSION COLLEGES.
- NOTES.

JANUARY, 1892.
- A STEP FORWARD.
- THE UNIVERSITY EXTENSION LECTURER.—I.
- THE UNIVERSITIES AND THE ELEMENTARY SCHOOLS.
- ECONOMICS.—I.
- THE IDEAL SYLLABUS.
- NOTES.

FEBRUARY, 1892.
- UNIVERSITY EXTENSION, WHY?
- THE EDUCATION OF CITIZENS.
- THE UNIVERSITY EXTENSION LECTURER.—II.
- ECONOMICS.—II.
- NOTES.
- THOUGHTS FROM THE NATIONAL CONFERENCE.

MARCH, 1892.
- THE CHICAGO SOCIETY FOR UNIVERSITY EXTENSION.
- THE CLEVELAND SOCIETY FOR UNIVERSITY EXTENSION.
- UNIVERSITY EXTENSION IN THE SOUTHWEST.
- ECONOMICS.—III.
- NOTES.
- UNIVERSITY EXTENSION IN NEW YORK.

APRIL, 1892.
- CLASS WORK IN UNIVERSITY EXTENSION.
- EXTENSION TEACHING IN WISCONSIN.
- UNIVERSITY EXTENSION WORK IN MATHEMATICS.
- AN UNKNOWN QUANTITY AND THE POSSIBLE VALUE.
- NOTES.

UNIVERSITY EXTENSION SYLLABI.

The following is a list of the syllabi thus far published by the American Society. They are all arranged for six lectures, except those marked thus *. They may be had post-free upon receipt of the price, and may be ordered by the numbers.

No. 3. Milton's Poetic Art	$0 10
" 5. Story of Faust	10
" 6. Electricity	10
" 7. Shakespeare's Tempest, with Companion Studies	10
" 8. Psychology	10
" 9. Stories as a Mode of Thinking	10
" 10. Euripides for English Audiences	10
" 12. Four Studies in Shakespeare	10
" 15. Animal Life. Considered as a Part of Universal Energy	10
" 16. Modern Essayists	10
" 17. Mathematics with Application to Mechanics	10
" 19. American Literature	10
" 20. Algebra *	15
" 21. Botany; Structural	10
" 22. Geology and Paleontology. Part I	20
A. No. 1. Political History of Europe since 1815. Part I. 1815–1848	10
Part II. 1848–1881	10
" " 2. Constitution of the United States	10
" " 3. English Literature—Chaucer to Tennyson	10
" " 4. Epochs in American History. 1620–1892	10
" " 5. Europe Finds America	10
" " 6. Civil Development of the United States	10
" " 7. Mathematics as Applied to Mechanics *	20
" " 8. Representative American Authors	10
" " 9. Earlier Plays of Shakespeare	10
" " 10. English Literature—Chaucer to Tennyson	10
" " 11. Political Economy	10
" " 12. Modern Novelists	10
" " 13. Central Europe in the Nineteenth Century	10
" " 14. Typical English Poets	10
" " 15. Modern Industrial History	10
" " 16. Poets of America	10
" " 17. Dynamical Geology. Part I	10
Part II	10
" " 18. Economic Condition of the People of the United States, between 1789 and 1816	10
" " 19. American Literature	10
" " 20. English Literature in the Nineteenth Century	10
" " 21. Structural Botany	20
" " 22. The Brook Farm Community	10
" " 23. Electricity	10
" " 24. Prose Fiction in America	10
" " 25. The Strength of Materials	10
" " 26. Political Economy. (With an outline of reading.)	10
" " 27. American History—Administration of Government	10
" " 28. Robert Browning	10
" " 29. Studies in English Poetry of the Nineteenth Century	10
" " 30. The Modern View of Energy	10
" " 31. English Poets of the Revolution Age	10
" " 32. A Bird's-eye View of European History, from the Battle of Marathon to the Fall of the Eastern Empire	10
" " 33. Literature of the Queen Anne Period	10
" " 34. History and Theory of Money. (With an outline Course of Study.)	40
" " 35. Plant Forms and Plant Functions. Parts I and II. (With outline Course of Study.)	20
" " 36. The Renaissance. Historically Considered	15
" " 37. Light	15
" " 38. Shakspere. The Man and his Mind	15
" " 39. Revolutions in Commerce	10
" " 40. Socialism—Past, Present, and Future. (With outline Course of Study.)	20
" " 41. The Change in Political Economy. (With outline Course of Study.)	20
" " 42. The Literary Study of the Bible	10

UNIVERSITY EXTENSION
Books and Pamphlets.

Any of the following publications will be sent post-free upon receipt of the price. They may be ordered by the numbers.

☞ A package containing pamphlets, specimen syllabi, and copies of UNIVERSITY EXTENSION, giving a fairly complete idea of the whole movement, will be sent post-free upon receipt of $1.00.

1. Proceedings of The First National Conference, containing in full all the addresses and reports. (pp. 292.) $1 50
2. An Address before the American Society. By R. G. MOULTON, Cambridge University Extension Lecturer. (pp. 19.) 10
3. Lecturer's Notes on the Working of University Extension. By R. G. MOULTON. (pp. 8.) 10
4. The University Extension Movement in England (1885). By R. G. MOULTON. (pp. 61.) 20
5. University Extension: Its Definition, History, System of Teaching, and Organization. (pp. 8.) 10
6. What should be the Position of University Extension? By SIDNEY T. SKIDMORE. (pp. 12.) 10
7. University Extension as seen by a Lecturer. By C. HANFORD HENDERSON. (pp. 15.)........................ 10
8. Report on the Movement in England. By GEORGE HENDERSON, General Secretary of the American Society. (pp. 31.) 10
9. University Extension as viewed by Prominent American Educators. (pp. 44.) 15
10. The Development of the University Extension Idea. By MICHAEL E. SADLER, Secretary Oxford Delegacy. (pp. 20.) 10
11. The University Extension Lecturer. By DR. E. J. JAMES, President of the American Society. (pp. 18.) 15
12. The Function and Organization of a Local Centre. By MICHAEL E. SADLER. (pp. 8.) 10
13. The Y. M. C. A. and University Extension. By MR. WALTER C. DOUGLAS, General Secretary of the Philadelphia Y. M. C. A. (pp. 7.) 10
14. The Church and University Extension. By the REV. DR. J. S. MACINTOSH. (pp. 7.) 10
15. The Class in University Extension. By MR. EDWARD T. DEVINE, Staff Lecturer of the American Society. (pp. 6.) 10
16. The Place of University Extension in American Education. By HON. WILLIAM T. HARRIS. (pp. 14.) 15
17. The First Annual Report of the American Society 15

SPECIAL NOTICE.

HAND-BOOK OF UNIVERSITY EXTENSION (being Vol. I., July, 1891-July, 1892, of UNIVERSITY EXTENSION), containing a full description of the movement, with reports of experiments in the United States and abroad. Octavo. 416 pp. Black Cloth.

READY JULY 1.   *PRICE, $1.00.*

THE NEW
CHAMBERS'S ENCYCLOPÆDIA.

*New Type, New Subjects, New Illustrations,
New Maps.*

A COMPLETE DICTIONARY OF ART, SCIENCE, HISTORY, LITERATURE, FABLE, MYTHOLOGY, BIOGRAPHY, GEOGRAPHY, ETC. HANDSOMELY ILLUSTRATED WITH MAPS - - - AND NUMEROUS WOOD-ENGRAVINGS - - -

---

Eight volumes now ready. The two remaining volumes to be issued during 1892.

Price per vol. : Cloth, $3.00 ; Cloth, uncut, $3.00 ;
Sheep, $4.00 ; Half morocco, $4.50.

"Every article has been written with reference to the needs of readers of the present generation. Not only are latest discoveries in science, natural history, and archæology to be found in it, but matters of a purely temporary and, we might even say, local importance are, in many cases, very fully treated. A similar liberality is shown in the illustrations, particularly in the department of Natural History, the cuts in which are numerous, extremely well done, and well printed."—*N. Y. Critic.*

"'Chambers's Encyclopædia' is a publication that is entitled to every consideration as an educational factor."—*Philadelphia Ledger.*

"'Chambers's Encyclopædia,' in spite of the claims of other similar works, still continues to hold its own as a standard reference for the home or school. The new revision brings its articles well up to date, and introduces a large number of entirely new subjects. No expense has been spared in obtaining the co-operation of the best authorities in the special lines, and the result is a complete and comprehensive dictionary of useful knowledge. 'Chambers's' has an undisputed title to be considered one of the most accurate, reliable, convenient, and useful encyclopædias now on the American market."—*Boston Journal of Education.*

"All who are interested with respect to persons and places, questions of art and religion, politics and science, and who in these busy days are anxious to find the latest information on any subject lying ready to hand, should possess themselves of these volumes as they are published."—*Liverpool Mercury.*

Specimen pages mailed free to any address.

J. B. LIPPINCOTT COMPANY, Publishers,
715 and 717 Market Street, Philadelphia.

COMPLETE AND AUTHORIZED
EDITION OF THE WORKS OF

WILLIAM H. PRESCOTT,

WITH NOTES BY JOHN FOSTER KIRK.

"Mr. Prescott was by far the first historian of America, and he may justly be assigned a place beside the very greatest of modern Europe. Compare what he has written with the most of what others have left on the same subjects, and Prescott's superiority beams upon you from the contrast. The easy flow of his language and the faultless lucidity of his style may make the readers forget the unremitting toil which the narrative has cost; but the critical inquirer sees everywhere the fruits of investigation rigidly and most perseveringly pursued, and an impartiality and soundness of judgment which give authority to every statement and weight to every conclusion."—GEORGE BANCROFT.

THE STUDENT'S EDITION,

Just issued, is intended to meet the increasing demand for such standard authors as are now required by recent courses in English in our leading schools and colleges. It is published in five volumes, with illustrations and maps that have appeared in other editions.

SOLD SEPARATELY, $1.00 PER VOLUME.

"*THE CONQUEST OF MEXICO,*"
"*HISTORY OF FERDINAND AND ISABELLA,*"
"*CONQUEST OF PERU,*" and "*MISCELLANIES,*"
"*THE REIGN OF CHARLES V.,*"
"*THE REIGN OF PHILIP II.*"

PER SET:

CLOTH, $5.00;   HALF CALF, GILT TOP, $12.50;
EXTRA CLOTH, GILT TOP, $6.25;   HALF CALF, MARBLED EDGES, $12.50.

J. B. LIPPINCOTT COMPANY, Publishers,
715 and 717 Market Street, Philadelphia.

LIPPINCOTT'S BIOGRAPHICAL DICTIONARY.

By JOSEPH THOMAS, M.D., LL.D.

Bound in sheep, $12.00 ; half Russia, $15.00.

Memoirs of the Eminent Persons of all Ages and Countries, and Accounts of the Various Subjects of the Norse, Hindoo, and Classic Mythologies, with the Pronunciation of their Names in the Different Languages in which they occur.

It is really a cyclopædia within itself, including every character that has strong claims to our notice, either from public notoriety or lasting celebrity, and from it may be gathered a knowledge of the lives of those who have made the world's history famous.

OPINIONS OF THE PRESS.

"'Lippincott's Biographical Dictionary,' according to the unanimous opinion of distinguished scholars, is the best work of the kind ever published."—*Philadelphia Ledger.*

"No other work of the kind will compare with it."—*Chicago Advance.*

"This work presents a very wide range of treatment, great compactness and perspicuity, wonderful accuracy, and a typographical execution that is absolutely perfect."—*N. Y. Evening Post.*

"There is nothing like it in the English language. . . . It may be fairly esteemed a credit to the age and country which have produced it."—*Philadelphia Press.*

TESTIMONY OF DISTINGUISHED SCHOLARS.

"In the judicious brevity of its articles, the comprehensiveness of its selections of topics, the nice exactness in matters of orthography and pronunciation, as well as for its admirable typography, it promises to take a very high place among our books of reference."—*From* PROFESSOR NOAH PORTER.

"It is a work which I shall be glad to possess, both on account of the fulness of its matter, and because the pronunciation of names, so far as it can be represented by the alphabet of our language, is given. The work will be a valuable addition to the books of reference in our language."—*From* WILLIAM CULLEN BRYANT.

"It is universal in fact as in name, doing like justice to men prominent in science, literature, religion, general history, etc. The author knows how to put a large number of facts into a very small compass, and in a manner remarkable for system, fairness, precision, and easy diction."—*From* PROFESSOR JAMES D. DANA, M.A., LL.D.

⁎ For sale by all Booksellers, or will be sent by mail, post-paid, on receipt of the price by

J. B. LIPPINCOTT COMPANY, Publishers,

715 and 717 Market Street, Philadelphia.

".... Supplement to

Allibone's Dictionary

"The complete work ought to be not only in every library, but in every school in which English literature is taught."
—*New York Nation.*

. of English Literature and British and .
.... American Authors ....

By JOHN FOSTER KIRK.

Two volumes. Imperial 8vo. Nearly 1600 pages. Cloth binding, $15.00; sheep, $17.00; half Russia, $20.00; half calf or half morocco, $22.00.

"We have no hesitation in declaring our conviction that it is by far the most satisfactory work of the kind with which we are acquainted. It is ample in its information; it is accurate to a degree very rarely attained; it is catholic as to the persons included; and it is, with all this, eminently readable."
—*London Saturday Review.*

"Mr. Kirk's volumes contain not only the results of the years of painstaking labor directed to the task in hand, but also show the work of a life spent in literary studies, and that scholarship of the very highest order of excellence has been used in perfecting and completing a book that is now more than ever valuable to every one who needs a reference handbook for the names and works and life of all who have contributed to the vast stores of English literature."—*Philadelphia Public Ledger.*

.. Allibone's Dictionary and Supplement ..
Complete in Five Volumes.

The entire work containing the names and history of over 83,000 authors. Cloth, $37.50; sheep, $42.50; half Russia, $50.00; half calf, $55.00; half morocco, $55.00.

"It can hardly be doubted that Allibone's Dictionary of English Literature and British and American Authors, taken as a whole, embracing as it does in its original three volumes the names of over 46,000 authors, and in its Supplement those of 37,183 authors—with notices of their several hundred thousand books—will long remain without a rival as a bibliography of the literature of the English tongue."—*Boston Literary World.*

"No dictionary of the authors of any language has ever before been undertaken on so grand a scale. For convenience and trustworthiness this work is probably not surpassed by any similar production in the whole range of modern literature."—*New York Tribune.*

J. B. LIPPINCOTT COMPANY,

..... Publishers .....

715 and 717 Market St., Philadelphia.

*** For sale by all Booksellers, or will be sent, post-paid, on receipt of the price.

WORCESTER'S DICTIONARY

Is the standard authority on all questions of orthography, pronunciation, or definition, and is so recognized by all the colleges of the country, by the principal newspapers and periodicals, and by such leaders of American thought as Phillips Brooks, Edward Everett Hale, George Bancroft, Oliver Wendell Holmes, Irving, Marsh, Agassiz, Henry, etc. Leading book-publishers recognize Worcester as the highest authority, and millions of school-books are issued every year with this great work as the standard.

WORCESTER'S SCHOOL DICTIONARIES.

WORCESTER'S NEW ACADEMIC DICTIONARY.

WORCESTER'S NEW COMPREHENSIVE DICTIONARY.

Adopted and used in
New York City, Philadelphia, Boston, Cambridge, Chicago, St. Louis, Worcester, Lowell, Salem, Washington, and hundreds of cities and towns throughout the United States and Canada. Recently adopted for North Carolina, West Virginia, and Virginia.

WORCESTER'S NEW ACADEMIC DICTIONARY

Is designed especially for the use of the *higher schools and seminaries of learning*, but is well adapted in its scope and range to the needs of families and individuals.

The *distinctive feature* of the book is its treatment *of the etymology of words*. In no other work of its size and class (so far as is known to the editors) is there anything approaching it in fulness and completeness in this regard.

Printed from entirely new plates. 688 pages. 264 Illustrations.

WORCESTER'S NEW COMPREHENSIVE DICTIONARY

Contains a full vocabulary of 48,000 words. The design has been to give the greatest quantity of useful matter in the most condensed form, to guard against *corruptions in writing and speaking the language*, to adapt the work to the use *of the higher schools and seminaries* of learning, and also to make it a convenient manual for families and individuals.

Printed from entirely new plates. 688 pages. 577 Illustrations.

For sale by all Booksellers. Circulars sent on application to the Publishers.

J. B. LIPPINCOTT COMPANY,
715 AND 717 MARKET ST., PHILADELPHIA.

www.ingramcontent.com/pod-product-compliance
Lightning Source LLC
Chambersburg PA
CBHW022117230426
43672CB00008B/1411